JAVA™ 2 PROGRAMMER'S INTERACTIVE WORKBOOK

KEVIN CHU

AND

ERIC BROWER

90000

9 780130 166388

 Prentice Hall PTR
Upper Saddle River, New Jersey 07458
www.phptr.com

Acquisitions editor: *Mark Taub*
Editorial assistant: *Michael Fredette*
Cover design: *Anthony Gemmellaro*
Cover design director: *Jerry Votta*
Manufacturing manager: *Alexis Heydt*
Marketing manager: *Kate Hargett*
Development editor: *Ralph Moore*
Project coordinator: *Anne Trowbridge*
Compositor/Production services: *Pine Tree Composition, Inc.*

 © 2000 by Prentice Hall PTR
Prentice-Hall, Inc.
Upper Saddle River, New Jersey 07458

Printed in the United States of America
10 9 8 7 6 5 4 3 2

ISBN 0-13-016638-3

Prentice-Hall International (UK) Limited, *London*
Prentice-Hall of Australia Pty. Limited, *Sydney*
Prentice-Hall Canada Inc., *Toronto*
Prentice-Hall Hispanoamericana, S.A., *Mexico*
Prentice-Hall of India Private Limited, *New Delhi*
Prentice-Hall of Japan, Inc., *Tokyo*
Pearson Education Asia Pte. Ltd.
Editora Prentice-Hall do Brasil, Ltda., *Rio de Janeiro*

To Rochelle, for being my world.

To Helen and Cole, for your unfailing patience and support.

CONTENTS

INTRODUCTION

Welcome to the *Java 2 Programmer's Interactive Workbook*. This book will help guide you as you learn the Java programming language, which is regarded as the future of computer programming. Never before has a computer language so successfully combined a powerful object-oriented language with all of the graphical tools needed to create a fully functional program that can run on any system and in any Web browser. With the advance of the Internet, Java has become the language of choice for developers who need to create and distribute their applications quickly.

Java was developed by Sun Microsystems in the early 1990s and has been gaining popularity every since. Prior to Java, the two main languages used by the computer industry were C, and C++. C is simple, powerful, and sometimes elegant, but it is also a procedural language. C++ is object-oriented, but also hugely complex and requires a great deal of overhead to maintain a program. Both languages are also *machine-dependent*, meaning that their programs only run on one type of computer (PC, Mac, Unix). The program must be recompiled, and sometimes rewritten, to work on a different computer. This can lead to long development times for projects.

Likewise, neither C nor C++ have built-in graphical utilities. Both must use special *libraries* that allow the program to use the windowing features of the computer. These libraries can be vastly different on various computer platforms, requiring more rewriting of the programs.

Java provides programmers the power and flexibility of C, while at the same time, allowing them to build true object-oriented programs without the overhead of C++. Additionally, the graphics utilities are built-in to Java, so no writing is ever needed. With Java 2, the "look and feel" of the program can be changed to match the local windowing system without any rewriting or recompiling. This means the same program can look like a Mac program when running on a Mac, and also look like a Windows program when running on a PC. All of this is possible after just writing and compiling the program just one time.

One additional feature of Java is that all of the objects created in Java are truly reusable. This means that every program can build on past programs, greatly reducing the time it takes to develop programs. No longer do programmers have to keep reinventing the wheel with every new project.

WHO THIS BOOK IS FOR

This book is for the beginning programmer. It teaches computer programming using Java as the first language. Almost every other Java book out there assumes that you've programmed in some other language before (usually C). This book does not make that assumption. If you have never programmed before, then this book is for you. If you have programmed in an "older" language, such as Fortran, Pascal or Cobol, then this book is also for you. If you have programmed extensively in C or C++, then this book is probably *not* for you—it may be too basic for you.

In addition to covering the basics of the Java programming language, this book will also cover topics that apply to any programming language. Such topics include general programming terms, Boolean logic, and basic program design. There are many books that show you how to do something in Java, but the authors feel that it's just as important to know why and when to do it.

This book is also not intended to be the *end-all* of Java books. Far from it! However, the unique format of the Interactive Workbook series makes this book an excellent tool to get you started down the path of learning Java. You won't be a Java expert when you're done with this book, but you will have a solid foundation on which to become an expert. The authors recommend that you follow-up this book with at least two other books on Java (you know, the ones that assume you already know the language!). One book should be a general Java reference book, and the other should be a *Swing* book. You'll learn about *Swing* is this book, but for now, know that *Swing* is the toolkit used to create graphical user interfaces (GUIs). There are many such books out there today, and most of them are very good, but as *reference* books. This book is meant to fill that gap between knowing nothing, and being able to use the reference books.

HOW THIS BOOK IS ORGANIZED

The Interactive Workbook series offers a unique and challenging program to "learn by doing." Only by engaging your brain in exercises can you truly learn anything. The creators of the Interactive Workbook series understand this concept, so these books offer more than just reading.

CHAPTERS, LABS, AND EXERCISES, OH MY!

Every chapter is divided into several labs. Each lab targets a specific topic. You should try and complete a lab in a single sitting, so allow yourself some time. As you begin each lab, you will be given some instruction followed by the exercises. Make sure you do the exercises! The exercises are the key to learning. The authors also provide answers to the exercises, as well as follow-up discussion.

It is crucial that you actually do the exercises and then read the answers. It is also crucial that you read the discussion that follows. Unlike most books, the "chapter" is not over when the labs begin. The labs are not just a regurgitation of the chapter instruction. The exercises in the lab will reinforce the instruction in the chapter, but they will then challenge you to build on that knowledge. The answers to the exercises may contain *new information* not presented in the chapter instruction. This new information will make much more sense to you if you have done the exercises first.

SELF-REVIEW QUESTIONS

At the end of each chapter are a series of *Self-Review Questions*. These questions also help to reinforce that you have learned what you needed to learn from the chapter. The answers to these questions can be found in Appendix A of this book.

TEST YOUR THINKING

The end of each chapter also has a *Test Your Thinking* section. This section contains more advanced projects than those contained in the labs. If you can handle these exercises, then you have really started to master the subject! The answers for the *Test Your Thinking* projects are not in the book, but they can be found on the Web page for this book.

WEB COMPANION

As with all of the books in the Interactive Workbook series, this book has a companion Web site, which is located at the following site:

```
http://www.phptr.com/phptrinteractive
```

This companion Web site is closely integrated with the content of this book, and we encourage you to visit it early and often. At the Web site, you will find all of the source code used in this book, answers to the *Test Your Thinking* exercises, the Self-Review questions and answers, and more!

You can also send e-mail to the authors because they just don't get enough!

WHAT YOU WILL NEED

In order to program in Java, and use this book, you will need a few things.

A COMPUTER

This may seem obvious, but you will need one. Java, being a platform-independent language, will run on most current computers. Java is supported on the following systems:

- Window 95, 98, or NT or better.
- MacOS 8.1 or better
- Solaris 2.5.1 or better.

For the other flavors of Unix, including Linux, you'll need to check the Web page that follows.

THE JAVA 2 SOFTWARE DEVELOPERS KIT (SDK)

For this book, you will need to obtain the *Production* Release of the Java 2 SDK *Standard Edition*. This is also known as the JDK 1.2. At press time, this was actually known as JDK 1.2.2. There may be a more recent release by the time the book goes to print.

The Solaris and Windows version of Java 2 are free from Sun Microsystems at the following URL:

```
http://java.sun.com/java2
```

At this URL you will find both the Java 2 software and the documentation. We recommend that you get both. You may not be able to understand the documentation at first, but . . .

Sun may require that you register yourself for the download, but the software is free.

At press time, the actual download URL is the following:

```
http://java.sun.com/products/jdk/1.2
```

From this location you can download the Windows or Solaris releases of Java. If you have a Mac, or different flavor of Unix, click on the *Platform Ports* link to direct you to the version you need.

In Chapter 1, we will cover the download process and make sure that you can compile and run a Java program. Then in Chapter 2, we'll start learning some Java!

CONVENTIONS USED IN THIS BOOK

There are several conventions that we've used in this book to try and make your learning experience easier. These are explained here.

 This icon is used to flag notes or advice from the authors to our readers. This might be some philosophy or useful piece of advice that the authors feel might be helpful. Remember, free advice is worth the price you paid for it!

 This icon is used to flag tips or tricks that will save you time or trouble. The authors have been around the block a few times. Example: Measure twice, cut once.

 If you're ever on the verge of doing something dangerous, we will warn you with this icon. Example: never eat anything bigger than your head. You have been warned!

 This icon is used to flag passages in which there is a reference to the book's companion Web site, which once again is located at:

```
http://www.phptr.com/phptrinteractive/
```

The Whole Truth

One of the necessary evils of teaching a beginning-level subject is having to simplify certain topics. When this happens, we can put the *whole truth* into a sidebar like this one. If you're thirsting for knowledge, this is the place to come!

ACKNOWLEDGMENTS

A book like this takes many people to be successful. As authors, we get our names on the front, but we had a great deal of help from some very talented and understanding people. We would first like to thank Mark Taub for having faith in us and for giving us those extensions. If Mark is grayer or balder than when we started, it's due to us.

We are also indebted to Ralph Moore who helped shape us into writers and also oversaw the production of the book. If you ever have the chance to work with Ralph, take it!

Likewise, this book would not have been as good without the technical reviews of Marc Loy. Marc kept us honest and had some brilliant insights of his own. If you're looking for a book on *Swing*, there's a great one with Marc's name on it.

We would also like to thank Patty Donovan and the production staffs at Prentice Hall and Pine Tree Composition for the work they put in. You're holding the fruits of their labor.

Finally, and most importantly, we must thank the extremely loving, amazingly patient, and infinitely forgiving women in our lives, Rochelle and Helen. We can't begin to express our gratitude and love for all of the support you've given us, but it's sure going to be fun to try!

CHAPTER 1

GETTING STARTED

 The longest journey begins with a single step.

CHAPTER OBJECTIVES

In this chapter, you will learn about:

✔ Compiling and Running a Java Program   Page 2

To attain proficiency with a computer programming language, you must get your hands dirty. In order to get your hands dirty, you must have appropriate tools at your disposal. Within this chapter, we will introduce the tools needed to create and run Java programs, and show you how to obtain and configure these tools on your system.

With these tools installed on your computer, this interactive workbook offers you the opportunity to both read about Java programming and become an active participant in your Java education as well. There is no substitute for experience, so let's hit the ground running!

L A B   1 . 1

COMPILING AND RUNNING A JAVA PROGRAM

LAB OBJECTIVES

After this lab, you will be able to:

- Install and Configure the Java Development Kit
- Compile and Run a Java Program
- Compile and Run a Java Applet

Before the introduction of the Java programming language, most software development was done in a platform-specific manner. Programs written in languages such as Fortran, C, and C++ were run through *compilers* to generate platform-specific executables. PCs, Macintoshes, and UNIX workstations all required their own version of an executable and often the programs would have to be specifically tailored for each platform.

Java programs must be run through a compiler as well. However, the Java compiler does not generate platform-specific code—it generates platform-independent *bytecodes*. These bytecodes can then be executed by a *Java Virtual Machine* (JVM). Strictly speaking, Java is not "Write Once, Run Anywhere" as claimed by Sun; realistically, it is "Write Once, Run on Any System With a JVM." Because JVMs are available for most interesting platforms (and even a few not-so-interesting ones), the language has fulfilled its promise of cross-platform compatibility.

To foster development with the Java programming language, Sun Microsystems provides a free software development kit (SDK), which includes a compiler, virtual machine, debugger, and a host of other useful development tools. This is called the Java Development Kit, or JDK, and the latest Windows and Solaris versions are always available from the Sun Web site at:

```
http://java.sun.com/products/jdk/1.2/index.html
```

If you are developing on a platform other than Windows or Solaris (good for you!), you can find information regarding JDKs for other platforms on the Web at:

```
http://java.sun.com/cgi-bin/java-ports.cgi
```

The JDK is free of charge and free of frills. There is no graphical user interface provided to these tools, so you can only use them from a command-line interface such as a DOS window or UNIX shell. The benefit of the JDK is that it is a reference implementation—if you can successfully compile and run programs using Sun's JDK, you can be sure your programs will run under any compatible JVM. If you have done previous software development with an integrated development environment (IDE), you may find this adjustment difficult. Many commercial Java IDEs are available, and there are even a few free IDEs (like Sun's Java Workshop product), but they will not be addressed within this text—use them at your own peril.

Do not confuse the JDK with the Java Runtime Environment (JRE). The JRE contains only the virtual machine and supporting code necessary to run (not develop) Java programs. The computer industry has an affinity for ambiguous acronyms, and if you install the JRE instead of the JDK you will find yourself DOA without an SDK.

LAB 1.1 EXERCISES

1.1.1 INSTALL AND CONFIGURE THE JAVA DEVELOPMENT KIT

The latest version of Sun's Java2 JDK can be found on the Web at:

```
http://java.sun.com/products/jdk/1.2/index.html
```

Download the JDK version appropriate for your platform and install it. The Windows version will attempt to install itself into **C:\JDK1.2.x**, where **x** indicates the dot-version of the current JDK. The Solaris version will attempt to install itself into your current working directory.

The JDK documentation, known as the Java API documentation or "Javadocs," can be downloaded from the same Web site. Download the HTML-formatted documentation and install it. The Javadocs are an excellent example of documentation done right, and we will be referring to this documentation throughout the text.

You didn't neglect to install the documentation, did you? Consider it a requirement for learning the language.

As you will shortly discover, Javadocs will become your second-best friend during your forray into the depths of Java. Your best friend, of course, is this interactive workbook!

Once the JDK is installed on your system, you must modify your **PATH** environment variable to include the location of your development tools. For those unfamiliar with the **PATH** variable, it tells your operating system where to look within your filesystem for programs.

ON WINDOWS 95, 98 OR NT . . .

If you are running Windows 95 or 98, you can modify your **PATH** within the **autoexec.bat** file in a manner similar to the following. Be sure to change the **JDK1.2.x** in the following line to match the location where you installed the JDK on your system.

```
PATH=%PATH%;C:\JDK1.2.x\Bin
```

This change will take effect next time you reboot Windows—like that is news to any Windows user.

Users of WindowsNT can make this modification within the Console application available within the Control Panel.

To double-check that your **PATH** modification has been successful, you can input the following from an MS-DOS Prompt window:

```
C:\WINDOWS>path
```

If your **PATH** was modified successfully, you should see the location of the **Bin** subdirectory of your JDK installation, similar to the following:

```
PATH=C:\WINDOWS;C:\WINDOWS\COMMAND;C:\JDK12~1.2\BIN
```

ON SOLARIS, UNIX OR LINUX OS . . .

If your default shell is a Bourne-shell derivative, you can modify your **PATH** similar to the following in your **.profile** file. Modify the **/usr/local/jdk1.2.x/bin** below to reflect the **bin** subdirectory where you installed the JDK.

```
PATH=$PATH:/usr/local/jdk1.2.x/bin
export PATH
```

To double-check your modification, open a new shell and input the following:

```
echo $PATH
```

If the modification was successful, you should see the location of the **bin** subdirectory of your JDK installation, similar to the following:

```
/bin:/usr/bin:/usr/local/bin:/usr/local/jdk1.2.x/bin
```

IF YOU HAVE ALREADY INSTALLED A PREVIOUS VERSION OF THE JDK ON EITHER PLATFORM . . .

Similar to the **PATH** environment variable used by your operating system, Java uses another environment named **CLASSPATH**. The **CLASSPATH** environment variable informs the JVM where it should look for Java program files (classes). If you do not have this defined on your system, don't worry about it. If you do have this defined on your system, be sure to remove an entry for **classes.zip** if it is present—this entry is needed for older Java1.1 releases, but will only confuse matters with Java2. Use the same steps as outlined previously for your **PATH** environment variable.

CONGRATULATIONS!

You have just installed and configured the JDK. Answer the following questions:

From an MS-DOS prompt or UNIX shell, type the following:

```
java -version
```

a) What was displayed?

_____

_____

1.1.2 COMPILE AND RUN A JAVA PROGRAM

Java source code can be written with whatever editor you are most comfortable. On Windows systems this might be notepad, edit, or brief. On UNIX systems this is probably vi, emacs, or pico.

Java source code files adhere to a strict naming convention. This will be discussed in following chapters, but it is important to know that filenames are case-sensitive (*MyApp* is not the same as *myapp*) and all end with a **.java** extension.

Create your first Java program by firing-up your favorite editor and entering the following code exactly as it is written. Save this file as **Welcome.java**:

```
import javax.swing.*;
public class Welcome
{
    public static void main(String[] argv)
    {
        JOptionPane.showMessageDialog(
            null,
            "Welcome to the wonderful world of
Java!",
            "Welcome, new Programmer",
            JOptionPane.PLAIN_MESSAGE);
        System.exit(0);
    }
}
```

Once the file is saved, start up an MS-DOS Prompt or UNIX shell. Navigate to the directory that contains Welcome.java and run the following command:

```
javac Welcome.java
```

a) What were your results from running this command?

Welcome to the wonderful world of Java

Without changing directories, run the following command:

```
java Welcome
```

b) What were your results from running this command?

1.1.3 COMPILE AND RUN A JAVA APPLET

Fire up your favorite editor and create the following file, named **WelcomeApplet.java**:

```
import java.awt.*;
import java.applet.*;
public class WelcomeApplet extends Applet
{
    Label textLabel;
    public void init()
    {
            textLabel = new Label(
                "Welcome to the wonderful world of Java!");
            textLabel.setAlignment(Label.CENTER);
            this.add(textLabel);
    }
}
```

Start an MS-DOS Prompt or UNIX shell and navigate to the directory that contains WelcomeApplet.java. Run the following command:

```
javac WelcomeApplet.java
```

a) What were your results from running this command?

Once again, start an editor and create the following file named **Welcome-Applet.html**:

```
<HTML>
<TITLE>Welcome</TITLE>
<APPLET CODE="WelcomeApplet.class" WIDTH=400
HEIGHT=200>
If you can read this, your browser does not support
Java!
</APPLET>
</HTML>
```

From within the same directory, run the following command:

```
appletviewer WelcomeApplet.html
```

b) What were your results from running this command?

_____

_____

LAB 1.1 EXERCISE ANSWERS

1.1.1 ANSWERS

From an MS-DOS prompt or UNIX shell, type the following:

```
java -version
```

a) What was displayed?

Answer: If everything worked properly, you should have seen output similar to the following:

```
java version "1.2.2"
Classic VM (build JDK-1.2.2-W, native threads,
symcjit)
```

The **java** program is responsible for starting a JVM. The argument **-version** indicates that you are only interested in the version of the JVM, and do not care to run a Java program.

Depending upon the current version of the JDK, you may be running a slightly newer version than shown in the output above. So long as your version string is of the format **1.2.x**, where **x** represents the dot-release of the JDK, you are doing well. If by some chance an older version was displayed, such as **1.0.x** or **1.1.x**, you may have an old version of Java on your system. If you do not wish to remove the old version of Java, you should modify your **PATH** environment variable so that the 1.2 JDK entry is placed before any other JDK entries.

If you received an error message similar to

> **Bad command or file name**

or

> **java: command not found**

your **PATH** environment variable may not be set correctly. Review the Lab and double-check that the JDK bin directory is in your **PATH**.

1.1.2 ANSWERS

Once the file is saved, start up an MS-DOS Prompt or UNIX shell. Navigate to the directory that contains Welcome.java and run the following command:

> **javac Welcome.java**

a) What were your results from running this command?

Answer: If all went well, you should have received no output to your console.

The **javac** program is the Java compiler. It translates source code into Java bytecodes. If the compiler was successful, it translated your **Welcome.java** source code into Java bytecodes and stored them in a new class file named **Welcome.class**.

If you received any error messages from the **javac** command, check the source code to be sure it was input exactly as shown in the Lab. Java is case-sensitive, so be sure you did not mix character cases.

Without changing directories, run the following command:

> **java Welcome**

b) What were your results from running this command?

Answer: You should have been greeted by a popup window that contained the text "Welcome to the wonderful world of Java!".

The **java** command started a JVM that ran the **Welcome** program. This simple program merely created a popup window that contained a friendly welcome message similar to the following:

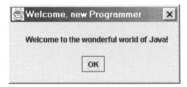

If you received an error from the java command similar to the following:

```
Exception in thread "main" java.lang.NoClass
DefFoundError: Welcome
```

the JVM was unable to locate the **Welcome.class** file. Try running the command again, from the same directory which contains the **Welcome .class** file.

1.1.3 ANSWERS

Start an MS-DOS Prompt or UNIX shell and navigate to the directory which contains WelcomeApplet.java. Run the following command:

```
javac WelcomeApplet.java
```

a)   What were your results from running this command?

Answer: Similar to the previous lab section, you should have received no output if all went well.

If the WelcomeApplet.java source code compiled properly, you received no messages from the Java compiler. If you did receive error messages from the compiler, double-check the source code to be sure it appears exactly as shown within the lab. You don't think *we* made a typo, do you?!

From within the same directory, run the following command:

```
appletviewer WelcomeApplet.html
```

b) What were your results from running this command?

Answer: You should have been greeted by an applet that displayed the text message "Welcome to the wonderful world of Java!"

The **appletviewer** program is included with the JDK as an alternative to running applets within a web browser, and provides an interface that makes testing of applets much less cumbersome than within a web browser.

More importantly, at the time of this writing, neither Netscape Navigator nor Microsoft Internet Explorer include standard support for Java2. For this reason, we will assume throughout the workbook that **appletviewer** will be used to run all the example applets.

If you did not see an applet displayed, check your **WelcomeApplet.html** file to be sure it does not deviate from that which is shown within the Lab. Also, be sure that both the **WelcomeApplet.html** and **Welcome-Applet.class** files exist within the same directory from which you ran **appletviewer**.

What do you mean Java2 is not supported by my browser?!

Relax—in an effort to provide an upgrade to the JVM of your browser, Sun has created a free browser plug-in which allows you to run the JVM of your choice within the web browser.

Check your browser documentation to see if it supports Java2. If it does not, check Sun's Java Plug-In web site for details:

http://java.sun.com/products/plugin

LAB 1.1 SELF-REVIEW QUESTIONS

In order to test your progress, you should be able to answer the following questions.

1) The Java compiler transforms source code into what platform-independent format?
   a) _____ opcodes
   b) _____ bytecodes
   c) _____ virtual machines
   d) _____ applets

**LAB
1.1**

2) What command runs the Java compiler?
   a) _____ java
   b) _____ appletviewer
   c) _____ jdb
   d) _____ javac

3) Which of the following commands is used to run a Java application?
   a) _____ java
   b) _____ appletviewer
   c) _____ jdb
   d) _____ javac

4) Which of the following commands is used to run a Java applet?
   a) _____ java
   b) _____ appletviewer
   c) _____ jdb
   d) _____ javac

5) The freely-available collection of tools which can be used to create Java programs is known as what?
   a) _____ JRE
   b) _____ JDK
   c) _____ JVM
   d) _____ JNI

Quiz answers appear in Appendix A, Section 1.1.

C H A P T E R   1

TEST YOUR THINKING

The purpose of this chapter was just to make sure you could run a Java program. There's not much point in learning a computer language if you can't use it.

1) Since you are going to be programming frequently in this book, we suggest that you setup a "programming environment" for yourself. A programming environment is a configuration of your computer, or computer account, which allows you to write, compile, and run computer programs. We recommend that you setup your login environment to allow you to write, compile, and run Java programs. Once you have successfully completed the labs of this chapter, you should "lock in" that configuration so the next time you login to use your computer, you don't have to worry about the configuration again. This will save you a great deal of time in the future.

C H A P T E R 2

BASIC SYNTAX OF A JAVA PROGRAM

Parts is parts.

Country Wisdom

Previously, you learned how to execute a Java program. Hopefully, this has whet your appetite for creating a Java program of your very own. While this chapter is not intended to cover everything you need to know about creating your own programs, it will introduce the structure of a basic Java program and introduce key concepts essential to understanding Java. When finished with this chapter, you will have a basic understanding of how Java programs are structured and how objects are used as the basis of modeling and solving problems.

This chapter focuses on Java applets, rather than applications. The reasons for this are many, but suffice it to say that the differences between the two are minimal in most circumstances and applets will allow you to do more in less time.

15

L A B   2 . 1

THE STRUCTURE OF A SIMPLE JAVA PROGRAM

LAB OBJECTIVES

After this lab, you will be able to:

- Identify the Components of a Program
- Modify an Already-Written Program

Unless you have been living in a cave for the last few years, you probably know that Java is an *object-oriented* (OO) programming language. If you are already familiar with a *procedural* language such as C or Visual Basic, you may find this concept difficult to understand.

Procedural programs enumerate the steps necessary to solve a problem or perform a task—basically, they are a list of code statements which are executed in order until the program is complete. Object-oriented programs are modeled differently—each part of the problem or task is identified as an object, and the program simply handles the interactions between these objects. The benefits of object-oriented program include the ability to use objects in many different programs because they need not be specific to a single task. This can be a difficult concept to understand at first, and this book only attempts to teach you enough to become productive with basic Java programming. It is highly recommended that you follow this text with a book on object-oriented design.

The best way to learn basic OO concepts is to examine a basic Java applet, which is the focus of this chapter.

THE QUICK INTRODUCTION TO CLASSES

Being object-oriented, Java deals strictly with objects (well, this is about 99-percent true, but good enough for now) and the interactions between them. So, you may ask, how does one create an object in Java? The answer is "with the definition of a *class.*"

A *class* is nothing more than a definition of an object. From this definition, your program can create *instances* of this object as determined by the class itself. Let's take a look at it this way—the class is a blueprint of an object, and your application can then create objects from this blueprint. When a builder plans a community of homes, many homes within the neighborhood share the same floor plan. Think of the various floor plans as classes, and the finished homes as the "realization" of these classes—objects. If the builder were to plan another community of homes, the same blueprints could be used, greatly reducing the amount of time it would take to plan subsequent communities. This introduces one of the many benefits of OO programming — that classes, if properly written, can then be reused in many other applications.

A Java program is nothing more than one or more classes. In turn, each of these classes is comprised of data and operations that can be carried out upon that data. Does this seem too simple? It does not have to be any more complicated of a concept than has just been described, but keep in mind a very fitting phrase from the classic board game *Othello* by Parker Brothers: "An afternoon to learn. A lifetime to master."

■ *FOR EXAMPLE:*

Tradition dictates that the very first program to be analyzed in a programming text must be a "Hello World" program. So as not to break the laws of tradition, and alienate ourselves from the programming community, let's take a look at such an example first.

```
import java.applet.Applet;
public class HelloWorldApplet extends Applet
{
    String myOutput;
    // This is a comment
    public void init()
      {
          myOutput = "Hello World!";
          doOutputMessage();
      }
  /*
```

```
 * This is also a comment.
 */
    public void doOutputMessage()
    {
            System.out.println(myOutput);
    }
}
```

Well, it does not get much simpler than this. This applet is comprised of a single class, named **HelloWorldApplet**. This class describes an object that defines data:

```
String myOutput;
```

and operations that pertain to that data:

```
public void init()
public void doOutputMessage()
```

Even the most complex applet you may encounter follows the same basic principles—definitions of classes, which are nothing more than data and operations that pertain to the data.

If you have not already done so, take the time now to run **Hello-WorldApplet**. Be forewarned that this is not going to be one of the more impressive applets you have experienced in your life, but it does contain the basics upon which we will build. The output from this applet goes to the Java Console of your browser, or to the window from which you invoked *appletviewer*. For simplicity, it is not displayed within the applet itself.

RUN THE PROGRAM

Here is the HTML that can be used to launch the applet:

```
<HTML>
<HEAD>
<TITLE>HelloWorldApplet</TITLE>
</HEAD>
<BODY>
<APPLET CODE="HelloWorldApplet.class"WIDTH=100
HEIGHT=100>
If you can read this, your browser does not support
Java!
</APPLET>
</BODY>
</HTML>
```

Save this to a file named **HelloWorldApplet.html**. You should, by this point, have no difficulties in getting the applet to run. If you encounter difficulties, refer to the previous chapter that discusses this process.

LAB 2.1 EXERCISES

2.1.1   IDENTIFY THE COMPONENTS OF A PROGRAM

a) What is the output from **HelloWorldApplet**?

_____

_____

b) Which line tells the Java compiler where it can find a class that is referenced within the current class?

_____

_____

c) Which line names the class and tells the compiler that the class is an extension of an existing class?

_____

_____

d) Which line defines a variable name that belongs to the class?

_____

_____

e) How many "actions" are defined for this class, and what are the names of those actions?

_____

_____

2.1.2 MODIFY AN ALREADY-WRITTEN PROGRAM

a) Which line would you modify to have the program print "*This is not very exciting*" instead of "*Hello World?*"

_____

_____

b) What modification could you make to have the program print the previous phrase twice?

_____

_____

c) What is another way to have the program print the phrase twice?

_____

_____

d) What modifications would you have to make to change the name of the class from `HelloWorldApplet` to `NotVeryExciting-Applet`?

_____

_____

LAB 2.1 EXERCISE ANSWERS

2.1.1 ANSWERS

a) What is the output from this program?

Answer: The following text should be displayed either within the Java Console of your Web browser or in the terminal window from which you launched the appletviewer:

```
Hello World!
```

The `System.out.println()` statement in the program is responsible for the output to your console. There are many other ways in which we could display the text within the applet itself, but for simplicity we have opted to print only to the console.

If you did not see the output in your console, do not become discouraged. Please re-read the previous chapter and be sure you have a good understanding of how to invoke either the appletviewer or your Web browser in the context of this applet.

b) Which line tells the Java compiler where it can find a class that is referenced within the current class?

Answer: The following line informs the compiler that your class is referencing another class in whole or in part:

```
import java.applet.Applet;
```

This line is called an *import statement* because it informs the compiler that you are referencing external classes. In this instance, we are informing the compiler that we will be using the **java.applet.Applet** class, which provides our class with basic applet functionality.

Alternatively, you could use the following import statement:

```
import java.applet.*;
```

What this statement does is import all of the classes in the java.applet package. The ***** acts as a wildcard character and matches everything, including the **Applet** class.

We will return to the **import** statement later in the book, as it becomes quite important when you are designing your own classes.

c) Which line names the class and tells the compiler that the class is an extension of an existing class?

Answer: The following line provides a name for the class and also tells the compiler that this class is an extension of the basic Applet class:

```
public class HelloWorldApplet extends Applet
```

There is really a lot going on in this line. First, we declare our class as **public,** which simply means that we don't place any restrictions on which other classes can reference this class. Next we name the class **HelloWorldApplet**. Finally, we tell the compiler that this class is an extension of the class named **Applet**. Ultimately, all programs written as applets are an extension of the existing **Applet** class. You needn't worry much about this now, but we will definitely cover this topic in greater detail when we progress to basic object-oriented programming concepts.

d)   Which line defines a variable name that belongs to the class?

Answer: The following line defines a variable that is used within the class:

```
String myOutput;
```

This line simply declares a variable of type **String** that is named **myOutput**. By default, no value is provided for the String; it is set later in the program.

e)   How many "actions" are defined for this class, and what are the names of those actions?

Answer: There are two "actions" defined for this class. They are:

```
public void init()
public void doOutputMessage()
```

All class "actions" are called *methods*. A method is a set of directions that the class knows how to follow. As we described earlier, a class consists of state and of ways to represent or modify that state. Methods allow for the representation or modification of the class state.

The **init** method simply sets a default value to the String variable **myOutput** and then requests that the class represent its state by calling the other method, **doOutputMessage**. The **doOutputMessage** method prints the value of **myOutput** to the console.

Now that we have briefly introduced a basic class, let's take another look at this class and identify all the components. Figure 2.1 labels all of the components of a Java program.

IMPORT STATEMENTS

The import statements are used to inform the Java compiler that you are making use of other classes outside your current class. In our current example, the **HelloWorldApplet** is an applet so we must inform the compiler that we are basing our class on functionality present in the already-defined **Applet** class.

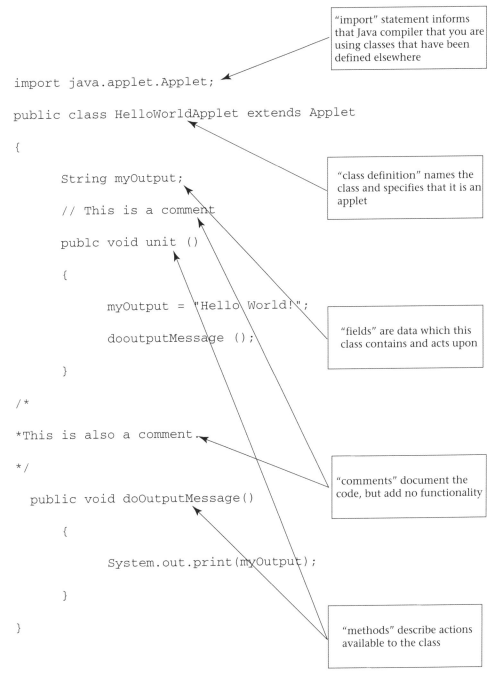

```
import java.applet.Applet;

public class HelloWorldApplet extends Applet

{

        String myOutput;

        // This is a comment

        publc void unit ()

        {

                myOutput = "Hello World!";

                dooutputMessage ();

        }

/*

*This is also a comment.

*/

   public void doOutputMessage()

        {

                System.out.print(myOutput);

        }

}
```

"import" statement informs that Java compiler that you are using classes that have been defined elsewhere

"class definition" names the class and specifies that it is an applet

"fields" are data which this class contains and acts upon

"comments" document the code, but add no functionality

"methods" describe actions available to the class

Figure 2.1 ■ The Components of a Java Program

CLASS DEFINITION

The class definition gives a name to your class. People refer to you by your name every day, and Java classes are no different. In addition, if your class is based upon another class (we will discuss this in much more detail later), the class definition is where you inform the Java compiler. In the current example, **HelloWorldApplet** is an extension of the existing class **Applet**, as are all applets.

FIELDS

Fields are nothing more than data that belong to the class. This data describes the state of your object, and it is upon this data that your methods will operate. In the current example, we have only one field, a String (this is simply text, if you have not figured that out already) named **MyOutput**, which is not initially assigned any value.

METHODS

Methods are actions that your class knows how to perform. These methods are usually used to describe or modify the state of your object, in conjunction with the fields. In our example, we have two methods, **init** and **doOutputMessage**.

COMMENTS

Comments are text that can be inserted into the source code, but do not actually affect the program. Java will ignore comments when it reads the source code file. Comments are used to insert notations into the code to help a human who is reading the code to understand what is going on.

There are two ways of adding a comment:

- **// The double slash comment**
- **/* The slash-star star-slash comment */**

The "double slash" comment is a one-line comment. Everything after the double slash is considered a comment. Java will ignore everything after the double slash up until the last line.

The "slash-star star-slash" comment is a multiline comment. The start of the comment is the **/*** sequence of characters. Java will ignore everything it reads until it gets to the ***/** sequence, which ends the comment.

2.1.2 ANSWERS

a) Which line would you modify to have the program print *This is not very exciting* instead of *Hello World*?

Answer: The following line assigns the value "Hello World!" to the variable myOutput:

```
myOutput = "Hello World!";
```

This line shows a simple assignment of a String value to the variable *myOutput*. To modify the program to output *This is not very exciting,* we need only modify this assignment as follows:

```
myOutput = "This is not very exciting!";
```

If you are still awake following this riveting exercise, please continue on.

b) What modification could you make to have the program print the previous phrase twice?

*Answer: Because the output is performed by the **doOutputMessage** method, calling this method twice would produce the desired result.*

The **doOutputMessage** method does one thing, and one thing only—it prints the value of the variable **myOutput** to the console. Every time it is called, it performs the one and only task that it knows how to accomplish. If you wanted to see the output 10 times (though we can't imagine why), simply call the method 10 times. Though a simplification, this method presents a powerful concept within object-oriented programming; the variable **myOutput** contains state, and the method **doOutputMessage** represents that state. This is enough functionality to be considered an object, though it is of admittedly little use.

c) What is another way to have the program print the phrase twice?

Answer: Instead of calling the method twice, you can simply have the method perform the same task twice.

In the previous question, we determined that calling the **doOutputMessage** method twice would result in the same action being performed twice. However, if your object was designed to always report its state *n* times, it may be preferable to simply modify the method to take the appropriate action *n* times. To always output the value of **myOutput** twice, we can modify **doOutputMessage** in the following manner:

```
public void doOutputMessage()
{
    System.out.println(myOutput);
    System.out.println(myOutput);
}
```

d) What modifications would you have to make to change the name of the class from **HelloWorldApplet** to **NotVeryExcitingApplet**?

Answer: Probably more changes are necessary than you might have suspected. In addition to the obvious change to the class definition, you will also need to rename the file that contains the class. As well, if you expect to see this class function as an applet, you will also need to modify the HTML file that calls the applet.

Let's take a look at the necessary changes. The most obvious change is to the class definition, where you simply need to modify the name of the class from:

```
public class HelloWorldApplet extends Applet
```

to:

```
public class NotVeryExcitingApplet extends Applet
```

What is not so obvious is that the name of the file that defines the Java class must be renamed as well. Java strictly enforces that all classes be defined within a file that is named after the class. In this instance, the class name is **NotVeryExcitingApplet**, so the definition of this class must be contained within a file named **NotVeryExcitingApplet.java**, which is then compiled into a class named **NotVeryExciting-Applet.class**. If you attempted to modify the class name without modifying the name of the file, you probably saw an error from the compiler that looked similar to the following:

```
HelloWorldApplet.java:2: Public class
NotVeryExcitingApplet must be defined in a file
called "NotVeryExcitingApplet.java".
```

Strictly speaking, that is the extent of the modifications that need to be done to the class. However, because this is an applet, you must also modify the HTML file from which this applet is called. Otherwise, the Web browser or appletviewer will not be able to locate the class. So, to finish things off, you should modify the following line in the HTML file from:

```
<APPLET CODE="HelloWorldApplet.class" WIDTH=100
HEIGHT=100>
```

to:

```
<APPLET CODE="NotVeryExcitingApplet.class" WIDTH=100
HEIGHT=100>
```

Now you can sleep easy at night.

LAB 2.1 REVIEW QUESTIONS

In order to test your progress, you should be able to answer the following questions.

1) The blueprint, or definition, of an object is called which of the following?
    a) _____ field
    b) _____ method
    c) __X__ class
    d) _____ applet

2) Data stored within an object are called which of the following?
    a) _____ import statements
    b) _____ blocks
    c) __X__ variables
    d) _____ fields

3) The basic definition of an object is which of the following?
    a) __✔__ A collection of data and operations that can be performed on that data
    b) _____ Any Java program that can be run in a browser or the appletviewer
    c) _____ A collection of files that combine to form a complete application
    d) _____ A class file

4) The purpose of a method is which of the following?
    a) _____ To store data that represents the state of an object
    b) __✓__ To perform operations upon the data of an object
    c) _____ To declare external classes used within the current class definition
    d) _____ To print text messages to the screen or appletviewer console

5) The purpose of a field is which of the following?
    a) __✓__ To store data that represents the state of an object
    b) _____ To perform operations upon the data of an object
    c) _____ To declare external classes used within the current class definition
    d) _____ To print text messages to the screen or appletviewer console

**LAB
2.1**

6) The purpose of an import statement is which of the following?
   a) _____ To store data that represents the state of an object
   b) _____ To perform operations upon the data of an object
   c) ___✓___ To declare external classes used within the current class definition
   d) _____ To print text messages to the screen or appletviewer console

Quiz answers appear in Appendix A, Section 2.1.

LAB 2.2

A BASIC OVERVIEW OF VARIABLES

> ## LAB OBJECTIVES
>
> After this lab, you will be able to:
>
> - Understand Variable Declaration, Assignment, and Scope

After taking a cursory look at a Java program, it's time to delve deeper into the definition of a class and examine the concept of variables. If you already program in another computer language, you may wish to glance this lab or skip it altogether. This lab briefly introduces variables, and successive chapters expand on what is presented here.

As mentioned in the previous lab, a Java *class* defines an object. An object is simply data and operations that manipulate or represent that data. Variables are "holders" of data within a class. Just to confuse things a bit, variables are also referred to as *fields*.

DECLARING VARIABLES

Before variables can be used, your class must define both a variable type and a name for the variable; this is called a *declaration*. In the previous lab, you saw one declaration:

```
String myOutput;
```

Here, a variable type of **String** has been specified with the name **myOutput**. Note the trailing semicolon—no expression in Java is complete without ending in a semicolon. Don't worry about the variable types just yet; they will be discussed in a following chapter.

There are few restrictions on variable names. Variables cannot have the same name as a Java reserved word, and they must begin with an alphabetic character, the *$* or _ characters, or a *Unicode* character that denotes an alphabetic character in any language. Variable names are case sensitive, which means that capitalization counts—the variable names **myValue** and **myvalue** refer to different variables and are not interchangeable. The limit on variable name length is large enough that nobody should exceed the threshold; so for all intents and purposes, it is unlimited.

You can declare a variable at any point within your code, provided that another variable with the same name does not already exist within that block of code. A block of code is simply the space between two curly-braces; a method is considered a block of code, as is the entire class definition. Good programming practice, however, dictates that all variables be declared at the top of the block in which they are used. We'll investigate this a bit later when we tackle *variable scope*.

VARIABLE ASSIGNMENT

After declaring a variable, you should initialize it to a default value. This *assignment* of a value can be done simply with the = operator; the variable name should be on the left of the = sign and the value on the right. Any valid Java expression can be used to set a value.

■ *FOR EXAMPLE:*

Let's declare a few variables. Once again, the variable types are not important right now, only the syntax:

```
String myName;
int _height;
char $middleInitial;
```

Now we can assign values to these variables:

```
myName = "Java Joe";
_height = 71;
$middleInitial = 'J';
```

In fact, we can combine the declaration and assignment onto one line:

```
String favoriteDrink = "Latte";
int _cupsPerDay = 5;
boolean $takes3lumps = true;
```

The leading $ is legal, but not encouraged in Java programs.

VARIABLE SCOPE

Variable *scope* defines where a variable exists, and where it doesn't. When a variable is defined, it is only defined for a certain area, or *scope*. Outside of that scope, the variable does not exist, and you will get an error ("Undefined variable") if you try and access it.

Every variable is valid only within the block of code in which it is declared, and any blocks that are subsequently contained within that block. Outside of that area, the variable does not exist and cannot be referenced. Variable scope is an important feature of object-oriented programming; unlike in many procedural languages, there is no such concept as a *global* variable that has a scope of the entire program. However, it is possible to simulate such a global variable in Java, but you'll have to wait until Chapter 10 before you see that.

■ *FOR EXAMPLE:*

Let's examine variable scope in greater detail. Following is a simple class that contains four variables. You should be able to recognize the scope of each of the variables by identifying within which block they are defined.

```
import java.applet.Applet;
public class scopeTest extends Applet
{
    String myString = "Hello";
    public void init()
    {
        doPrintSomething();
        doPrintSomethingElse();
    }
    public void doPrintSomething()
    {
        String notPrinted;
        notPrinted = "Hi!";
        String localString = "World!";
        System.out.println(myString + " " + localString);
    }
    public void doPrintSomethingElse()
    {
```

```
            String localString = "Everybody!";
        System.out.println(myString + " " + localString);
    }
}
```

The output of this code is as follows:

```
Hello World!
Hello Everybody!
```

The String variable **myString** has scope throughout the class definition, from the point at which it is declared until the end of the block in which it was declared. As you can see, both **doPrintSomething()** and **doPrintSomethingElse()** are within the scope of **myString** and reference the variable. However, the scope of **localString** is restricted to the block in which it is defined. In this case, it is defined once in **doPrintSomething()** and once in **doPrintSomethingElse()**. This may look confusing at first, but it's important to realize that there are *two* separate and distinct variables, both of which are named **localString**. Just because they have the same name, doesn't mean that they are the same variable. They are not. Because each of those methods represents a block of code, the separate variables are visible only within their respective methods.

Likewise, the variable named **notPrinted** in **doPrintSomething()** can only be referenced within that method. If you tried to reference **notPrinted** from **doPrintSomethingElse()**, you would get an error.

Later in this book, we will examine conditional statements; these too can comprise blocks within methods, and thus limit variable scope as well.

LAB 2.2 EXERCISES

2.2.1   UNDERSTAND VARIABLE DECLARATION, ASSIGNMENT, AND SCOPE

a) Which of the following are valid variable names?

```
FirstName
_last_name
<weight>
$height
AGE
1HairColor
hairColor1
```

b) Show the code necessary to declare a variable of type **String** with the name **someString** and assign the value *Hello Everybody* to this variable.

c) If you completed the preceding question with two lines of code, do it in one line of code. If you completed the question in one line of code, break it into two lines of code. Show the modified code.

d) Using the following class, describe the scope of the variables **someVar1**, **someVar2**, and **someVar3**. The syntax may be unfamiliar to you, but do your best to recognize the blocks.

```
import java.applet.Applet;
public class scopeTest2 extends Applet
{
    String someVar1 = "the applet says: ";
    public void doSomethingManyTimes()
    {
        String someVar2 = "Hello!";
        for(int ctr = 0; ctr < 5; ctr++)
        {
            System.out.println(someVar1 + someVar2);
        }
    }
    public void doSomethingOnce()
    {
        String someVar3;
        SomeVar3 = someVar1 + "Heya!";
        System.out.println(someVar3);
    }
}
```

LAB 2.2 EXERCISE ANSWERS

**LAB
2.2**

a)   Which of the following are valid variable names?

Answer: The following variable names are valid.

```
FirstName
_last_name
$height
AGE
hairColor1
```

Recall that variables must begin with either an alphabetic character, the **$** character, or the _ character. For this reason, the examples **<weight>** and **1HairColor** are invalid. Variables may not contain the **<** or **>** characters, nor may they begin with a numeral. Numerals are permitted within names, however. Example: **HairColor1** would be a valid variable name.

b)   Show the code necessary to declare a variable of type String with the name *someString* and assign the value *Hello Everybody* to this variable.

Answer: If we separate the declaration and the assignment, we would have the following code:

```
String someString;
someString = "Hello Everybody";
```

Be sure that each of your lines of code ends with a semicolon, and that the case of the variable name matches as shown. You may have combined these two steps into one line of code. If this is what you have done, check your code against the following answer.

c)   If you completed the preceding question with two lines of code, do it in one line of code. If you completed the question in one line of code, break it into two lines of code. Show the modified code.

Answer: If you combined the declaration and assignment, you should have the following code:

```
String someString = "Hello Everybody!";
```

Be sure that your statement ends with a semicolon and that the case of the variable name matches as shown. You may have split the declaration

```
import java.applet.Applet;

public class scopeTest2 extends Applet

{

        String someVar1 = "the applet says: ";

        public void doSomethingManyTimes()

        {

                String someVar2 = "Hello!";

                for(int ctr = 0; ctr < 5; ctr++)

                {

                        System.out.println(someVar1 + someVar2);

                }

        }

        public void doSomethingOnce()

        {

                String someVar3;

                SomeVar3 = someVar1 + "Heya!";

                System.out.println(someVar3);

        }

}
```

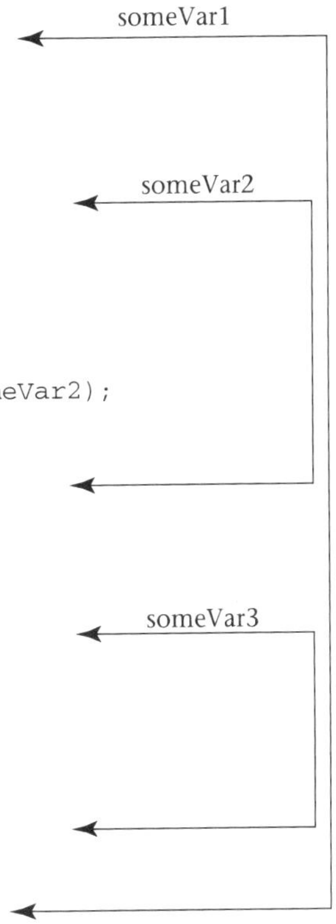

someVar1

someVar2

someVar3

Figure 2.2 ■ Variable Scope

and assignment of the variable onto two separate lines. If this is what you have done, check your code against the previous answer.

Either manner is correct—splitting the declaration and assignment into two lines or combining them into one line. It is very important, however, that you do not attempt to use a variable before it has been assigned an initial value.

LAB 2.2

It is highly recommended that you declare all variables at the top of the enclosing block of code in which they are to be used. This is simply good programming practice, as other programmers can scan the top of each block of code and see what variables are used within. However, the Java compiler does not enforce this convention—you can declare variables wherever you like within a block of code so long as they are initialized before you attempt to use them.

d) Using the following class, describe the scope of the variables **someVar1**, **someVar2**, and **someVar3**. The syntax may be unfamiliar to you, but do your best to recognize the blocks.

*Answer: The scope of variable **someVar1** extends throughout the entire class, including both methods. The scope of **someVar2** is limited to the method **doSomethingManyTimes** but extends within the **for** block within that method. The scope of **someVar3** is limited to the method **doSomethingOnce**.*

Without knowing the entire syntax presented, you should still be able to determine the scope of these variables. By examining the curly braces, you can determine the boundaries of code blocks. Let's take another look at this class and highlight the scope of the variables. Figure 2.2 shows the scope of each variable.

LAB 2.2 REVIEW QUESTIONS

In order to test your progress, you should be able to answer the following questions.

1) Variable names can be comprised of any characters.
    a) _____ True
    b) _____ False

2) Another name for a variable is which of the following?
    a) _____ Function
    b) _____ Method
    c) _____ Field
    d) _____ Modifier

3) Variable declaration and assignment must occur within separate lines of code.
  a) _____ True
  b) _____ False

4) Variable scope is which of the following?
  a) _____ The maximum amount of data that can be stored in a variable
  b) _____ The absolute range of data values that can be stored in a variable
  c) _____ The code contained within any pair of curly braces in a class
  d) _____ The visibility of a variable within or between classes
  e) _____ A way of keeping your variables "minty fresh"

5) A variable can hold any type of data.
  a) _____ True
  b) _____ False

6) Which of the following is true of global variables?
  a) _____ They are technically not supported by the Java language
  b) _____ They are inherently dangerous and should not be used
  c) _____ They are convenient and may be used if necessary
  d) _____ They promote good object-oriented design

Quiz answers appear in Appendix A, Section 2.2.

L A B   2 . 3

A BASIC OVERVIEW OF METHODS

LAB OBJECTIVES

After this lab, you will be able to:

* Understand Method Definitions

To conclude your brief introduction to the structure of basic Java programs, we'll take a look at methods. Methods perform the vital task of "doing things." This may sound ambiguous, but that is purposeful—methods are definitions of what actions your class is able to take, and how those actions are performed. Without methods, your classes would not be able to manipulate or represent state to other classes. The term *function* is a synonym for method, though *method* is the preferred term in object-oriented parlance. Get the lingo straight, and you'll be able to mingle with the OO crowd without problem!

As mentioned in the previous lab, this lab is not expected to be an exhaustive tome encompassing all that is to be known about methods. Rather, they are briefly introduced here and the topic will be expanded upon as the book progresses.

Methods are usually classified into one of three categories:

* *Mutators—methods that accept input to modify internal variables*

* *Accessors—methods that return the value of internal variables*

* *Effectors—methods that perform an action*

Keeping these terms in mind will help you when you begin to design your own classes and methods. Better still, it will make you look like a OO veteran at parties!

DEFINING METHODS

You have already seen quite a few method definitions, so let's take another look at and identify the components of the definition:

```
public void doPrintSomething(String something)
{
    System.err.println(foo);
}
```

The action performed by this method is unimportant right now, so let's concentrate on the line that names the method:

LAB
2.3

```
public void doPrintSomething(String something)
```

This line contains four important parts:

- modifier
- return type
- name
- argument list

The modifier specifies the visibility of this method to other classes. We will discuss this in greater detail as the book progresses. For now, we have used the modifier **public**, which simply means that any other class has permission to call this method.

When an action has been taken by a method, it has the ability to return a value to the caller of the method; this return value is specified in the method definition as the return type. In the method above, no value is returned (this method was designed solely to perform an action, not to report state), so we use the keyword **void** to indicate that no value will be returned to the caller of this method. A return type can be any valid Java class or data type. It is important to note that the return type becomes a pact between the programmer and the Java compiler—if you define a method as returning a certain type, it must return an object of the specified type. If not, the compiler will complain loudly and refuse to compile your class.

The name of the method is fairly straightforward—**doPrintSomething**. This is the name by which the method is known. In Java, it is perfectly acceptable to have many methods that share the same name, so long as the type of arguments specified are unique for each method. Naming is pretty much at the discretion of the programmer, similar to the naming of variables; however, there are additional naming conventions we will discuss later that you may wish to consider.

The argument list specifies what objects must be passed into this method. Callers of the method must provide arguments as specified in the argument list. In the example above, the single argument is a String object that will be available to the method for internal use with the name **something**. As mentioned previously, so long as the argument list differs, you can have several methods that use the same name. The Java compiler is smart enough to determine which method your code wishes to call by examining the *signature* of each method.

When you make a purchase with your credit card, your signature is used to verify that you are whom you purport to be. Java is not so different— each method is identified not solely by name, but by signature. The term *signature* is used to define the name and arguments of a given method. The signature for the method we have been examining would be:

```
public void doPrintSomething(String someString)
```

Amazing—it looks very much like what we have been investigating all along! There is no magic here, folks.

LAB 2.3 EXERCISES

2.3.1 UNDERSTAND METHOD DEFINITIONS

a) Which of the following are valid method names?

```
someMethod
1stStep
Step2
$doThis
get%OfIncome
```

Use the following method to answer the remaining questions:

```
private String getSomeValue()
{
    String someValue = "I Love Java!";
    return(someValue);
}
```

b) What modifier is specified for this method?

_____

_____

c) What is the name of this method?

_____

_____

d) What is the return type of this method?

_____

_____

e) What is the argument list for this method?

_____

_____

f) What is the signature for this method?

_____

_____

2.3.1 ANSWERS

a) Which of the following are valid method names?

Answer: **someMethod, Step2** *and* **$doThis**.

As with variables, method names must begin with an alphabetic character, the **$** character, or the _ character. They may not begin with numer-

als, nor may they contain other non-alphanumeric character other than those just mentioned—many of the non-alphanumeric characters are operators, such as +, -, %, and so forth.

As with variables, the names are case sensitive. The method names **someMethod** and **somemethod** are not equivalent. Java would consider these two different method names.

**LAB
2.3**

b)   What modifier is specified for this method?

*Answer: The modifier for this method is **private**. This means that other classes will not be able to call this method—it is visible internally to that particular class (in fact, to a particular object of that class) and cannot be called by others.*

There are many modifiers for methods; some limit the scope of which other classes or objects can call the method, while others are used by the compiler for optimization. These modifiers will be introduced throughout the book as appropriate to the topics covered.

c)   What is the name of this method?

*Answer: The answer is a no-brainer: **getSomeValue**.*

This is a good time to introduce naming conventions for methods. Though not enforced by the compiler, there are a few naming conventions that may be very worthwhile for you to use when selecting names for your methods.

First, give the method a name that represents what action it performs. This may sound silly, but if you spend enough time looking at other people's code, you will quickly learn that this is not so much of a self-evident truth than you might imagine. For example, you would know the purpose of a method named **incrementCounter** instantly, but not if it was named **cntrOp**.

Another way to help other people understand your code (and sometimes help yourself!) is to insert comments into your code.

Second, begin method names with a lower-case letter, and capitalize letters that demarcate word boundaries. We have done this throughout the chapter—**dosomethinginteresting** is a lot more difficult to read than **doSomethingInteresting**.

Third, if your method is an *accessor* (it exists simply to return a value or object), prefix the name with *get*. An example would be **getCounter-**

`Value` instead of `counterValue`. This becomes important if you wish to program using the *JavaBeans* component model, which is not within the scope of this book.

Fourth, if your method is a *mutator* (it exists simply to set values internal to the class), prefix the name with *set*. An example would be `set-CounterValue` as opposed to `counterValue`. As well, this is another convention that will serve you well if you progress to using *JavaBeans*.

Finally, if your method is an *effector* (it exists simply to perform some task, without returning a value), prefix the name with *do*. An example would be `doStartTimer` instead of `startTimer`. This is simply a matter of preference, but the authors have found this convention very helpful.

LAB 2.3

d) What is the return type of this method?

> *Answer: This method returns a **String** to the caller.*

When this method is called, the caller will be returned a `String` object. Remember, this is a pact that you make with the compiler—if you say you will return a `String` object, then you must do so.

e) What is the argument list for this method?

> *Answer: This was a feeble attempt at tricking you, although you probably saw right through it. This method does not take any arguments.*

A method does not need to take arguments. If no arguments are needed, the argument list within the parentheses should be empty. If, on the other hand, the method takes multiple arguments, they should be listed within the parentheses delimited by commas.

The signature for a method that takes two `String` objects as arguments would look like the following:

```
public void doPrintAFewThings(String stringOne,
String stringTwo)
```

Realistically, there is no limit to the number of arguments you can specify in a method definition. However, if you consistently define methods that take a lot of arguments, you may wish to reconsider the design of your methods and of the entire class.

f) What is the signature for this method?

> *Answer: The method signature is as follows:*

```
private String getSomeValue()
```

Remember that the method signature is merely a convenience for relaying the important information about a method. It is common practice to have more than one method with the same name that takes different arguments to perform the same task. The compiler consults the signature of each method to determine which one is used when a method by that name is called. Many other languages do not have this feature, and you cannot have many methods that share the same name regardless of the argument list. Thank goodness for Java!

LAB 2.3

LAB 2.3 REVIEW QUESTIONS

In order to test your progress, you should be able to answer the following questions.

1) A method that returns the value of an internal variable can be classified as which of the following?
   a) _____ An accessor method
   b) _____ A mutator method
   c) _____ An effector method
   d) _____ An internal method

2) A method that exists to modify the value of an internal variable can be classified as which of the following?
   a) _____ An accessor method
   b) _____ A mutator method
   c) _____ An effector method
   d) _____ An internal method

3) A method that exists to perform an action can be classified as which of the following?
   a) _____ An accessor method
   b) _____ A mutator method
   c) _____ An effector method
   d) _____ An internal method

4) Multiple methods with the same name can be defined if which of the following is true?
   a) _____ The return type is different for each method
   b) _____ The argument list is different for each method
   c) _____ The modifier is different for each method
   d) _____ Pigs fly—you simply can't do that!

5) Which of the following is true of method naming conventions?

a) _____ They are strictly enforced by the compiler

b) _____ They are optional, but highly recommended

c) _____ They allow the compiler to optimize your code

d) _____ They dictate that all methods should begin with an upper-case letter

6) Which of the following statements is true?

a) _____ Modifiers change the return value of a method

b) _____ `void` is an example of a Modifier

c) _____ Multiple modifiers can be used with a single method

d) _____ Modifiers can be used to limit access to a method

Quiz answers appear in Appendix A, Section 2.3.

LAB
2.3

C H A P T E R   2

TEST YOUR THINKING

If you haven't already done so, please visit the Web site for this book. It contains additional material and information. You will also find the code used in this book, both in the examples and in the exercises.

The Web page for this book can be found at the following location:

`http://www.phptr.com/phptrinteractive`

1) Go to the Web site and download the source code to the **`Thinking2-1.java`** program. Modify this program to print your own name instead of the "John Smith" name.

2) Modify your program from question 1 to print your name five times.

3) Add comments to any of your programs.

CHAPTER 3

DATA TYPES

"You're not my type."

Every woman who has rejected the authors

CHAPTER OBJECTIVES

In this chapter, you will learn about:

There are two primary parts to a computer program: the *instructions* and the *data*. This chapter is all about data (the next will be about instructions). To a computer, the world is just data and nothing more. It is our jobs as programmers to represent the real world as structured data. Data means information, and in Java there are many different kinds of information. Java organizes all data into different categories, or *types*. Whenever you define a variable in Java, you need to define its type, that is, the type of information that is being stored in this variable.

Before discussing how Java operates, let's look at how we store information in our everyday lives. A piece of information (data) could be either a *number* or a *word*, or even a *picture* or a tape *recording*. In these cases, *number*, *word*, *picture*, or *recording* would all be considered different types of data. Java takes this concept and goes even further. There are hundreds of Java data types, but this chapter will introduce you to the basic data types and show you how to use them. In later chapters, we will see other types and even learn how to make our own data types.

47

L A B   3 . 1

PRIMITIVE DATA TYPES

LAB OBJECTIVES

After this lab, you will be able to:

- Use Primitive Data Types
- Convert Between Data Types

Just as atoms are the building blocks of the entire universe, primitive data types are the fundamental building blocks of all other data types in Java. We've said that Java is an object-oriented programming language and that everything in Java is an object. Well, we lied. Everything is an object, except for the primitive data types. None of the types covered in this lab is an object. This means that primitive data types have a value that you can *set* or *get,* but these variables do not have *fields* or *methods* like an object has. Primitive variables would just be considered "normal" variables in other languages such as C, Basic, Fortran, Cobol, and Pascal.

SUMMARY OF PRIMITIVE DATA TYPES

Table 3.1 is a complete list of all primitive data types. We will not be discussing all of them in this chapter, just the most common ones, which are in **bold** type. If you have programmed before then Table 3.1 is probably all you need and you can skip this lab. If the concepts of *variables* and *types* are new to you, then keep reading!

THE int DATA TYPE

We've seen the **int** data type in the previous lab on variables, and we said that an **int** is just a number. Officially, the **int** data type represents an *integer,* or whole number. Integers are also called "counting numbers" because they are the numbers we count with: 1, 2, 3, 4, and so on. Integers can also be negative numbers like –3, –10, and –100. However, integers cannot be decimal numbers like 2.3 or 3.14. Decimal numbers are another type that we will cover later.

Table 3.1 ■ Summary of Primitive Data Types

Type	Meaning	Description	Examples
byte	8-bit integer	Any whole number	0, 1, 2, 3, ...
short	16-bit integer	Any whole number	-2, 0, 1, 2, 3, ...
int	32-bit integer	Any whole number	-2, 0, 1, 2, 3, ...
long	64-bit integer	Any whole number	-2, 0, 1, 2, 3, ...
float	single-precision floating point number	Any decimal number	4.21, 3.141592
double	double-precision floating point number	Any decimal number	4.21, 3.141592
char	16-bit Unicode character	Any keyboard character	'a', 'k', '%', '?'
boolean	Boolean	True or false	true, false

Let's look at some examples of using the **int** data type. We will also re-visit some of the concepts of using variables because they may make a little more sense now.

■ *FOR EXAMPLE:*

Here is how we define and use an **int** variable:

```
int x;
x = 5;
System.out.println(x);
```

This yields the following output:

```
5
```

We have done three things here. First, we *defined* the variable **x** as an **int**. Next, we *assigned* **x** the value of **5** using the = (*equals*) symbol. Last, we *used* the value of **x**. The **System.out.println()** command gets the value of **x**, which is 5, and then prints it to the screen.

The value 5 (and any other number) is called a *constant*. A *constant* is just a value that never changes, as opposed to a *variable* whose value can

**LAB
3.1**

change. Variable **x** can be assigned the value of any integer number because **x** is of type **int**.

■ *FOR EXAMPLE:*

The following code shows how you can define and assign a variable at
the same time.

```
int x = 5;
System.out.println(x);
```

This will print the following:

```
5
```

This example is functionally the same as the previous example. The only
difference is that we assigned the value to **x** at the same time we defined
it. This is just a convenient feature of Java. We will be using the "define
and assign" style more in this book just in the interest of space.

■ *FOR EXAMPLE:*

We will now update the value of **x** and see what happens.

```
int x = 5;
System.out.println(x);
x = 5 + 20;
System.out.println(x);
```

This will print the following:

```
5
25
```

There are two things to notice in this example. First, notice that the value
of **x** can change. The **System.out.println(x)** command is the same
both times but since the value of **x** has changed, so did the output. Second, notice that the right-hand side of the second assignment expression
is an equation. Java adds 5 and 20 to get 25 and then assigns the value 25
to **x**.

THE float DATA TYPE

Whereas **int** variables store integers, variables of type **float** store *float-
ing*-point numbers, or decimal numbers. Examples would be numbers like
2.21 and 0.1234. For example, if you need a variable to represent the

price of something, then **float** is the type to use. Using a float variable is just like using an **int**, except that the constant values can have a decimal point.

■ FOR EXAMPLE:

The following example will print the total price of five movie tickets that cost $7.25 each.

```
float price = (float) 7.25 * 5;
System.out.println(price);
```

The output is as follows:

> **36.25**

The way to do multiplication in Java is with the ***** symbol (called *star*). Use the *star* where you would normally use an **x** to multiply two numbers together.

We could bore you with more **float** examples, but we won't. In the real world, you may never actually use a **float**. Instead you would use the **double** type that will be discussed next. Later, we will also explain why you need to put the word **(float)** before the **7.25**.

THE double DATA TYPE

The **double** data type is exactly like the **float** data type, that is, a floating-point number. The only difference is that a **double** uses twice the computer memory to represent a number than a **float** does. The name **double** comes from "double-precision, floating-point number." If you don't know what that means, then you probably don't care. In fact, even if you *do* know what that means, you probably don't care. Read the sidebar if you really want to know more.

■ FOR EXAMPLE:

The following example will add 7/9ths and 2/9ths.

```
double val1 = 7.0 / 9.0;
double val2 = 2.0 / 9.0;
double val3 = val1 + val2;
System.out.println(val1);
System.out.println(val2);
System.out.println(val3);
```

The Whole Truth about `doubles` and `floats`

Deep inside the computer, all numbers are represented by a series of bits (values of 0 or 1). For integers, this is a straightforward representation. However, for floating-point numbers, it gets a little more complicated. If a number is very long (not necessarily big, just long), it takes more and more bits to represent the number accurately. For example, the decimal equivalent of 1/9 is 0.11111111111... with the 1s repeating forever. It is technically impossible to represent that number *exactly*, but we can get very close. The **double** type uses twice as many bits to represent a number than a **float** does so the **double** type is more accurate.

By default, all floating-point numbers in Java are **double** types. In the previous section on the **float** type, we had to put the word **(float)** in front of the number **7.25** or else we would get an error when we compiled the program. The reason for this is that **7.25** is actually a **double,** and we need to convert it into a **float** for use in a **float** variable. Converting data types is called *casting*. Most of the time, Java does the casting for us, but not in this case. As we mentioned before, most people always use **double** variables and never use **float** variables because you don't have to worry about casting your results since everything is already a **double**. We will discuss more on casting in the last section of this lab.

The output is as follows:

```
0.777777777777778
0.222222222222222
1.0
```

Notice that we don't have to cast any of the results to **double** like we did with the **float** type. This is because floating-point math operations yield **double** results by default.

Because the use of **double** is the same as **float**, we put in a few new things to make this example more interesting. The first is to show that you use the / (*slash*) to divide in Java. The second (and more important) thing to notice is that we can use variables in our assignment expression. **val3** is assigned the value of **val1** plus **val2**. This practice is quite common, if not unavoidable, in any programming language. Almost all data is represented by variables, and variables are usually defined in terms of other variables.

SUMMARY OF MATHEMATICAL OPERATORS

We're going to take a small break from defining the data types to summarize the mathematical operators we introduced here. One of the primary purposes of a computer program is to do mathematical computations (it might also explain where the word *computer* came from). Table 3.2 summarizes the basic operators that Java provides. Except where noted, these operators work on all of the *number* types that we just covered.

We now return you to your normal programming.

THE char DATA TYPE

Up until now, all of our data have been numbers. The **char** data type is used to represent letters, also called *characters*. A variable of type **char** represents a single letter, and by "letter" we mean any character that you can type on your keyboard. This includes characters like "@" and "$" and even "5". Yes, the character "5" is different from the number 5. The technical term for a **char** is *alphanumeric character*.

■ *FOR EXAMPLE:*

Here is how we define and use a **char** variable:

```
char letter = 'a';
System.out.println(letter);
```

This yields the following output:

```
a
```

Table 3.2 ■ Summary of Mathematical Operators

Operator	Meaning	Example	Remarks
+	plus	`op1 + op2`	Adds op1 and op2
-	minus	`op1 - op2`	Subtracts op2 from op1
*	multiply	`op1 * op2`	Multiplies op1 and op2
/	divide	`op1 / op2`	Divides op1 by op2
%	modulo	`op1 % op2`	Remainder of dividing op1 by op2. Only works with **int** type.

All **char** constants must have the single quotes around them. This is to distinguish them from variables and numbers. By themselves, **char** variables are not very interesting. You can't do math on a **char**. However, they are part of a larger and more interesting object, called **String**, which we will see in the next lab.

THE boolean DATA TYPE

In the world of Java, the word *boolean* means "true or false." Perhaps then it won't be too surprising to learn that a variable of type **boolean** can only have two possible values: **true** or **false**. By the way, **boolean** is pronounced *BOOL-ee-ann*. If you were to say "boo-LEAN" to someone, he or she might think you were talking about a new, spooky weight-loss program.

■ *FOR EXAMPLE:*

Here is how we define and use a **boolean** variable:

```
boolean value = true;
System.out.println(value);
```

This yields the following output:

true

When assigning a **boolean** variable, you can only use **true** or **false**. Do not use any quotes! The word "true" is different from the *keyword* **true**. The **println()** command knows how to print the value of a **boolean** variable.

CONVERTING BETWEEN DATA TYPES

In your programming journeys, you may find the need to combine several different data types together. You have already seen a case where we had to convert (*cast*) a **double** into a **float**. The most common need for

---

The Whole Truth about *boolean*

The word *boolean* does not actually mean "true or false," although it has started to take on that meaning. The word is really *Boolean* and comes from mathematician George Boole. The mathematical ideas he developed are *Boolean* ideas. Among these ideas are Set Theory and how objects with only two possible values can be combined. We will actually explore some Boolean math later in the book.

conversion is between the number types, such as converting an **int** into a **float.** In some cases, Java will do this automatically, but there are times when you will need to do it yourself.

■ *FOR EXAMPLE:*

Let's say we want to put the value of an **int** into a **float**. First, let's look at the **incorrect** way of doing this. The following example is wrong:

```
int apples = 10;
float oranges = apples;
```

Java will complain about the preceding code because the two variables are of different types (you are comparing apples to oranges). Here is the correct way of converting an **int** into a **float**.

```
int apples = 10;
float oranges = (float) apples;
```

Variable **oranges** will now have the value of 10.0. This process of converting a value is called *casting*. We *cast* the value of **apples** to a **float**. The concept of casting will be very important in the future.

LAB 3.1 EXERCISES

3.1.1 USE PRIMITIVE DATA TYPES

a) What is the output of the following code?

```
int i = 10;
System.out.println(i);
i = 15;
System.out.println(i);
```

_____

_____

b) What are the two mistakes in the following code?

```
int i;
System.out.println(i);
```

```
int i = 15;
System.out.println(i);
```

c) Is there anything wrong with the following code?

```
double x = 15.0;
x = x * 10;
System.out.println(x);
```

d) Assume you have two **int** variables named **mulder** and **scully**. Write code to swap their values with each other.

3.1.1 CONVERTING BETWEEN DATA TYPES

Using the following code for the next question:

```
double almostFour = 3.99999999;
int intAlmostFour = (int) pi;
```

a) What is the value of **intPi**?

b) Write code to print out a baseball player's batting average (the number of hits divided by the number of batting attempts).

c) Run your code from question d. Did you get the results that you expected?

_____

_____

LAB 3.1 EXERCISE ANSWERS

3.1.1 ANSWERS

a) What is the output of the following code?

```
int i = 10;
System.out.println(i);
i = 15;
System.out.println(i);
```

Answer: The output is as follows:

```
10
15
```

You only need to define a variable once. However, you can assign and reference it any number of times, as this program does.

b) What are the two mistakes in the following code?

```
int i;
System.out.println(i);
int i = 15;
System.out.println(i);
```

*Answer: Mistake #1 is using the variable **i** before it has a value. Mistake #2 is defining variable **i** a second time.*

If you don't assign a value to a variable before you use it, then the variable is considered "undefined." This is bad, and Java will give you an error when you compile the program. Some other programming languages don't care and will let you make this kind of mistake (called *shooting yourself in the foot*). Other languages have default values like *zero* or *null* that get assigned to undefined variables (called *getting unexpected results at the worst possible time*). Java, however, is very strict and will not let you make this kind of mistake. Think of Java as that strict, but loving, parent who is just trying to protect you.

The second mistake, redefining *i*, is a common mistake that people make, especially if they use the *cut & paste* feature of their editor. Again, Java will catch this error for you, but you still need to know what is wrong so you can fix it.

c)   Is there anything wrong with the following code?

```
double x = 15.0;
x = x * 10;
System.out.println(x);
```

*Answer: Nope, nothing is wrong. **x** is first assigned the value of 15.0. Then **x** is given a new value of 150.0 (15.0 * 10).*

First of all, an expression like **LHS = RHS** is always an *assignment statement*. We are assigning the value of the right-hand side (**RHS**) to the left-hand side (**LHS**). The LHS is always a variable, no exceptions. The RHS, however, can be any expression that results in the same type as the LHS variable. The entire RHS expression is evaluated first, and then assigned to the LHS.

Looking at the code from this question, Java first looks at the right side. **x** has the value 15.0, so 15.0 * 10 is 150.0. The new value of 150.0 replaces the old value of **x**. At this point, the old value of **x** (15.0) is lost, and we can't get it back.

d)   Assume you have two **int** variables named **mulder** and **scully**. Write code to swap their values with each other.

Answer: The following code will switch the values.

```
int mulder = 10;
int scully = 15;
System.out.println(mulder);
System.out.println(scully);
int tmp = scully;
scully = mulder;
mulder = tmp;
System.out.println(mulder);
System.out.println(scully);
```

The output of this code follows:

```
10
15
15
10
```

To successfully swap the values, we need a third variable to act as a temporary holding area. The following code is wrong!

```
mulder = scully;
scully = mulder;
```

If we try to switch the code in this manner, we don't actually switch the values of the two variables. Instead, we end up with both variables having the same value (15, the original value of **scully**). Additionally, we lose the value originally contained in **mulder**.

3.1.2 ANSWERS

a) What is the value of **intPi**?

Answer: 3

When we cast the value of a **double** (or **float**) into an **int**, the new value is *truncated,* not rounded.

b) Write code to print out a baseball player's batting average (the number of hits divided by the number of batting attempts).

Answer: The following code is one example:

```
int hits = 40;
int atBats = 100;
double battingAverage = (double) hits / (double) atBats;
System.out.println(battingAverage);
```

The output of this code is as follows:

```
0.4
```

Baseball purists would say the output should be **.400**. However, *mathematically* the output is correct. Batting averages are always a number less than 1.0 since you can't have more *hits* than *at bats*. What is important to learn here is that if you need to get a floating-point result from two **int** values, you need to cast the two **int** values to **double** values first (or **float**). If you don't do the casting, then the division result would be an **int,** and the result would be truncated. The **0.4** result would be truncated to **0**, which is not what you want.

c) Run your code from question d. Did you get the results that you expected?

Answer: We can't tell you how your code did, but we can anticipate a mistake that you may have made. If your output is always 0, regardless of the input, then read the answer to question d for a possible explanation.

When you divide an **int** by an **int**, the result is going to be an **int**. Since **int** values can only be whole numbers, any value that is between 0 and 1 is going to be truncated to 0. By casting the **int** values to **double**, the result is now a **double**.

LAB 3.1 SELF-REVIEW QUESTIONS

In order to test your progress, you should be able to answer the following questions.

1) Which data type(s) can store the value 1.75? Check all that apply
 a) _____ int
 b) _____ boolean
 c) _____ char
 d) _____ float
 e) _____ double

2) Which data type(s) can store the value 10? Check all that apply
 a) _____ int
 b) _____ boolean
 c) _____ char
 d) _____ float
 e) _____ double

3) Which data type would you use to store a stock-market price?
 a) _____ int
 b) _____ boolean
 c) _____ char
 d) _____ float
 e) _____ double

4) Which data type would you use to store the value of π (pi)?
   a) _____ int
   b) _____ boolean
   c) _____ char
   d) _____ float
   e) _____ double

5) Which of the following are legal values for a **char**? Check all that apply.
   a) _____ A
   b) _____ 'A'
   c) _____ 5
   d) _____ '5'
   e) _____ **None of the above**

6) Which of the following are legal values for a **boolean**? Check all that apply.
   a) _____ true
   b) _____ false
   c) _____ 'true'
   d) _____ 0
   e) _____ 1

7) What is the value of the following statement:

   ```
   (int) 9.9;
   ```

   a) _____ 9
   b) _____ 10
   c) _____ 9.9
   d) _____ an error

Quiz answers appear in Appendix A, Section 3.1.

L A B 3 . 2

THE STRING CLASS

LAB OBJECTIVES

After this lab, you will be able to:

• Use the String Class

In this lab, we will learn about the **String** class. Starting with this lab, all of the data types covered will be objects. Since these types are objects, it is more accurate to call them *classes* instead of *types*. Remember that a *class* is a description of an object just like blueprints are a description of a house. You can build many houses from a single set of blueprints. The blueprints would be the *class* definition, and the houses would be the constructed objects (another word for constructed is *instantiated*). The primitive types have no such class description. They just exist as the basic building blocks of Java.

THE STRING CLASS

When we introduced the **char** type, we said that you would have to wait until the **String** Section before you could store words in a variable. Well, your wait is over! The **String** class is here. **String** comes from the term character string, because when you create words and sentences, you *string* together a bunch of *characters*.

CONSTRUCTING STRINGS

The first thing we need to do is build a **String**. There are actually two ways of constructing a new **String.**

■ *FOR EXAMPLE:*

This example will demonstrate the two ways of constructing a **String**.

```
String firstName = "George";
String lastName = new String("Washington");
```

```
System.out.println(firstName);
System.out.println(lastName);
```

We cannot tell a lie. This prints the following output:

```
George
Washington
```

In the preceding code, we constructed two **String** variables called **firstName** and **lastName** with the values "George" and "Washington," respectively. Each variable was constructed using a different method of building a **String.**

Strings are special in that there are two ways of constructing a **String**. Every other object only has one way (as we'll see). The "George" line in the preceding example shows the most common way **Strings** are created. To create a **String**, just place double quotes around your text and you have a **String**. This is what you did in Chapter 1 when you compiled and ran your "Hello World" program.

The second line ("Washington") shows the actual **String** constructor. The normal way of constructing an object is with the **new** operator. Every other object, besides **String**, must be constructed using the **new** operator. That is, either of the two following forms:

```
Class variableName = new Class();
Class variableName = new Class(parameters);
```

You would replace *Class* with the object's class name. A *parameter* is information that you give to a new class to help it build the object. In the preceding example, the *parameter* is **"Washington"** since that information is needed to construct the **String.** There can be more than one parameter passed into the constructor, but we will see that later.

COMBINING STRINGS

It is also possible to build a **String** from two or more other **Strings**. In technical terms, this is called *concatenation,* but all it really means is joining multiple **Strings** together to make another **String**.

■ FOR EXAMPLE:

Let's extend the previous example by adding the following code:

```
String fullName = firstName + lastName;
System.out.println(fullName);
```

This additional code would print the following:

```
GeorgeWashington
```

In this example, it looks like we are adding two variables together. In essence, that is exactly what we are doing. However, we are not adding them mathematically, we are adding **lastName** to the end of **firstName.** The result is a new **String** ("GeorgeWashington") which is assigned to **fullName**.

Note that there is no space between *George* and *Washington.* The concatenation of Strings is very literal; you only get out what you put in. Think of it as Java Karma.

■ *FOR EXAMPLE:*

Now let's fix that missing space problem. Add the following code to the previous example. This will add a space between the two names.

```
fullName = firstName + " " + lastName;
System.out.println(fullName);
```

The new and improved output is as follows:

```
George Washington
```

Just as you can add three numbers together, you can also add three (or more) **Strings** together. We just inserted a space between the two variables.

STRING METHODS

Now that we have a **String,** what can we do with it? In the *Introduction to Objects* section, we said objects have both *data* and *methods* associated with them. The *data* part of a **String** object is the text (like "George"). The *methods* for a **String** give us more information about the data in the **String.** If you have programmed before, then a *method* is analogous to a *subroutine* or a *function.*

THE LENGTH METHOD

The first method we will look at is the **length()** method. It will tell us how long a **String** is.

■ *FOR EXAMPLE:*

The following code will give us the length of a **String**.

```
String title = "Get Rich Quick by Writing Java Books";
int len = title.length();
System.out.println(len);
```

This yields the following output:

```
36
```

The **length()** method will return the *length* of its **String**. If you count the letters (including the spaces) in **title**, you should find that there are 36 characters in it. Note that the length value is returned as an **int** so we need an **int** variable to hold the result.

The Application Programming Interface (API) definition of the **length()** method:

```
public int length()
```

Let's look at how to interpret this definition. For now, ignore the word *public*. It just means that everyone has access to the method (public access). The **int** means that this method returns an **int** value. The name of the method is *length*, and the empty set of parentheses means that this method does not take any parameters.

THE INDEX OF METHOD

Every character in a **String** has a position, or *index*, in that **String**. For example, when you go to the opera (and we know you do!), you are given an assigned seat like *Row 24, Seat 15*. In a **String**, every character's *index* is its assigned "seat." The first character in a **String** has *index* 0, the second character has *index* 1, and so on. It is important to realize that the index values start at *zero*.

Figure 3.1 shows a **String** and the *index of* each character in that **String**.

Let's say that we want to find a word within a **String**. To do this, we can use the **indexOf()** method. It will give us the *index of* the word we are looking for.

■ *FOR EXAMPLE:*

The following code will find the word "Rich" in the title of our next book.

```
String title = "Get Rich Quick by Writing Java Books";
int index = title.indexOf("Rich");
System.out.println(index);
```

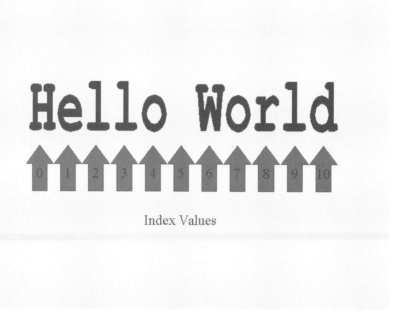

Index Values

Figure 3.1 ■ Diagram of a String index.

This yields the following output:

4

The index of "Rich" is 4 because the word "Rich" starts at index 4 of **title**. Notice that we passed in the word "Rich" as a parameter to **indexOf()**. We needed to tell the method what to look for, and the way to do that is by passing in a parameter.

The definition of the **indexOf()** method:

```
public int indexOf(String findMe)
```

THE SUBSTRING METHOD

A *substring* is part of a **String**. In the previous example, "Rich" was a *substring* of **title**. If we want to access a *substring* of a **String**, we can use the **substring()** method.

■ *FOR EXAMPLE:*

Let's take our previous example and split the value of **title** into its first half and its second half. The following code will split **title** into two new **String** values.

```
String title = "Get Rich Quick by Writing Java
Books";
String firstHalf = title.substring(0, 18);
String lastHalf = title.substring(18);
System.out.println(firstHalf);
System.out.println(lastHalf);
```

This prints the following output:

```
Get Rich Quick by
Writing Java Books
```

The **substring()** method has two forms, one that takes one parameter and a second that takes two parameters. Let's start with the two-parameter version.

First of all, whenever a method takes more than one parameter, we must separate them with commas. The two parameters in this case are the *starting* and *ending* indices of the substring. In the preceding example, **firstHalf** is the substring between index 0 and index 18. The result is the **String** "Get Rich Quick by " (note the space at the end).

Now let's look at the single-parameter version of **substring()**. To get the value of **lastHalf,** we only pass in the index of the middle character (18). When there is only one index parameter, **substring()** will return everything from that index to the end of the **String**. In the preceding example, **lastHalf** is the substring of **title**, starting at index 18, and ending at the last character of **title**.

The definitions of the **substring()** methods:

```
public String substring(int startIndex)
public String substring(int startIndex, int endIndex)
```

Note that the parameters are **int** values and the return value is a **String**.

SUMMARY OF STRING METHODS

Here is a quick summary of the **string** methods covered in this lab:

```
public int length()
public int indexOf(String findMe)
public String substring(int startIndex)
public String substring(int startIndex, int endIndex)
```

There are many more **String** methods that we did not cover. To see all of the methods available for the **String** class, and any other Java class, you can view the Javadoc Web pages that might have come with your Java Developer's Kit (JDK). These Web pages are also available from Sun Microsystems at the following URL:

**LAB
3.2**

```
http://java.sun.com
```

You will want to find the API for the version of Java you are using.

LAB 3.2 EXERCISES

3.2.1   THE STRING CLASS

a) Write code that defines a **String** variable **name** and assigns it the value "Rochelle".

_____

_____

b) Using the **String** from Question a, write code that has output like the following:

Hello, my name is Rochelle.

_____

_____

c) Given the following code:

```
String str1 = "The quick brown fox";
String str2 = "jumped over";
String str3 = "the lazy dogs.";
```

Write additional code that has the following output:

**Length of 'The quick brown fox' is 19
Length of 'jumped over' is 11
Length of 'the lazy dogs.' is 14**

_____

_____

Use the following code for the next three questions:

```
String force = "Use the force, Luke!";
String key = "Luke";
int index = force.indexOf(key);
System.out.println("Found key at " + index);
```

d) What is the output of this code?

_____

_____

e) If we change the value of **key** to "Leia", what is the output?

_____

_____

f) Write code that uses the **substring()** method to extract the word "Luke" from the **force** variable.

_____

_____

g) Can you write another solution to question f that does not use any *fixed* values like **15** and **19**?

_____

_____

LAB 3.2 EXERCISE ANSWERS

3.2.1 ANSWERS

a) Write code that defines a **String** variable **name** and assigns it the value "Rochelle".

*Answer: The following code shows two ways of defining a **String**.*

```
String name = "Rochelle";
String name = new String("Rochelle");
```

Both of these constructors will create a new **String.** The first method is really just a shortcut that Java allows us to do. The fact is that Java actually does the "new String" command for us. **String** is the only class that has a shortcut like this, so don't get spoiled!

b) Using the **String** from question a, write code that has output like the following:

Hello, my name is Rochelle.

Answer: This code will work:

```
String name = new String("Rochelle");
System.out.println("Hello, my name is " + name);
```

Remember that we can construct a new **String** by joining two **Strings** together. Note that there is a space between the word *is* and the closing quote mark. This is to make sure that there is a space before *Rochelle* in the output.

c) Given code […] write additional code that has the following output:

Length of 'The quick brown fox' is 19
Length of 'jumped over' is 11
Length of 'the lazy dogs.' is 14

Answer: The following code will work:

```
String str1 = "The quick brown fox";
String str2 = "jumped over";
String str3 = "the lazy dogs.";
int len = str1.length();
System.out.println("Length of '" + str1 + "' is " + len);
len = str2.length();
System.out.println("Length of '" + str2 + "' is " + len);
len = str3.length();
System.out.println("Length of '" + str3 + "' is " + len);
```

Again, we are using concatenation to join several **Strings** into one **String** for printing. This time we are also setting the **len** variable to the length of each **String** before printing the value.

Since Java requires the use of the double quote to delimit a String, we put single quotes in our String to avoid the conflict. However, it is possible to have double quote characters in a String. What you need to do is put a backslash (\) before the double quote. The backslash character is a special character that tells Java to accept the next character as part of the String.

This code:

```
String hasQuotes = "\"quoted text\"";
System.out.println(hasQuotes);
```

Has this output:

"quoted text"

Use the following code for the next three questions

```
String force = "Use the force, Luke!";
String key = "Luke";
int index = force.indexOf(key);
System.out.println("Found key at " + index);
```

d) What is the output of this code?

Answer: The output is as follows:

Found key at 15

The index of **key** is 15 because the word "Luke" starts at index 15 in the **force** variable. Remember that the first character of a **String** has an index position of 0.

e) If we change the value of **key** to "Leia", what is the output?

Answer: The output is as follows:

Found key at –1

Okay, what happened here? First of all, we hope you noticed that the word *Leia* does not appear in the **force**. Since there is no index value for *Leia*, the **indexOf()** method returns the value **–1** to signify a "not found" response. If you read the Javadoc definition for **indexOf()**, it will tell you this.

Any method that returns a value may also return an *error value* if it can't give you what you asked for. We will cover error handling in a later chapter, but it is important to realize that you don't always get what you ask for. Such is life.

f) Write code that uses the **substring()** method to extract the word "Luke" from the **force** variable.

Answer: The following code will work:

```
String force = "Use the force, Luke!";
String subStr = force.substring(15, 19);
System.out.println("Substring is " + subStr);
```

This code has the following output:

Substring is Luke

This code may seem simple, but there is a subtle concept that is important to learn here. Let's take another look at the definition of the **substring()** method:

```
public String substring(int startIndex, int endIndex)
```

If you read the Javadoc reference for the **substring()** method, it tells you that **substring()** returns the **String** starting at index *startIndex* and ending at *endIndex*. However, what may not be clear is that **String** includes the character at *startIndex,* but does *not* include the character at *endIndex*. We passed in 15 and 19 for the values of *startIndex* and *endIndex*. Look again at **force** and count out the indices for each letter. The 'L' character is at index 15, but the character at index 19 is the exclamation point. The **String** returned is everything from the 'L' up to, but not including, the '!'. While this may seem a little strange, there is a good reason for this. The length of "Luke" is 4 characters and 15 plus 4 is 19. Thus, you can always be sure that the following is true:

```
startIndex + length = endIndex
```

Question g will demonstrate an alternate solution that takes advantage of this fact.

g) Can you write another solution to question f that does not use any *fixed* values like **15** and **19**?

Answer: The following code is an alternate solution:

```
String force = "Use the force, Luke!";
String findString = "Luke";
int findStringLenth = findString.length();
int startIndex = force.indexOf(findString);
int endIndex = startIndex + findStringLength;
String subStr = force.substring(startIndex, endIndex);
System.out.println("Substring is " + subStr);
```

This code demonstrates the relationship between a substring's length, starting index, and ending index. Note that once we define the values of **force** and **findString,** we leave the rest of the work to Java. We don't have to count letters or figure out how long a **String** is. We don't even have to find the starting or ending indices. And while this example doesn't actually do anything useful, it does demonstrate some very useful principles that can be used down the road.

LAB 3.2 SELF-REVIEW QUESTIONS

In order to test your progress, you should be able to answer the following questions.

1)   Which of the following are **String** values? Check all that apply.
   a) _____ **I'm a String**
   b) _____ **"No, I'm a String."**
   c) _____ **new String()**
   d) _____ **'Ha! I am the only real String.'**
   e) _____ **new String("I am not a String")**

2)   What is the result of the following:

   `"Green eggs" + "Ham"`

   a) _____ **"Green eggs + Ham"**
   b) _____ **"Green eggs Ham"**
   c) _____ **"Green eggsHam"**
   d) _____ **an error**
   e) _____ **indigestion**

3)   Given the **String** "Drum" what is the *index of* "rum"?
   a) _____ **0**
   b) _____ **1**
   c) _____ **2**
   d) _____ **3**
   e) _____ **-1**

4) Given the **String** "Chocolate" what is the *index of* "bloom"?
   a) _____ 0
   b) _____ 1
   c) _____ 2
   d) _____ 3
   e) _____ −1

5) Which method returns the number of characters in a **String**?
   a) _____ size()
   b) _____ length()
   c) _____ width()
   d) _____ girth()
   e) _____ **None of the above**

6) What is the output of the following code?

```
String rhyme = "Twinkle, twinkle little star";
System.out.println(rhyme.substring(10,14));
```

   a) _____ **wink**
   b) _____ **winkl**
   c) _____ **twin**
   d) _____ **twink**

Quiz answers appear in Appendix A, Section 3.2.

L A B   3 . 3

ARRAYS

> ## LAB OBJECTIVES
>
> After this lab, you will be able to:
>
> • Define an Array
> • Access Array Elements

So far, we have learned how to represent different kinds of data. We can store numbers and words in variables and perform some operations on them. Now it is time to learn how to structure some of this data. Let's look at the **String** class again. What makes a **String**? A **String** is just a *collection* of ordered **char** variables. This structure is called an *array*. An *array* is actually a collection of any similar things, not just letters. In Java, we call these similar things *elements*.

Definition: An array is an ordered collection of similar elements.

For an array, all of the elements must be the same type. Technically, a **String** contains an *array* of **char** variables. We can also have arrays of **ints**, **doubles**, even **Strings**. You can have an array of anything, just as long as everything is the same type.

DEFINING AN ARRAY

Array variables are named like any other variable. However, we use the square brackets ([ ]) to denote that the variable is an array. There are three ways of defining an array, as follows.

■ *FOR EXAMPLE:*

Let's define three **int** arrays.

```
int firstArray[];
int secondArray[] = new int[10];
int thirdArray[] = {10, 12, -10, 100};
```

**LAB
3.3**

firstArray is a *null* array. This means that the variable **firstArray** exists, but it has no value (thus a *null* value).

Contrast this with **secondArray,** which is an *empty* array. **secondArray** is an **int** array with space for ten **int** values. These values can be filled in at a later time.

Finally, **thirdArray** is an array of four **int** values that we have preloaded to 10, 12, –10, and 100. We must use the curly braces to contain the array elements, and a comma must separate each element.

ACCESSING AN ARRAY

Now that we have our arrays, what can we do with them? Let's start with **thirdArray** from the preceding example.

■ *FOR EXAMPLE:*

Let's add the following code to the previous example:

```
System.out.println(thirdArray[0]);
System.out.println(thirdArray[1]);
System.out.println(thirdArray[2]);
System.out.println(thirdArray[3]);
```

We now get the following output:

```
10
12
-10
100
```

Just like a **String** variable's first character has an index of zero, the first element in an array also has an index of zero (no surprise since the **String** class uses an array of **char** to hold the text). Note that **thirdArray** is an array of **int**, but **thirdArray[0]** is actually an **int**. You can use it wherever you could use any **int** variable.

ARRAY LENGTH

All arrays have a built-in field called *length,* which is the number of elements in the array.

■ *FOR EXAMPLE:*

The following code shows how to use the **length** field.

```
char letters[] = { 'a', 'b', 'c' };
System.out.println(letters.length);
```

The output of this code is:

> 3

Hopefully it is not too surprising to see that **letters** has three elements. Note that the array **length** is always in **int**, regardless of the array type (**char** in this case).

**LAB
3.3**

LAB 3.3 EXERCISES

3.3.1 DEFINING ARRAYS

a) How would you define an array of 100 **double** values?

_____

_____

b) Create a **string** array called **months** that contains the names of all of the months in a year.

_____

_____

c) Using your array from question b, what is the index of "January"?

_____

_____

3.3.2 ACCESSING ARRAYS

Use the following code for all of the questions:

```
String names[] = { "Jeffrey", "Brandon", "Katelyn" };
String people[];
people = names;
```

a) What is the value of **names[1]**?

**LAB
3.3**

_____

_____

b) What is the value of **people[2]**?

_____

_____

c) What is the output of the following code:

```
System.out.println(names);
```

_____

_____

d) Update **names** by changing the value of "Jeffrey" to "Jeff"?

_____

_____

e) Now that you have changed **names**, did **people** change too?

_____

_____

f) How would you *copy* the values in **names** to a new variable?

_____

_____

LAB 3.3 EXERCISE ANSWERS

3.3.1 ANSWERS

a) How would you define an array of 100 **double** values?

Answer: The following code is one possible answer:

```
double myArray[] = new double[100];
```

This code defines an array named **myArray** with 100 elements. However, none of the elements have been defined. That is okay as they can be filled in later.

b) Create a **String** array called **months** that contains the names of all of the months in a year.

Answer: The following code is one possible answer:

```
String months[] = {"January", "February", "March",
"April", "May", "June", "July", "August",
"September", "October", "November", "December"};
```

We have pre-loaded the values of **months** with the month names. Since we are dealing with a **String** array, we must use double-quotes around each **String** constant.

c) Using your array from question b, what is the index of "January"?

Answer: The index of "January" is 0 since all array indices start at 0 and "January" is the first element.

Details like this are important because most people associate January with the number 1 since January is the first month. A common mistake would be to assume that January is **month[1],** but that would be incorrect.

3.3.2 ANSWERS

Use the following code for all of the questions:

```
String names[] = { "Jeffrey", "Brandon", "Katelyn" };
String people[];
people = names;
```

a) What is the value of **names[1]**?

*Answer: **names[1]** is "Brandon".*

Again, remember that the array index starts at 0. We know that we keep saying this, but the idea is to drive this point home.

b) What is the value of **people[2]**?

*Answer: **people[2]** is "Katelyn".*

When we assigned **names** to **people,** the **people** array is now the same as the **names** array. Arrays can be assigned just like any other variable. There is one important difference that we will see shortly.

c) What is the output of the following code:

```
System.out.println(names);
```

Answer: The output will look something like the following but will have a different value:

[Ljava.lang.String;@f6751870

Unlike the previous types and classes we have seen, the **println()** method does not know how to print an array. The best it can do is print a unique but not very useful key string. In the next chapter, we will learn how to write code to print all of the values of an array.

d) Update **names** by changing the value of "Jeffrey" to "Jeff"?

Answer: The following code will do what we want:

```
names[0] = "Jeff";
```

Remember that while **names** is a **String** array, **names[0]** is a **String** variable and can be treated just like any **String** variable, including reassigning it.

e) Now that you have changed **names**, did **people** change too?

*Answer: Yes. Now **people[0]** also has the value of "Jeff".*

All object variables in Java are considered *reference* variables. This means that the variable name *refers* to the data it represents. A single data object can have more than one reference to it. In this case, the array of names has two references to it, **names** and **people**. If you change one, then the other also changes.

f) How would you *copy* the values in **names** to a new variable?

Answer: The following code will make a copy of **names**.

```
String names[] = { "Jeffrey", "Brandon", "Katelyn" };
String children[] = new String[3];
children[0] = names[0];
children[1] = names[1];
children[2] = names[2];
```

What we have done here is create a whole new empty array called **children**. This new array has three slots for **String** data and we copy each element from **names** into **children**. However, unlike the case in question e, we can edit one array without affecting the other array.

This method of copying an array is for demonstration purposes only. We will explore better ways of copying data later in this book.

LAB 3.3 SELF-REVIEW QUESTIONS

In order to test your progress, you should be able to answer the following questions.

1) Which of the following variables is an array?
  a) _____ winners
  b) _____ losers()
  c) _____ quitters{}
  d) _____ cheaters[]

2) Which command defines an array of 50 **int** values?
  a) _____ int numbers[50];
  b) _____ int numbers = int[50];
  c) _____ int numbers[] = new int[50];
  d) _____ int numbers = new int[50];
  e) _____ int numbers[50] = new int[50];

3) Which of the following would be the first element of an array?
  a) _____ prices[1]
  b) _____ prices(0);
  c) _____ prices{0}
  d) _____ prices[0]
  e) _____ prices{1}

4) Which of the following would be the last element of an array?
    a) _____ **prices[prices.last]**
    b) _____ **prices[0];**
    c) _____ **prices[prices.length – 1]**
    d) _____ **prices[prices.length]**
    e) _____ **prices[prices.last + 1]**

5) Which of the following is not a legal type for an array?
    a) _____ **boolean**
    b) _____ **String**
    c) _____ **int**
    d) _____ **float**
    e) _____ **None of the above**

6) The **System.out.println()** method will print the contents of an array.
    a) _____ **True**
    b) _____ **False**

7) Once you have defined an array, it is possible to change its size.
    a) _____ **True**
    b) _____ **False**

Quiz answers appear in Appendix A, Section 3.3.

**LAB
3.3**

L A B   3 . 4

VECTORS

LAB OBJECTIVES

After this lab, you will be able to:

- Use Vectors
- Use the Wrapper Classes
- Use an Enumeration

A **Vector** is similar to an array, but can contain a mixture of any objects. Also, the size of a **Vector** will grow and shrink as you add and remove elements. The only restriction on a **Vector** is that the elements must be objects. You cannot add any of the primitive data types, at least not directly. After we show you the **Vector** class in action, we will show you the wrapper classes, which let you add primitive types into a **Vector**.

Definition: A Vector is a collection of objects.

USING A VECTOR

The first thing we have to do is import the **java.util.Vector** package. The Vector is not included in the default set of classes available. If we forget to import this package, then the Java compiler will not understand it and will generate lots of error messages!

■ *FOR EXAMPLE:*

The following example will define a **Vector** and add two **String** values into it. We have included more of the program to show the **import** line. The remaining examples won't show this, but you still need to do it.

Remember, all **import** statements come at the beginning, before the outer-class definition.

```
import java.util.Vector;
public class MyClass
// [ etc ]
    Vector v = new Vector();
    String s = new String("Hello");
    v.add(s);
    v.add("Goodbye");
    System.out.println(v);
    System.out.println(v.size());
```

**LAB
3.4**

This code has the following output:

```
[Hello, Goodbye]
2
```

As you can see, the **println()** method can print the values in a **Vector**. This is another advantage of a **Vector** over an array. Note that the words *Hello* and *Goodbye* appear in the same order in which we added them. The entire list of elements is enclosed in square braces as well.

Unlike an array, we must use the **add()** method to add objects to the **Vector**. We can also query how many elements are in a **Vector** using the **size()** method. In this case there are two elements in **v**.

■ *FOR EXAMPLE:*

Add the following code to the previous example. This will remove the variable **s** from the **Vector** using the **remove()** method.

```
boolean success = v.remove(s)
System.out.println(v);
System.out.println(success);
System.out.println(v.size());
```

This code has the following output:

```
[Goodbye]
true
1
```

We can see that variable **s** has been removed. The **boolean** variable **success** is set to **true** to show that the removal was successful. If we had tried to remove something that wasn't in the **Vector,** then the value of **success** would have been **false**. We can also see that the size of the **Vector** is now one.

The add() *and* remove() *methods are new starting with Java 2. For older versions of Java, you need to use the* addElement() *and* removeElement() *methods. All of these methods are available in Java 2, for backwards compatibility.*

Here is a quick summary of the API definitions for some of the useful methods of the **Vector** class:

```
public boolean add(Object o);
public boolean remove(Object o);
public int size();
public Enumerator elements();
```

Stay tuned for an explanation of the **Enumerator** class, but first we need to discuss the wrapper classes.

As with most of the classes we discuss in this book, we will only mention the most common and useful methods in a class. For a list of all of the methods, see the *Javadoc* API specifications for the **java.util.Vector** class.

You might have noticed that the add() *method also returns a boolean value, in this case* true *for success and* false *for failure. It is not re-quired that we save the return values from a method. However, this in-formation is sometimes useful and shouldn't be ignored without reason. Since we are still learning Java at this point, we will defer this topic until the end of the book. For a* Vector, *you almost never need to save the return value of the* add() *method.*

USING THE WRAPPER CLASSES

We will now visit the object cousins of the primitive data types. Since we cannot place any of the primitive types inside a **Vector**, the authors of Java created new classes called *Integer, Float, Double, Character,* and *Boolean*. These classes contain, or wrap, the primitive data types and allow us to treat these primitive types as objects. Additionally, each of the wrapper classes contains helpful methods and fields that apply to each class. The wrapper classes are sometimes called *reference* classes or *object* classes because they *refer* to primitive data and because they are *objects*.

Let's start with the **Integer** class. Once we understand it, the other wrapper classes are pretty much the same.

■ FOR EXAMPLE:

The following code will construct an **Integer** variable that wraps the **int** value 2112. Then we extract the actual **int** value into an **int** variable.

```
Integer I = new Integer(2112);
int i = I.intValue();
```

It is important to realize that **I** only contains the value 2112. We must use the **intValue()** method to actually access it. Each wrapper class has its own special method to access its primitive type. Table 3.3 summarizes all of the wrapper classes and their *accessor* methods.

As you can see, the pattern is pretty consistent. To construct a wrapper object, you must pass in its corresponding primitive value. Likewise, to retrieve the primitive value, you must call the similarly named method.

Now that we can construct a wrapper object, let's use them with a **Vector**.

■ FOR EXAMPLE:

We can now add our new wrapper objects into a **Vector**. The following example creates a personnel record for an employee and stores his name, age, and salary.

Table 3.3 ■ Summary of Wrapper Classes

Class	Constructor	Accessor Method
Integer	new Integer(int i)	public int intValue()
Float	new Float(float f)	public float floatValue()
Double	new Double(double d)	public double doubleValue()
Character	new Character(char c)	public char charValue()
Boolean	new Boolean(boolean b)	public boolean booleanValue()

```
String name = new String("John Bigbooty");
Integer age = new Integer(30);
Double salary = new Double(82312.44);
Vector record = new Vector();
record.add(name);
record.add(age);
record.add(salary);
System.out.println(record);
```

This code has the following output:

[John Bigbooty, 30, 82312.44]

We have now succeeded in combining different types together in one **Vector**. Without a **Vector**, it would be very difficult to link these objects together.

ENUMERATIONS

The **Enumeration** class allows us to cycle through the values of a **Vector**. We get an **Enumeration** from the **elements()** method of a **Vector**. Once we have the **Enumeration** object, we can use the following methods:

```
public boolean hasMoreElements();
public Object nextElement();
```

Let's look at how to use these methods.

■ *FOR EXAMPLE:*

The following code will create a **Vector** containing some dog names and then use an **Enumeration** to display each element (each dog's name).

```
Vector dogs = new Vector();
dogs.add("Rambo");
dogs.add("Feisty");
Enumeration names = dogs.elements();
System.out.println(names.hasMoreElements());
System.out.println(names.nextElement());
System.out.println(names.hasMoreElements());
System.out.println(names.nextElement());
System.out.println(names.hasMoreElements());
```

This will print the following:

```
true
Rambo
true
Feisty
false
```

Notice that we do not pass in any arguments to either of the **Enumeration** methods. Yet each time we call **nextElement()**, we get a different element (the *next* one! Go figure!). Likewise, **hasMoreElements()** keeps returning **true** until we have cycled through all of the dog names. The **Enumeration** object accomplished this by maintaining its own *state* information. It keeps track of which element is the next element and how many elements are left.

One more important piece of information: Because a **Vector** can hold any object, **nextElement()** always returns an **Object** type (look again at that API definition). If you need to assign this value to a variable, you must cast it to the proper class.

■ *FOR EXAMPLE:*

Here is an example of casting a value from **nextElement()**.

```
String name = (String) names.nextElement();
```

Just like when we casted the value of an **int** into a **float**, we have cast the value of the **Object** into a **String**. We can do this since **String** is a subclass of the **Object** class. If we don't do this, Java will give us an error message.

LAB 3.4 EXERCISES

3.4.1 VECTORS

The following questions build on each other so keep reusing the same piece of code.

a) Write code that creates a **Vector** called **stooges** containing the names *Larry, Curly,* and *Moe.*

b) Using **stooges**, write code to remove *Curly* and add *Shemp*.

_____

_____

c) Print out the value of **stooges**. In what order do you expect the names to be listed?

_____

_____

d) Using **stooges**, write code that generates the following output:

```
The 3 Stooges
```

LAB
3.4

_____

_____

e) Create a second **Vector** called **actors** that contains the names *Bob, Ted,* and *Alice.*

_____

_____

f) What happens if we do the following?

```
actors.add(stooges);
```

_____

_____

g) What will be the output of the following code? And why?

```
System.out.println(actors.size());
```

_____

_____

3.4.2 WRAPPER CLASSES

a) How would you add the numbers 2.5 and 2.75 into a **Vector?**

_____

_____

Use the following code for the next question:

```
Double length = new Double(50.4);
Double width = new Double(20.5);
Double area;
```

**LAB
3.4**

b) Set **area** to be the product of **length** times **width.**

_____

_____

c) Enter the following code and run it. What is the output?

```
char letter = 'f';
boolean lowerCase = Character.isLowerCase(letter);
System.out.println("Is letter lower case? " + lower-
Case);
```

_____

_____

3.4.3 ENUMERATIONS

Use the following code for the questions in the Exercise:

```
Vector disasters = new Vector();
disasters.add("earthquake");
disasters.add("flood");
disasters.add("tornado");
disasters.add("macarena");
```

As you answer each question, append your code to this original code
since each question builds on the one before it.

a) Construct an **Enumeration** object called **e1** from **disasters** and use it to build an array that contains all of the values in **disasters**.

_____

_____

b) After you have finished building the array, what value would **e1.hasMoreElements()** return?

_____

_____

c) Construct a second **Enumeration** object called **e2** from **disasters**. What value would **e2.hasMoreElements()** return?

_____

_____

d) Likewise, what value does **e2.nextElement()** return? Why?

_____

_____

LAB 3.4 EXERCISE ANSWERS

3.4.1 ANSWERS

The following questions build on each other so keep reusing the same piece of code.

a) Write code that creates a **Vector** called **stooges** containing the names *Larry, Curly* and *Moe.*

Answer: The following code works:

```
Vector stooges = new Vector();
stooges.add("Larry");
stooges.add("Curly");
stooges.add("Moe");
```

We must add each stooge separately. We cannot initialize the **Vector** with any values.

b) Using **stooges**, write code to remove *Curly* and add *Shemp*.

Answer: The following code works:

```
stooges.remove("Curly");
stooges.add("Shemp");
```

In this case, we did not check the return value of the **remove()** method. This is fine in this situation.

c) Print out the value of **stooges**. In what order do you expect the names to be listed?

Answer: The output should be as follows:

```
Larry
Moe
Shemp
```

Since we removed *Curly,* the **Vector** automatically shrank to two elements. When we added *Shemp,* he was added to the end of the element list.

d) Using **stooges**, write code that generates the following output:

```
The 3 Stooges
```

Answer: We can use the **size()** *method, as follows:*

```
System.out.println("The " + stooges.size() +
" Stooges");
```

We are simply constructing a **String** by concatenating a **String,** and **int,** and another **String**.

e) Create a second **Vector** called **actors** that contains the names *Bob, Ted,* and *Alice.*

Answer: The following code is very similar to Question a.

```
Vector actors = new Vector();
actors.add("Bob");
actors.add("Ted");
actors.add("Alice");
```

There is nothing new to learn here; we are just setting up the next question. It is important to have two **Vector** objects.

f) What happens if we do the following?

```
actors.add(stooges);
```

*Answer: We have added one **Vector** to another **Vector**.*

It is perfectly legal for one **Vector** to contain another. Remember that a **Vector** can contain *any* object, including another **Vector**. It is also possible to have a **Vector** of arrays or an array of **Vectors**! Structuring your data is a very important part of programming. You can find entire books and courses on *data structures* so we won't cover too much of the theory in this book. Just remember that it is possible for you to organize and structure your data in all kinds of ways.

**LAB
3.4**

g) What will be the output of the following code? And why?

```
System.out.println(actors.size());
```

Answer: This line generates the following output:

4

If you thought the answer was six, you're wrong. The **Vector** called **actors** only contains four elements: three **String** objects and one **Vector** object (**stooges**). Even though **stooges** contains three elements itself, it only counts as one element inside of **actors**.

If we print **actors**, it looks like this:

```
[Bob, Ted, Alice, [Larry, Moe, Shemp]]
```

Notice how the inner **Vector** is enclosed in its own set of square braces.

3.4.2 ANSWERS

a) How would you add the numbers 2.5 and 2.75 into a **Vector**?

Answer: You must place the values into a wrapper class first, either a Float or a Double, as follows:

```
Vector v = new Vector();
v.add(new Double(2.5));
v.add(new Double(2.75));
```

We could have taken some extra steps and assign the values to **Double** variables first, and then added the variables to the **Vector**, but it is not necessary.

b) Set **area** to be the product of **length** times **width**.

Answer: Adding the following code will work:

```
double l = length.doubleValue();
double w = width.doubleValue();
area = new Double(l * w);
```

Since we cannot actually multiply two **Double** variables together, we must first extract the primitive values out first, and then construct a new **Double** based on the product.

c) Enter the following code and run it. What is the output?

```
char letter = 'f';
boolean lowerCase = Character.isLowerCase(letter);
System.out.println("Is letter lowercase? " + lower-
Case);
```

Answer: The output is as follows:

Is letter lowercase? true

Do you remember when we said that the wrapper classes also contained useful fields and methods? This is an example of one of them. The **Character** class contains a *class method* that can be called at any time to test the value of a char to see if it is a lowercase letter. There are many of these class methods that can be called so read the Javadoc reference for a list of all of them.

3.4.3 ANSWERS

a) Construct an **Enumeration** object called **e1** from **disasters** and use it to build an array that contains all of the values in **disasters**.

Answer: The following code will do this:

```
Enumeration e1 = disasters.elements();
String disastersArray[] = new
String[disastes.size()];
disastersArray[0] = (String) e1.nextElement();
```

The Truth about Class Methods

You might not have realized it, but you have been using a class method for a long time now. There is a class called **System**, which contains an object called **out**, which contains a class method called **println()**. Herein lies the true power of Java. While Java does contain many useful functions, it is also completely extensible. New methods and objects can be added to your Java environment at any time. Classes can, and should, be shared by the whole programming community. The hope is that everyone can build on the work of everyone else. Since no one has to keep "reinventing the wheel," the time it takes to develop software can be significantly reduced.

```
disastersArray[1] = (String) e1.nextElement();
disastersArray[2] = (String) e1.nextElement();
disastersArray[3] = (String) e1.nextElement();
```

First we construct an array that is the same size as **disasters**. Next we add each element in the **Vector** into its own space in the array. We also must cast the **Vector** value to a **String** because the array can only hold **String** objects.

We will see a much better way of iterating through an **Enumeration** in the next chapter, but for now this will do. Additionally, there is even a method in a **Vector** that will convert itself into an array, but the point of this exercise it to learn how to use the **Enumeration** object.

b) After you have finished building the array, what value would **e1.has-MoreElements()** return?

Answer: false

Since you have called **e1.nextElement()** four times, there are no more elements left in the **Vector**.

c) Construct a second **Enumeration** object called **e2** from **disasters**. What value would **e2.hasMoreElements()** return?

Answer: true

Even though **e1** has already cycled through all of the elements in **disasters, e2** has not. Each **Enumeration** maintains its own *state,* and therefore contains it own *view* of the data in **disasters**. The actual data never changes, but the view from each of the **Enumeration** objects does.

d)   Likewise, what value does **e2.nextElement()** return? Why?

Answer: "earthquake"

Since this would be the first time we have called **e2.nextElement()** it would return the first element.

LAB 3.4 SELF-REVIEW QUESTIONS

In order to test your progress, you should be able to answer the following questions.

1)   Which data types can be stored in a **Vector**? Check all that apply
    a) _____ **int**
    b) _____ **Boolean**
    c) _____ **char**
    d) _____ **Float**
    e) _____ **double**
    f) _____ **String**

2)   All objects in a **Vector** must be the same type.
    a) _____ **True**
    b) _____ **False**

3)   How can you add a **boolean** variable to a **Vector**?
    a) _____ **Use a Boolean wrapper**
    b) _____ **Just add it**
    c) _____ **You can't**

4)   How would you extract the **char** value from a **Character** object **myChar**?
    a) _____ **myChar.getChar()**
    b) _____ **Just use myChar**
    c) _____ **getChar(myChar)**
    d) _____ **myChar.charValue()**

5)   Where is an object inserted into a **Vector** when you use the **add()** method?
    a) _____ **At the end**
    b) _____ **At the beginning**
    c) _____ **In alphabetical order**
    d) _____ **Undefined**
    e) _____ **You must specify the location**

6) An **Enumeration** object is used for what?
   a) _____ **Copying a Vector**
   b) _____ **Iterating through a Vector's contents**
   c) _____ **Counting the values in a Vector**
   d) _____ **Converting primitive types into Objects**
   e) _____ **Converting Objects to primitive types**

7) Using an **Enumeration** changes a **Vector.**
   a) _____ **True**
   b) _____ **False**
   c) _____ **Only if you call nextElement()**
   d) _____ **Only if you call hasMoreElements()**
   e) _____ **Both c and d**

8) You can only have one **Enumeration** object per **Vector?**
   a) _____ **True**
   b) _____ **False**
   c) _____ **You can only have one *at a time*, but you have more**

Quiz answers appear in Appendix A, Section 3.4.

LAB
3.4

C H A P T E R   3

TEST YOUR THINKING

As we said at the beginning of the chapter, our job as programmers is to represent the real world as structured data. Once we can accomplish this, then our battle is almost won. If we have well-structured data, then processing it becomes much easier. Look at how computers have jumped into the everyday lives of "regular" people now what we have been able to digitize pictures, music, video, and text. The World Wide Web has grown extremely quickly because the structure of the data (the web pages) is well-defined and standardized.

It's a simple task to represent someone's age as an integer, or a price as a floating-point number. However, more complex objects require more complex organization of the data.

1) Imagine that you are in charge of keeping score at a golf tournament. Assume that there are eighteen holes in the course, and that the players will play for three days. The number of players won't be known until the starting day since it's an open tourney. How would you structure your data to keep track of each player's score?

2) You did so well with your job at the golf course that you now work in a stadium selling tickets. Your stadium houses football games and rock concerts, and the prices of the tickets depend on the seat location and the event. Your job is to keep track of the ticket prices for each seat for each event and to keep track of which seats have been sold.

3) Your success at the stadium has catapulted you to the presidency of the United States. Congratulations! As president, it is your duty to write computer programs (the Constitution was amended by President Scott Adams before you were elected). You need to keep track of how each member of Congress voted on various issues and you need to know how many Republicans and Democrats are in each house of Congress.

CHAPTER 4

FLOW CONTROL

 Do you want fries with that?

Squeaky-voiced fast food employee

L ife is full of decisions. In this chapter we will learn about the decision-making process in Java. If you have programmed in another computer language before, this chapter, and the one that follows, may be a little basic for you, but we still recommend reading it to make sure you understand the few caveats that Java has.

Flow control is the decision-making part of a computer program. Up until now, we have been executing a series of commands. Each command is executed in order, one after the other. The "flow" of these programs has been linear, or in a straight line. In real life, there are always choices and decisions to be made—forks in the road, if you will. When writing a computer program, it is necessary to tell the computer how to make these

99

decisions (which path to take) and then what to do. Each choice can lead to a different set of commands, thus changing the flow of the program. Controlling this flow is the essence of computer programming. This chapter will cover some of the ways you can tell the computer "which path to take."

**LAB
4.1**

L A B   4 . 1

BOOLEAN TESTING

LAB OBJECTIVES

After this lab, you will be able to:

- Understand How to Compare Two Objects

As we said previously, the meaning of boolean is true or false. When it comes to flow control, we use tests that yield **boolean** values to make our decisions. Basically, we ask the question "Is this true?" The answer is either "yes" (true) or "no" (false). We then act accordingly based on the answer. In later labs, we will explore the "act accordingly" part, but this lab will concentrate on the "Is this true?" part.

COMPARING OBJECTS

One way of getting a boolean value is by comparing two objects. For example, we can ask if two objects are *equal* to each other. With numbers, we can also ask if one number is higher (*greater*) or lower (*less*) than another number.

EQUALS

The most basic question to ask is "Are these two values the same?" In Java, this is accomplished with the "equals" operator, which looks like this:

```
A == B
```

This is interpreted as "Does A equal B?" If A is equal to B then this statement evaluates to "true"; if not, then it evaluates to "false."

This is different from the assignment operator "=", which assigns the value to B to A. The "double equals" is the test to see if the value of A is the same as the value of B.

Also note that A or B can be variables, constants, or anything else in Java with a value.

■ FOR EXAMPLE:

Consider this code:

```
System.out.println("The statement 2 == 4 is");
System.out.println(2 == 4);
```

This yields the following output:

```
The statement 2 == 4 is
false
```

Java has evaluated the expression **2 == 4** and then printed the value. As we've already seen, the **println()** function will convert the values **true** or **false** into the words *true* or *false* for us.

A more common usage would be to check the value of a variable, as follows:

```
int x = 10;
System.out.println(x == 11);
```

This will print out:

```
false
```

The "==" operator should only be used on primitive data type such as int, float, char, boolean, and double. We will see the reason for this later.

THE EQUALS() METHOD

With object types such as **String**, **Integer**, and **Float**, there is a method you can call named **equals()**. The **equals()** method takes one parameter and returns **true** if the object's values are *equal* to the parameter's values.

■ FOR EXAMPLE:

```
Integer I1 = new Integer(2);
Integer I2 = new Integer(2);
System.out.println("Does I1 equal I2?");
System.out.println(I1.equals(I2));
```

This will print the following:

```
Does I1 equal I2?
true
```

We will explore why we must use the **equals()** method for object types in the exercises. Even if you already know programming, this is important to learn.

GREATER THAN / LESS THAN

The other two common comparison operators are "greater than" and "less than" which look like this:

```
A > B
A < B
```

These statements will evaluate to **true** if the value of A is greater than (or less than) the value of B, respectively. As with the **==** operator, only primitive types should be used.

GREATER EQUALS / LESS EQUALS

There is another form of these operators that looks like this:

```
A >= B
A <= B
```

These are combinations of the previous two operators. The first statement evaluates to true if A is greater than *or* equal to B. Likewise, the second statement evaluates to true if A is less than *or* equal to B. This is sometimes abbreviated "greater equals" and "less equals."

LAB 4.1 EXERCISES

4.1.1 COMPARING PRIMITIVE TYPES

Consider the following code:

```
int i = 10;
System.out.println(i == 10);
System.out.println(i > 10);
System.out.println(i >= 10);
System.out.println(i < 10);
System.out.println(i <= 10);
```

a) Just by looking at the code, what is the output?

_____

_____

Create this code and run it.

b) Did you get the results you expected?

_____

_____

Imagine if we changed the first line to "`int i = 9;`"

c) What would be the output now?

_____

_____

Make the change and run the program.

d) Did you get the results you expected?

_____

_____

Consider this code:

```
boolean b;
b = (12 < 10);
```

e) What is the value of b?

_____

_____

4.1.2 COMPARING OBJECT TYPES

Consider the following code:

```
Double d1 = new Double(1.23);
Double d2 = new Double(1.23);
Double d3 = new Double(4.56);
Double d4 = d1;
System.out.println(d1 == d1);
System.out.println(d1 == d2);
System.out.println(d1 == d3);
System.out.println(d1 == d4);
```

a) Just by looking at the code, what is the output?

_____

_____

Create this program and run it.

b) Did you get the results you expected?

_____

_____

Now add the following lines:

```
System.out.println(d1.equals(d1));
System.out.println(d1.equals(d2));
System.out.println(d1.equals(d3));
System.out.println(d1.equals(d4));
```

Run this program.

c) What are the results?

_____

_____

d) Do the new lines (the last four) match your expected answers from question a of this exercise?

e) How would you test to see if **d1** is less than **d3**?

f) Given a **String** **s**, how would you test if the value of **s** is **"Java"**?

LAB 4.1 EXERCISE ANSWERS

4.1.1 ANSWERS

Consider the following code:

```
int i = 10;
System.out.println(i == 10);
System.out.println(i > 10);
System.out.println(i >= 10);
System.out.println(i < 10);
System.out.println(i <= 10);
```

a) Just by looking at the code, what is the output?

Answer: The output should be as follows:

```
true
false
true
false
true
```

Create this code and run it.

b) Did you get the results you expected?

Answer: This should be the same as the answer to Question a.

Imagine if we changed the first line to **"int i = 9;"**

   c) What is the output now?

      Answer: The output should be as follows:

```
false
false
false
true
true
```

      Make the change and run the program.

   d) Did you get the results you expected?

      Answer: This should be the same as the answer to Question c.

      Consider this code:

```
boolean b;
b = (12 < 10);
```

   e) What is the value of **b**?

      Answer: false

This statement is both a test and an assignment. First the expression **(12 < 10)** is calculated (**false**). Then the value of **false** is assigned to the **boolean** variable **b.** Technically, the parentheses are not required, but they do make the code a little clearer.

4.1.2 ANSWERS

Consider the following code:

```
Double d1 = new Double(1.23);
Double d2 = new Double(1.23);
Double d3 = new Double(4.56);
Double d4 = d1;
System.out.println(d1 == d1);
System.out.println(d1 == d2);
System.out.println(d1 == d3);
System.out.println(d1 == d4);
```

a) Just by looking at the code, what is the output?

Answer: The output should be as follows:

```
true
false
false
true
```

We expect that most people said **true** for the second line. Keep reading to find out why it's really **false**.

Create this program and run it.

b) Did you get the results you expected?

Answer: The output should be the same as the answer to Question a. The authors expect that you answered "no" to this question. See Question d's answer for details on what's going on.

Now add the following lines:

```
System.out.println(d1.equals(d1));
System.out.println(d1.equals(d2));
System.out.println(d1.equals(d3));
System.out.println(d1.equals(d4));
```

Run this program.

c) What are the results?

Answer: The output should be as follows:

```
true
true
false
true
```

d) Do the new lines (the last four) match your expected answers from question a of this exercise?

Answer: We will assume so.

Explanation for Questions a though d:

The results from question c are probably the results that people expected from question a. The point of this exercise is to show the difference between using the **==** operator and the **equals()** method. Read the sidebar

---

The Difference Between == and equals()

OK, so why does Java say that **d1 == d2** is **false**? The answer is slightly technical, but here goes. Even though **d1** and **d2** have the same value (1.23), they are not the same object. Every time the **new** operator is used, a new *instance* of the object class is created. Imagine there are two people, both named "Marc." We now have two *instances* of people named Marc. Although their names are the same (i.e., their *values* are the same), they are not the same person. The **==** operator looks at the object (the person) and can see that they are not the same, so it returns **false**.

So, what about **d1** and **d4**? **d4** is essentially a nickname for **d1,** in the same way "Funky Mix Master M" could be a nickname for one of our friends named Marc. In this case, **d1 == d4** is **true** because **d4** was assigned the same object as **d1**.

The **equals()** method, on the other hand, looks at the *values* inside an object. It compares the **double** value inside a **Double**. Likewise, for our two friends, Marc and *Funky Marc,* **equals()** would return **true** because both of their real names are the same.

---

for more details. The key point to remember is: Use the **equals()** method when comparing two objects, and use **==** when comparing **ints**, **floats, doubles, chars,** and **booleans**.

e) How would you test to see if **d1** is less than **d3?**

   Answer: The following will do the trick.

```
d1.getDouble() < d3.getDouble()
```

Remember that the result of **getDouble()** is a **double** (not a **Double**) and can be used in the less-than comparison because **double** is a primitive type.

If you tried to do something like

```
d1 < d2
```

the Java compiler should have given you an error because the types are wrong. This is not a legal action in Java and the compiler will enforce this.

f) Given a **String s,** how would you test if the value of **s** is **"Java"**?

Answer: The following code will work:

```
S.equals("Java");
```

The type **String** is an object type, not a primitive type, so you must use the **equals()** operator. If you said **S == "Java"** that would be incorrect, although it may have seemed to work. The following example, shows why you need to use the **equals()** method.

```
String S = new String("Java");
System.out.println(S == "Java");
```

The output of this code is **false**, which would not be what you want. Read the sidebar from question d of this section if you want a more detailed explanation.

LAB 4.1 SELF-REVIEW QUESTIONS

In order to test your progress, you should be able to answer the following questions.

Use the following for the next two questions:

```
int x;
```

1) Which command tests if the value of **x** is equal to 100?
   a) _____x equals 100
   b) _____x.equals(100)
   c) _____x = 100
   d) _____x == 100

2) Which command tests if the value of **x** is greater than 100?
   a) _____100 > x
   b) _____x >= 100
   c) _____100 < x
   d) _____x < 100

Use the following to answer the next question:

```
Float f1 = new Float(6.6);
Float f2 = new Float(6.6);
```

3) Which of the following statements checks if **f1** and **f2** have the same value (6.6)?

a) _____`f1 == f2`
b) _____`f1 = f2`
c) _____`f1.equals(f2)`
d) _____`f1.getFloat() == f2.getFloat()`
e) _____(a) and (c)
f) _____(c) and (d)
g) _____All of the above
h) _____None of the above

4) The following is a legal Java statement:

```
boolean b = x == y;
```

a) _____True
b) _____False

5) Which of the following statements will generate a javac compiler error?

```
Double d1;
Double d2
```

a) _____`d1.equals(d2)`
b) _____`d1 < d2`
c) _____`d1 == d2`
d) _____`d1 = d2`

Quiz answers appear in Appendix A, Section 4.1.

L A B   4 . 2

IF-THEN-ELSE

LAB OBJECTIVES

After this lab, you will be able to:

- Use an if-then Statement
- Use an if-then-else Statement

In the previous lab, we learned how to perform a boolean test. In this lab, and the labs that follow, we will learn how to use these tests to control the flow of a program. That is, we will "act accordingly" based on a boolean test result. This section will look at the *if-then* statement and the *if-then-else* statement (both of which are sometimes simply abbreviated as *if* statement).

Figure 4.1 shows a path with a fork in the road. There are two choices and we must decide which one to take.

The *if* statements allow us to define a "fork in the road" and then tell Java how to choose which path to take.

IF-THEN

We will first cover the *if-then* statement. This statement lets us tell Java "**If** *something* is true, **then** do *this.*" There are two forms of an *if-then* statement: the *simple* form and the *complex statement block* form (also called the *block* form).

SIMPLE FORM

Here is the simple form of an if-then statement:

```
if (booleanValue)
    doSomething;
```

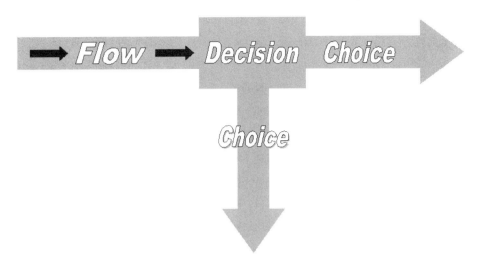

Figure 4.1 ■ Flowchart with a fork in the road.

This statement is read "If **booleanValue** is true, then **doSomething**." If **booleanValue** is **false**, then **doSomething** is not executed. Anything after **doSomething** is executed as usual.

Figure 4.2 shows the program flow of an *if* statement. Notice how the flow can take a detour to the **doSomething** code if **booleanValue** is **true**. After the *if-then* statement, the program returns to the original path.

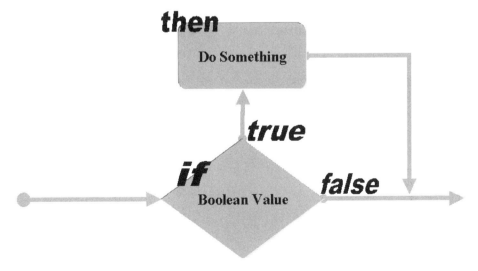

Figure 4.2 ■ Program flow showing if-then statement

■ *FOR EXAMPLE:*

```
int temperature = 95;
if (temperature > 90)
    System.out.println("It's too hot!");
System.out.println("Have a nice day.");
```

The output of this program would be:

```
It's too hot!
Have a nice day.
```

However, if we changed the first line to be **int temperature = 70,** then the output would look like:

```
Have a nice day.
```

The "It's too hot" sentence isn't printed because the boolean test was **false.** However, "Have a nice day" is still printed because it is not part of the *if-then* statement. The program flow always returns to the "Have a nice day" code regardless of the value of **temperature**.

COMPLEX STATEMENT BLOCK

What if you wanted to print more than "It's too hot!" if the temperature is too high? That is, you want to execute more than one command in the then-clause? The answer is to use a *complex statement block.* A complex statement block is just one or more simple statements enclosed with the curly braces: **{ }**. As previously mentioned, this is sometimes called the "block form" of an *if-then* statement.

Let's modify the previous example to print two lines of text.

■ *FOR EXAMPLE:*

```
int temperature = 95;
if (temperature > 90)
{
    System.out.println("It's too hot!");
    System.out.println("I want to go home!");
}
System.out.println("Have a nice day.");
```

The output of the code would be:

```
It's too hot!
```

```
I want to go home!
Have a nice day.
```

The complex block is considered (by Java) to be a single statement. While the block may contain many different commands, the entire block is considered the "then-clause" of the *if* statement. This is a common practice in all of the flow-control mechanisms in Java, so be sure to understand its use.

**LAB
4.2**

 It is considered good programming style to line-up the left and right brackets with the word "if" at the top. This makes it easier to tell where the if-then statement begins and ends.

IF-THEN-ELSE

There is one more optional part of an *if* statement called the "else" clause. Earlier, for the *if-then* statement, we gave the example: "**If** *something* is true, **then** do *this*." With the *if-then-else* statement, we can tell Java "**If** *something* is true, **then** do *this*, **otherwise (else)** do *that*." The else clause lets us define a path if the boolean test is **false**. Instead of one detour in our path, we now have two.

Figure 4.3 shows the flow of an *if-then-else* statement. Notice how it is similar to Figure 4.2 with the exception that we now have a second path to take. The program flow will take one of the two paths and then converge back to the original path.

As with the *if-then* statement, there are two forms of the *if-then-else* statement: the *simple* form and the *block* form.

SIMPLE FORM	BLOCK FORM

<pre>if (boolean)
     then-clause-statement
else
     else-clause-statement</pre>
	<pre>if (boolean)
	{
	     then-clause-block
	     more statements
	}
	else
	{
	     else-clause-block
	     more statements
	}</pre>

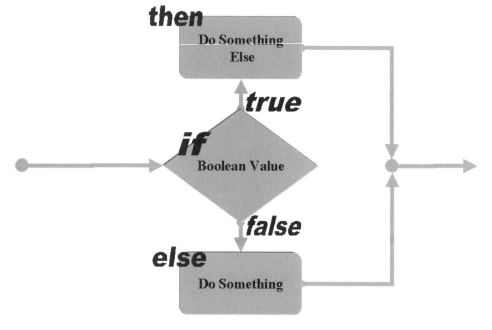

Figure 4.3 ■ Program flow showing if-then-else statement

■ FOR EXAMPLE:

```
int temperature = 70;
if (temperature > 90)
{
    System.out.println("It's too hot!");
    System.out.println("I want to go home!");
}
else
{
    System.out.println("It's a warm day.");
    System.out.println("Let's stay here.");
}
System.out.println("Have a nice day.");
```

The output of this program is:

```
It's a warm day.
Let's stay here.
Have a nice day.
```

We lowered the temperature to 70, so now it's a warm day. Java only executed the commands in the else block because the temperature test was **false**. As always, the "Have a nice day" message is printed because it is outside of the *if-then-else* statement.

LAB 4.2 EXERCISES

4.2.1   IF-THEN STATEMENT

Use the following code for the next three questions. The intent of the programmer was to print "Too small" and "Invalid Value" for any value that is less than 10.

```
if (i < 10)
    System.out.println("Too small.");
    System.out.println("Invalid Value.");
    System.out.println("Moving on.");
```

a) If variable **i** has the value of 5, what is the output?

_____

_____

b) If variable **i** has the value of 50, what is the output?

_____

_____

c) Based on questions a and b, how would you fix this program?

_____

_____

d) Write an if statement that prints the word "Valid" if a String **str** matches the value "abc".

_____

_____

Use the following code for the next two questions:

```
boolean b = (x > 10);
if (b)
    System.out.println("Too many.");
```

LAB 4.2

e) Is the preceding code valid Java code?

_____

_____

f) What happens if the value of **x** is 11?

_____

_____

g) Assume that you have a variable called **temperature** that represents the temperature of a glass of water. The temperature is measured in Fahrenheit. Write code that will do all of the following:

1) Print "warm" if the temperature is equal to or over 80 degrees.

2) Also, print "but not too hot" if the temperature is under 90 degrees.

3) Print nothing if the temperature is less than 80 degrees.

_____

_____

4.2.2 IF-THEN-ELSE STATEMENT

Use the following code for the next two questions:

```
if (price >= 10.0)
    System.out.println("The price is too high.");
else
    System.out.println("The price is OK.");
```

a) What is the output if `price` is 10.0?

_____

_____

b) What is the output if `price` is 9.0?

_____

_____

c) Write code that will

    1. Print "success" if a `String password` is equal to "peeka-boo".

    2. Print "Access denied" otherwise.

_____

_____

d) Write code that will print a message based on the value of `temperature` and the table below.

Temperature	Output
Less than 40	"Cold"
Between 40 and 60	"Chilly"
Between 60 and 80	"Warm"
Over 80	"Hot"

_____

_____

LAB 4.2 EXERCISE ANSWERS

4.2.1 ANSWERS

Use the following code for the next three questions. The intent of the programmer was to print "Too small" and "Invalid Value" for any value that is less than 10.

```
if (i < 10)
    System.out.println("Too small.");
    System.out.println("Invalid Value.");
System.out.println("Moving on.");
```

a) If variable **i** has the value of 5, what is the output?

Answer: The output should be as follows:

```
Too small.
Invalid Value.
Moving On.
```

This is what we wanted to do, but the code is actually incorrect, as the following questions and answers will show.

b) If variable **i** has the value of 50, what is the output?

Answer: The output should be as follows:

```
Invalid Value.
Moving On.
```

Now, this may be correct answer, but it's not what we wanted. See the answer to question c for more details.

c) Based on questions a and b, how would you fix this program?

Answer: First of all, the point of this exercise is to show that just indenting the "Invalid Value" line does not make it part of the then-clause. This is a common mistake that even advanced programmers make. If you answered question b correctly, then we congratulate you! The important thing to remember is that only the statement following the "if" line is the then-clause.

So, how do we fix this? We need to use the curly braces to make a statement block. We place every command that is part of the then-clause inside the curly braces.

```
if (i < 10)
{
    System.out.println("Too small.");
    System.out.println("Invalid Value.");
}
System.out.println("Moving on.");
```

Now this will do what we want. If **i** has the value of 50 then neither **println** statement is printed. Only the "Moving on" line is printed because it is not part of the *if-then* statement.

d) Write an if statement that prints the word "Valid" if a String **str** matches the value "abc".

Answer: The following code will do what we want.

```
if (str.equals("abc"))
{
    System.out.println("Valid");
}
```

We need to remember to use the **equals()** method. Otherwise, we may not get the results we expect. Remember that **equals()** returns a **boolean** value that can be used in the *if* statement. Also, even though we only have a *single then-clause-statement,* we still used the curly braces for no other reason than to show that it can be done. Some programmers always use them just to be clear.

Use the following code for the next two questions:

```
boolean b = (x > 10);
if (b)
    System.out.println("Too many.");
```

e) Is the preceding code valid Java code?

Answer: Yes, this is valid Java code.

The first line we have seen before. It defines a variable **b** that is of type **boolean** and then assigns **b** a value of either **true** or **false** (based on the value of **x**). The second line is also valid. The **if** statement requires a **boolean** value and **b** is of type **boolean**.

f) What happens if the value of **x** is 11?

Answer: The following would be printed:

```
Too many.
```

The number 11 is greater than 10 so **b** is set to **true**. The *if* statement checks the value of **b** (which is true) so the **println** statement is executed.

g) Assume that you have a variable called **temperature** that represents the temperature of a glass of water. Write code that will do all of the following:

Answer: While there is always more than one way of doing something, the following code is probably the simplest way. It also demonstrates nested if statements, which was the point of this question.

```
if (temperature >= 80)
{
    System.out.println("warm"");
    if (temperature < 90)
    {
        System.out.println(" but not too hot");
    }
}
// Done
```

"Nesting" means that something is inside of something else. The "90" *if* statement is nested inside the "80" *if* statement. Let's look at an example. If the value of **temperature** is 60, then none of the code inside the outer braces is ever executed. The program flow would jump to the "Done" line. However, if the value of **temperature** is 100, then the first *if* test would be **true**, so we enter the outer block. After printing "warm" the second *if* statement would test **false**, so the remaining code is skipped.

Now try stepping though this code using a value of 85 for **temperature**. This time we get to the inner code and get the following output:

```
warm
but not too hot
```

We will see a more detailed example of nested *if* statements in the next section.

4.2.2 ANSWERS

a) What is the output if **price** is 10.0?

Answer: The following should be the output:

The price is too high.

LAB
4.2

The *if* statement is **true,** so the then-clause is executed.

b) What is the output if **price** is 9.0?

Answer: The following should be the output:

The price is OK.

The *if* statement is **false** so the else-clause is executed.

c) Write code that will print "success" if a **String password** is equal to "peekaboo" an print "Access denied" otherwise.

Answer: The following code will meet the requirements:

```
if (password.equals("peekaboo")
    System.out.println("success");
else
    System.out.println("Access denied");
```

This is the simple form of the *if-then-else* statement and a fairly straightforward example. The variable **password** is a **String** which means that you must use the **equals()** method to test it. **equals()** returns **true** if the object (**password**) equals the value of the parameter (**"peekaboo"**). This is an oversimplified example of how a password-checking algorithm would work.

d) Write code that will print a message based on the value of **temperature** and the table below.

Answer: As always, there is more than one way of doing something, but the following code is what the authors believe is the best way of doing this.

```
if (temperature < 60)
{
    if (temperature < 40)
    {
        System.out.println("Cold");
    }
    else
    {
        System.out.println("Chilly");
    }
}
else
{
    if (temperature <= 80)
    {
        System.out.println("Warm");
    }
    else
    {
        System.out.println("Hot");
    }
}
```

As with question g from Exercise 4.2.1, the point of this question is to use nested *if-then-else* statements. If you haven't already done so, please review that question and its answer.

In the aforementioned question, we used nested *if* statements. In this case, we have two *if-then-else* statements nested inside of a third. If nothing else, this exercise demonstrates the importance of using the curly braces with consistent indentation. Without either the braces or the indentation, this code would be very difficult to read and could also be incorrect.

If you're having trouble figuring out how this code works, try running it with the following values for **temperature**: 35, 50, 75, 90. Do it both on the computer and in your head.

Figure 4.4 shows the flow of the previous program example.

We've tried to show the nested *if* statements in the light gray boxes. You can see how half of the code is bypassed after the first *if* statement since one code branch is eliminated after the first test. We then perform a second test and narrow the choices down again. In the end, only one of the four **System.out.println** statements is actually executed.

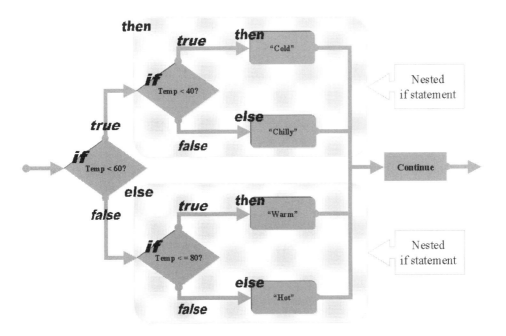

Figure 4.4 ■ Program flow of nested if-then-else statements.

LAB 4.2 SELF-REVIEW QUESTIONS

In order to test your progress, you should be able to answer the following questions.

Use the following code for the next two questions:

```
if (x < 10)
    y = 20;
else
    y = 30;
```

1) What will the value of **y** be if **x** is 10?
    a) _____30
    b) _____20
    c) _____10
    d) _____none of the above

2) For the same code, which line is the else-clause?
    a) _____if (x < 10)
    b) _____y = 20;
    c) _____else
    d) _____y = 30;

3)   The following is legal Java code:

```
if (x > 10)
    if (y < 10)
        z = 10;
```

a) _____True
b) _____False

4)   Properly indenting your *if-then-else* statements is . . .
a) _____required
b) _____recommended
c) _____for wimps
d) _____only used with curly braces

5)   The statement that follows an *if-then-else* statement . . .
a) _____is never executed
b) _____is always executed
c) _____is executed after the else-clause
d) _____is only executed if the test is true
e) _____is executed before the then-clause

Quiz answers appear in Appendix A, Section 4.2.

L A B   4 . 3

THE WHILE LOOP

LAB OBJECTIVES

After this lab, you will be able to:

- Use a while Loop

The key word in "the while loop" is the word *loop*. A *while* loop lets us repeat a section of code as many times as we want to. *Loop,* in this case, refers to the circular path that your code takes. Figure 4.5 shows the program flow of a *while* loop. The *while* loop also takes a detour from the path, but unlike the *if* statement, we keep taking the detour path as many times as we want.

WHILE LOOP SYNTAX

Just like the *if* statement, the *while* loop has both the simple and block forms depending on whether you need to loop through a single, or multiple commands. The block form is actually more commonly used in real life.

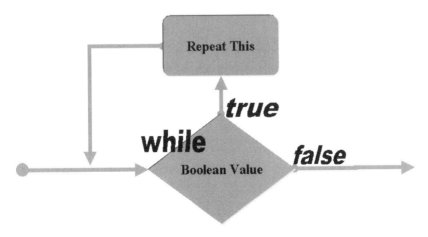

Figure 4.5 ■ Program flow of a while loop.

SIMPLE FORM	BLOCK FORM
```while (booleanValue) repeatThis;```	```while (booleanValue) { repeatThis; repeatThisToo; // etc. }```

LAB 4.3

The *while* loop will execute the **repeatThis** instruction again and again as long as **booleanValue** is true. It is important to realize that the **booleanValue** test is performed each time before each loop cycle. It is expected that the value of **booleanValue** can change within the loop.

The only difference between the two forms is the curly braces, which allow multiple commands to be repeated (Read Section 4.2 if you are not clear on the concept of using the curly braces). As you will see, almost every use of the *while* loop will need curly braces because more than one instruction will need to be run. The authors recommend that you get in the habit of always using curly braces for *while* loops. All of our examples will use the block form.

■ FOR EXAMPLE:

```
int x = 0;
while (x < 5)
{
    System.out.println(x);
    x = x + 1;
}
```

The output of this program would be:

```
0
1
2
3
4
```

Let's analyze what this program does.

1. First, we define an **int** called **x** with a value of zero.
2. We then test **x.** Is **x** less than 5?

3. Yes! So we enter the loop.

4. We print the value of **x.**

5. Then we increment the value of **x** by 1.

6. We now go back to the top of the *while* loop again (Step 2)

We will repeat steps 2 through 6 a total of five times. Each time the value of **x** is incremented by 1. However, when **x** has the value of 5, step 3 will be different. The boolean test (step 2) is **false**, so we don't enter the loop. The program will then skip over the loop block and continue with the next instruction after the *while* loop.

It is very, very important that you define the boolean test such that the while loop can end. If you fail to do this, your program will loop forever in what programmers call an "infinite loop." If this happens, you will need to break out of the Java program somehow. On some systems, this is done with the Control-C.

LAB 4.3 EXERCISES

4.3.1 WHILE LOOP

Use the following code for the next two questions:

```java
String s = "x";
while (s.length() < 4)
{
    System.out.println(s + " is too short.");
    s = s + "x";
}
System.out.println("All Done.");
```

a) What is the output?

_____

_____

b) When the while loop is done, what is the value of **s**?

_____

_____

c) Assume that you have access to a numeric combination lock. The lock will open if you enter in the correct number between 0 and 1000. You have access to this lock using a method (function) called **tryCombination()**, which is defined as follows:

```
public boolean tryCombination(int combination)
```

This method will return true if the combination is correct and false otherwise. Write code to "pick" this lock using a *while* loop. Make sure you print out the actual combination, too.

_____

_____

d) Write code to print out all of the elements of a **Vector**. Remember that an **Enumeration** has these methods defined:

```
public boolean hasMoreElements()
public Object nextElement()
```

_____

_____

LAB 4.3 EXERCISE ANSWERS

4.3.1 ANSWERS

Use the following code for the next two questions:

```
String s = "x";
while (s.length() < 4)
{
    System.out.println(s + " is too short.");
    s = s + "x";
}
System.out.println("All Done.");
```

a) What is the output?

Answer: The output is as follows:

```
x
xx
xxx
All Done.
```

Each time through the loop, the **s** is lengthened by one "x". The length of **s** therefore increases by one each time. When the length gets to 4, the test returns **false** and the loop exits.

b) When the while loop is done, what is the value of **s**?

*Answer: The length of **s** is 4, so the value of **s** is "xxxx".*

c) Write code to "pick" this lock using a *while* loop.

Answer: This code will work:

```
int combo = 0;
while (tryCombination(combo) == false)
{
    combo++;
}
System.out.println("The combination is " + combo);
```

First of all, remember that **combo++** is a shortcut for **combo = combo + 1** and will increase the value of **combo** by 1. This code will test every possible combination for this lock, starting at zero, until it finds one that works. Once it finds the combination [and **tryCombination**() returns **true**], it will stop and print the value of combo.

d) Write code to print out all of the elements of a **Vector.**

Answer: The following code will work. Note: This is a very common use for a while *loop.*

```
// Assume this exists somewhere:
Vector v = new Vector();
// Later . . .
Enumeration e = v.elements();
while (e.hasMoreElements())
{
    Object o = e.nextElement();
    System.out.println(o);
}
```

Remember that the **Vector** keeps track of which element is the "next Element" and automatically updates its reference. There is no need for you, the programmer, to update the **Vector** yourself. The **hasMore Elements**() method looks at this internal reference and only returns **false** if the reference points to the last element in the **Vector.**

LAB 4.3 SELF-REVIEW QUESTIONS

In order to test your progress, you should be able to answer the following questions.

Use the following code for the next two questions:

```
int x = 100;
int y = 0;
while (x > 0)
{
    y++;
    x = x - 10;
}
```

1) What will the value of **y** be after the loop completes?
   a) _____0
   b) _____10
   c) _____100
   d) _____none of the above

2) What will the value of **x** be after the loop completes?
   a) _____0
   b) _____10
   c) _____100
   d) _____none of the above

3) What is the biggest danger of a *while* loop?
   a) _____a while test that is always true
   b) _____no exit condition
   c) _____infinite loop
   d) _____all of the above

Use the following code for the next two questions:

```
int x = 0;
int y = 0;
while (moreWorkToDo)
{
```

```
        x = x + 2;
        y = y + 1;
    }
```

4) What is the type of variable **moreWorkToDo**?

   a) _____**int**
   b) _____**boolean**
   c) _____**Boolean**
   d) _____**true**

5) Assuming that **moreWorkToDo** is initially **true**, will the loop ever exit?

   a) _____**Yes**
   b) _____**No**

Quiz answers appear in Appendix A, Section 4.3.

LAB
4.3

L A B   4 . 4

THE FOR LOOP

LAB OBJECTIVES

After this lab, you will be able to:

- Use a for Loop

Again, the key word in "for loop" is *loop*. The *for* loop lets us loop through a block of code over and over again. A *for* loop is similar to a *while* loop, and in fact, is just a specialized version of a *while* loop.

FOR LOOP SYNTAX

Just like both the *while* loop and *if* statement, the *for* loop has two forms, the simple form and the block form.

SIMPLE FORM

Here is the syntax of a *for* loop. Don't worry if it looks a little confusing at first. The first example with real values will be much clearer.

```
for (initStatement; booleanValue; modificationStatement)
    repeatThis;
```

BLOCK FORM

As with the other flow control instructions we have seen, you need to use curly braces to define a block of commands within the loop:

```
for (initStatement; booleanValue; modificationStatement)
{
    repeatThis;
    repeatThisToo;
//  etc.
}
```

Before we define any of these terms, let's quickly look at a real *for* loop.

■ *FOR EXAMPLE:*

```
for (int x = 0; x < 5; x++)
{
    System.out.println(x);
}
```

Now, look back at the first *while* loop example. These two pieces of code will do the *exact* same thing. That is, the output of this program would be

```
0
1
2
3
4
```

Let's analyze what this code does.

1. First, we define a **int** called **x** with a value of zero.
2. We then test **x**. Is **x** less than 5?
3. Yes! So we enter the loop.
4. We print the value of **x**.
5. Then we increment the value of **x** by 1.
6. We now go back to the top of the while loop again (Step 2)

Do these steps look familiar? They should since the authors just cut and pasted them from the *while* loop section. The truth is that the *for* loop is just a specialized *while* loop. The **block form** of the *for* loop syntax could be rewritten as follows:

```
initStatement;
while (booleanValue)
{
    repeatThis;
    repeatThisToo;
    // etc.
    modificationStatement;
}
```

It is customary, although not required, that the **initStatement**, **booleanValue**, and **modificationStatement** be related, thus helping to ensure the loop actually exits.

> *Note that the initStatement does not have to define a variable, as in the example. It could just assign a value to an existing variable. Java, unlike other programming languages, lets us define variables almost anywhere. Also, it is important to realize that if you do define a variable within the for loop, then that variable is only defined in the block of the for loop. In the example, if you tried to use variable x after the for loop, you would get an error from the compiler that "x is not defined."*

Here is the same example as before, but this time we define **x** outside of the *for* loop.

■ FOR EXAMPLE:

```
int x;
for (x = 0; x < 5; x++)
{
    System.out.println(x);
}
System.out.println("x is now " + x);
```

This code will do the same thing as the previous example. The only difference is that **x** is defined outside of the *for* loop. The very last line of output would look like this:

x is now 5

Since **x** is defined outside of the *for* loop, we can reference its value outside of the loop. The concept of when a variable exists, and when it doesn't, is called "scope" and could fill a whole chapter. We won't go into that much detail in this book, but the important thing to remember is "If you define a variable in the *for* loop's **initStatement**, then that variable only exists inside the *for* loop."

LAB 4.4 EXERCISES

4.4.1 FOR LOOP

a) One of the most common uses of a *for* loop is to access all of the values of an array. Write code to print out all of the values of the following array:

```
String colors[] = {"red", "yellow", "blue",
"purple"};
```

b) Add the color "green" to the `colors` array as follows:

```
String colors[] =
    {"red", "yellow", "blue", "purple", "green"};
```

Now modify your program from the previous question so that it still prints out all of the colors, including "green."

c) Modify the code from Question a to only print the element that has the value of "blue". Also, print out the index of this element.

d) Write code to print out the squares of all numbers from 0 to 10 using a for loop. The "square" of a number is a number multiplied by itself (i.e., x*x).

e) Rewrite your code from question d as a *while* loop.

_____

_____

LAB 4.4 EXERCISE ANSWERS

LAB
4.4

a) One of the most common uses of a *for* loop is to access all of the values of an array. Write code to print out all of the values of the following array:

```
String colors[] = {"red", "yellow", "blue",
"purple"};
```

Answer: The following code will print the array:

```
String colors[] = {"red", "yellow", "blue",
"purple"};
for (int i = 0; i < colors.length; i++)
{
    System.out.println(colors[i]);
}
```

The preceding program would have the following output:

```
red
yellow
blue
purple
```

This program demonstrates one of the fundamental constructs of programming, so be sure you understand everything that is going on. It may seem obvious that **colors.length** is 4 because there are 4 elements in array. However, the *indices* of the elements are 0, 1, 2, and 3. The **length** of an array is always one more than the maximum index value. This is why we use the *less than* test (**i < colors.length**) instead of the *less-equals* test.

Alternatively, the *for* statement *could* have looked something like this:

```
for (int i = 0; i < 4; i++)
    System.out.println(colors[i]);
```

This code would work, too, since we know that there are four elements in the **colors** array. However, this is not a good idea, as the next question will demonstrate. If your program was similar to the alternative solution, then please pay particular attention to the next answer.

b) Add the color "green" to the **colors** array as follows:

```
String colors[] =
    {"red", "yellow", "blue", "purple", "green"};
```

Now modify your program from the previous question so that it still prints out all of the colors, including "green."

Answer: Other than modifying the **colors** *array, no changes are necessary to a well-written program. Such a program follows:*

```
String colors[] =
    {"red", "yellow", "blue", "purple", "green"};
for (int i = 0; i < colors.length; i++)
{
    System.out.println(colors[i]);
}
```

The code from the answer to Question a will *still* print out the entire array without having to make any changes. The lesson to learn here is that by using **colors.length** our program will automatically adjust the number of loops in the *for* loop.

Don't "hard code" Values in Your Programs.

In the answer to the question a, we mentioned that it was possible to just have used the number "4" instead of **colors.length**. If we had done that, then we *would* have had to change the code to handle the additional "green" array element. The "4" would have needed to have been changed to a "5" since there are now five elements in the array. This style of programming is called "hard coding" because the values are fixed or "hard." Hard coding is a bad programming practice because it is not flexible and can lead to bugs in your code. At the very least, hard coding can cause extra work for you, the programmer, if you need to modify your code. When you set the limits in the *for* loop, try your best to not hard code the limit values. Use the **length** field for arrays, the **size()** method for **Vectors**, and the **length()** method for **Strings**.

c) Modify the code from question a to print only the element that has the value of "blue". Also, print out the index of this element.

Answer: The following code will work:

```
String colors[] = {"red", "yellow", "blue",
"purple"};
for (int i = 0; i < colors.length; i++)
{
    if (colors[i].equals("blue"))
    {
            System.out.println("name = " + colors[i]);
            System.out.println("index = " + i);
    }
}
```

**LAB
4.4**

The output of this program would look like this:

```
name = blue
index = 2
```

Let's look at what we did. First, we added an *if* statement to test each element of the **colors** array. While **colors** is an array of Strings, **colors[i]** is just a single **String**. This means that you can print it or use its **equals()** method, which is what we did here. The second thing we did was to put the print statements inside the *if* block. Now these statements are only printed when we find the matching value of "blue".

The point of this exercise is to show that although we are looping through each element in the array, we can limit which elements we access (print out in this case). This code is an example of a *searching algorithm*. We had a "set of data" (the **colors** array) and we searched through all the data for a specific element ("blue"). When we found the element, we printed the element and some additional data (the index value). While this is a simple example, it is the same concept used in many database searches. When you dial the 411 directory assistance, they search for the name you give them, find it, and then give you some additional information which is the person's phone number. It's the same concept demonstrated here, just on a much larger scale.

d) Write code to print out the squares of all numbers from 0 to 10 using a for loop.

Answer: The following code will work:

```
int maximum = 10;
for (int i = 0; i <= maximum; i++)
```

```
{
    int square = i * i;
    System.out.println(i + " squared is " + square);
}
```

The output would be as follows:

```
 0 squared is 0
 1 squared is 1
 2 squared is 4
 3 squared is 9
 4 squared is 16
 5 squared is 25
 6 squared is 36
 7 squared is 49
 8 squared is 64
 9 squared is 81
10 squared is 100
```

This is a straightforward example. The point to learn here is that we can do a lot of work with just a little bit of code. If we wanted to find all of the squares from 0 to 1000, all we would have to do is change **maximum** from "10" to a "1000" and rerun the program. Whenever possible, let the computer do the busy work for you.

e)   Rewrite your code from question d as a *while* loop.

   Answer: The following code if functionally the same as the answer to question d:

```
int maximum = 10;
int i = 0;
while (i <= maximum)
{
    int square = i * i;
    System.out.println(i + " squared is " + square);
    i++;
}
```

The point of this exercise is to show that any *for* loop can be rewritten as a *while* loop. However, with the *for* loop, it is clearer that **i** is the key variable in the loop. As you program more, you will learn to appreciate the shortcut that the *for* loop allows over the *while* loop.

LAB 4.4 SELF-REVIEW QUESTIONS

In order to test your progress, you should be able to answer the following questions.

1) A *for* loop is a specialized . . .
   a) _____Infinite loop
   b) _____While loop
   c) _____Fruit loop
   d) _____If-then-else statement

2) How many times will this code loop?

```
for (int i = 0; i < 10; i++)
{
    System.out.println(i);
}
```

   a) _____0
   b) _____10
   c) _____100
   d) _____none of the above

3) Using the same code in question 2, what is the value of **i** after the loop exits?
   a) _____0
   b) _____10
   c) _____100
   d) _____i is not defined outside the loop and has no value

4) Using the same code in question 2, which instruction is executed at the end of each loop?
   a) _____ int i = 0
   b) _____ i < 10
   c) _____ i++
   d) _____ System.out.println(i)

5) Using the same code in question 2, which instruction is executed at the beginning of each loop?
   a) _____ int i = 0
   b) _____ i < 10
   c) _____ i++
   d) _____ System.out.println(i)

LAB
4.4

6) Using the same code in question 2, which instruction is executed at just one time?

a) _____ **int i = 0**

b) _____ **i < 10**

c) _____ **i++**

d) _____ **System.out.println(i)**

Quiz answers appear in Appendix A, Section 4.4.

L A B   4 . 5

SWITCH STATEMENT

LAB 4.5

The final flow control command is the *switch* statement. Unlike the *if-then-else* statement, which allows a program to choose between one of two possible paths, the *switch* statement allows a program to choose between one of many possible paths. Another name for a *switch* statement is "case statement." However, in this book we will use the term "switch statement."

LEARN BY EXAMPLE FIRST

We are going to break from the normal format and first show you an example *switch* statement before we show you the generic syntax. It will be easier to explain the *switch* statement once you have seen one.

INT EXAMPLE

■ *FOR EXAMPLE:*

```
int choice = 1;
switch (choice)
{
    case 0:
        System.out.println("Zero");
        break;
    case 1:
        System.out.println("One");
        break;
    case 2:
        System.out.println("Two");
```

```
            break;
      default:
            System.out.println("Unknown");
   }
```

The output of the preceding example is:

One

The *switch* statement looks at the value of **choice** and then looks for a match in all of the **case** labels. If it finds a match, it will then execute all of the instructions between the matching label and the first **break** statement. The **break** statement will cause the program to *break* and jump to the end of the **switch** statement.

 If none of the case *labels match the value of choice, then the* default *code is executed.*

In this example, **choice** has the value of 1, so the **case 1** code is executed. If **choice** had the value of 2 then the **case 2** code would output the word "**Two**".

Note that **choice** is an **int**, not a **boolean**. Booleans only have two possible values, so there are only two choices. Variables of type **int** can have many possible values so there can be many possible choices. *Switch* statements can take variables of type **int** or of type **char** as the "choice"

The Truth about char and int

The reason that a *switch* statement will take either an **int** or a **char** as the choice variable is that **ints** and **chars** are really the same things to Java. **ints** are just integer numbers, and the truth is, so are **chars**. Every letter is assigned a code number, just like a simple decoder ring. The letter A is given the code number 62. B is 63, C is 64, and so on. This code is called ASCII, which stands for the American Standard Character Information Interchange. It is not important to know this code, but it is useful to know that it exists and to remember that, to the computer, everything is a number.

For the sake of completeness, the following variables types are valid to use as the *switch* statement's variable: **boolean, char, byte, short, int,** and **long**.

variable. Most other types are not valid and will result in a compile error. See the sidebar for the reasons that **char** variables are allowed.

CHAR EXAMPLE

■ *FOR EXAMPLE:*

Here is an example of using a char as the "choice" variable:

```
char choice = 'c';
switch (choice)
{
    case 'a':
            System.out.println("alpha");
            break;
    case 'b':
            System.out.println("beta");
            break;
    case 'c':
            System.out.println("charlie");
            break;
    default:
            System.out.println("Unknown");
}
```

The output in this example would be:

charlie

The syntax is exactly the same as the **int** version. The only difference is that the **case** labels must specify **char** values.

THE BREAK IS OPTIONAL

In the previous examples, every **case** block had a **break** statement at the end. These **break** statements cause the program flow to jump to the end of the *switch* statement. However, the **break** is optional. If you don't have one, the program flow will "fall down" into the next **case** block. This may or may not be what you want, but it will happen.

MULTIPLE LABELS

Additionally, you can have more than one **case** label per block. If you had a situation where more than one choice should execute the same code, you can list all of the choices together. Technically, this is just an empty **case** block with no **break** statement.

■ *FOR EXAMPLE:*

This example demonstrates the "optional break" and "multiple label" situation. The idea behind this example is to print out "**even**" if a number (between 0 and 10) is even. Additionally, the word "**small**" should be printed if the number is less than five. For even numbers that are less than five, both words should be printed.

```
int x = 2;
switch (x)
{
    case 0:
    case 2:
    case 4:
            System.out.println("small");
    case 6:
    case 8:
            System.out.println("even");
            break;
    default:
            System.out.println("odd");
}
```

**LAB
4.5**

The output in this example is:

small
even

Let's look at what happened. Variable **x** has the value of 2. The *switch* statement finds a match with **case 2.** Java then starts executing any commands after the **case 2** label. It skips the **case 4** label because it's just a label. Then it prints the word "small." Because there is no **break** statement, Java continues on, skipping labels until it prints "even." Now there is a break statement, so the program flow jumps to the end of the *switch* statement.

GENERIC SWITCH SYNTAX

Now that you've seen a bunch of examples, here is the generic syntax of a switch statement.

```
switch (choiceVariable)
{
    case c1:
            [optional code;]
            [optional break;]
```

```
case c2:
        [optional code;]
        [optional break;]
    ...
    case cn:
        [optional code;]
        [optional break;]
    [optional default: label]
        [optional code;]
}
```

Where **choiceVariable** is either an **int** or a **char** variable. The **case** labels, **c1**, **c2**, through **cn** must be actual **int** or **char** *values*. You cannot put variables in the **case** labels. The **default** label is also optional, but if the *switch* statement cannot find a matching label, and there is no **default** block, then a Java error will be generated. It is recommended that you always include a **default** block, even if it doesn't do anything. The curly braces are required around the entire *switch* statement.

LAB 4.5 EXERCISES

4.5.1 THE SWITCH STATEMENT

Consider the following code:

```
char grade;
String rating;
// Later
switch (grade)
{
    case 'A':
        rating = "Excellent";
        break;
    case 'B':
        rating = "Good";
        break;
    case 'C':
        rating = "Average";
        break;
    case 'D':
        rating = "Poor";
        break;
```

LAB 4.5

```
     case 'F':
          rating = "Failure";
          break;
     default
          rating = "Confused";
}
```

a) What is the value of **rating** if **grade** is 'B'?

_____

_____

b) What is the value of **rating** if **grade** is 'K'?

_____

_____

c) On a telephone, most numbers have letters associated with them (e.g., The number '2' has 'ABC' on it). Write a switch statement to print the numeric value of the letters on a touch-tone phone. Given 'A' you would print '2', or given 'D' you would print '3', and so on.

_____

_____

d) Add a *for* loop to your code from Question c that will print the numeric telephone number given a String **phoneNumber,** which may contain letters (i.e., if **phoneNumber** has the value "800-GOJAVA", your code would print out the actual phone number "800-465282"). **Hint**: there is a method in **String** called **charAt**() that will return the **char** value of the character at **index**.

public char charAt(int index)

_____

_____

LAB 4.5 EXERCISE ANSWERS

4.5.1 ANSWERS

Consider the following code:

a) What is the value of **rating** if **grade** is 'B'?

Answer: The following is the output:

Good

The value of **grade** is **'B'** which matches the **case** **'B':** label so the code following this label is executed up to the break instruction.

b) What is the value of **rating** if **grade** is 'K'?

Answer: The following is the output:

Confused

Since 'K' does not match any of the labels, the **default** code is executed.

c) Write a switch statement to print the numeric value of the letters on a touch tone phone

Answer: Here is one example that works. In the interests of space, we compressed some lines into a single line. While technically valid, this is a bad programming style that only the authors of books should use!

```
switch (letter)
{
    case 'A': case 'B': case 'C':
        System.out.print('2'); break;
    case 'D': case 'E': case 'F':
        System.out.print('3'); break;
    case 'G': case 'H': case 'I':
        System.out.print('4'); break;
    case 'J': case 'K': case 'L':
        System.out.print('5'); break;
    case 'M': case 'N': case 'O':
        System.out.print('6'); break;
    case 'P': case 'Q': case 'R': case 'S':
        System.out.print('7'); break;
    case 'T': case 'U': case 'V':
```

```
              System.out.print('8'); break;
        case 'W': case 'X': case 'Y': case 'Z':
              System.out.print('9'); break;
    default:
              System.out.print(letter);
    }
```

This should be a straightforward example. Since each number has several letters associated with it, we use multiple **case** labels. The **default** block is very important as it handles all of the nonmatching cases. For normal numbers, or characters like '-' and '*', we just print the same **letter** value. This way we only "translate" the letters.

d) Add a *for* loop to your code from question c that will print the numeric telephone number given a String **phoneNumber**.

Answer: The following is one possible answer:

```
String phoneNumber = "1-800-GOJAVA";
for (int i = 0; i < phoneNumber.length(); i++)
{
    char letter = phoneNumber.charAt(i);
        switch (letter)
        {
        // Same code from Question c
        }
}
System.out.println();
```

**LAB
4.5**

This is another example of "letting the computer do the work for you." We cycle through each letter of the original phone number and then translate it using the code from Question c. If we want to translate a different phone number, all we have to do is change the value of **phoneNumber**.

LAB 4.5 SELF-REVIEW QUESTIONS

In order to test your progress, you should be able to answer the following questions.

1) What are the valid types of switch variables? Check all that apply.
   a) _____ float
   b) _____ int
   c) _____ Integer
   d) _____ char

2) What word identifies each switch choice?
a) _____ **choice**
b) _____ **switch**
c) _____ **case**
d) _____ **label**

3) What word identifies the choice used if no matches are found?
a) _____ **default**
b) _____ **any**
c) _____ **last**
d) _____ **none**

4) What word identifies the end of a block?
a) _____ **done**
b) _____ **jump**
c) _____ **last**
d) _____ **break**

For the remaining questions, use the following code:

```
switch (X)
{
    case 1:
            System.out.println("One");
    case 2:
            System.out.println("Two");
            break;
    case 3:
            System.out.println("Three");
    case 4:
            System.out.println("Four");
            break;
    default:
            System.out.println("Unknown");
}
```

5) What words are printed if **X** is 2? Check all that apply.
a) _____ **One**
b) _____ **Two**
c) _____ **Three**
d) _____ **Four**
e) _____ **Unknown**

6) What words are printed if **x** is 3? Check all that apply.
   a) _____ **One**
   b) _____ **Two**
   c) _____ **Three**
   d) _____ **Four**
   e) _____ **Unknown**

7) What words are printed if **x** is 7? Check all that apply.
   a) _____ **One**
   b) _____ **Two**
   c) _____ **Three**
   d) _____ **Four**
   e) _____ **Unknown**

Quiz answers appear in Appendix A, Section 4.5.

**LAB
4.5**

C H A P T E R   4

TEST YOUR THINKING

As you may have figured out by now, there are two kinds of flow-control operators: a branching operator (**if, switch**) and a looping operator (**for, while**). With these operators, it is possible to do a lot of work without doing a lot of coding.

1) Write code to find all of the prime numbers between 2 and 100. A prime number is a number that is evenly divisible **only** by itself and 1. The number 10 is **not** a prime because it is evenly divisible by 2 and 5.

2) Write code to find the *factorial* of a number. The *factorial* of a number is the product of multiplying the number by every whole number less than the number, all they way down to 1. For example, the factorial of 4 (written "4!") is 4 * 3 * 2 * 1 = 24. 3! = 3 * 2 * 1 = 6.

3) Write code to find average of all of the numbers in the **scores** array. Also, using the **names** array, print out the names of all of the students whose score is 70 or above. Assume that student's name has the same index as their score.

```
double scores[] = {50, 100, 75, 81, 90.5, 66, 33,
    99};
String names[] = {"David", "Mary", "Joannie", "Nancy",
    "Susan", "Elizabeth", "Tommy", "Nicholas"};
```

CHAPTER 5

BOOLEAN LOGIC

 To be, or not to be.

William Shakespeare

Hamlet had it easy. He only had two choices. In the real world, there are many choices and considerations. While the flow-control operators give you the basic tools to construct a network of *paths* your program can take, the boolean test that chooses which path to take can be an involved choice. Sometimes a simple *equals* or *greater-than* test is not enough. Sometimes you need to look at the values of more than one variable before you can make a decision. *Boolean math* is a technique that allows you to consider multiple factors in a single decision. With *boolean math,* you can build *boolean expressions* and give your flow-control operators some real power!

L A B   5 . 1

BOOLEAN MATH

LAB OBJECTIVES

After this lab, you will be able to:

- Understand the AND Operator
- Understand the OR Operator
- Understand the NOT Operator
- Understand the XOR Operator

Boolean math is actually very simple. In fact, boolean math is just common sense presented in mathematical terms. Try not to let the "mathematical" part throw you and try to focus on the commonsense part!

Here is an example of how something simple can sound complicated. You should understand the following simple equation:

```
1 + 2 = 3
```

The commonsense way of looking at this equation is "one plus two equals three." The mathematical way of saying this is that you *apply* the **plus** *operator* on the numeric values of 1 and 2 to get the numeric answer of 3. In *numeric* math, we apply *numeric* operators (such as plus, minus, multiply, or divide) to *numeric* values to get a *numeric* answer. In *boolean* math, we apply *boolean* operators to *boolean* values to get a *boolean* answer. Since boolean values consist of only **true** and **false**, we cannot "add" or "subtract" them, but we can combine two boolean values together with boolean operators.

BOOLEAN OPERATORS

There are four boolean operators: AND, OR, NOT, and XOR (pronounced eXclusive OR). We will cover each operator separately and then demonstrate how to build functions with these operators to better control the flow of your programs.

THE AND OPERATOR

The first operator we will cover is the AND operator. In Java, this looks like this:

```
X && Y
```

This is read as "X AND Y" where X and Y are **boolean** values. **X && Y** is **true** only if both **X** *and* **Y** are **true**. Table 5.1 describes the AND operator:

Table 5.1 ■ The AND Operator

X	Y	X && Y
false	false	false
false	true	false
true	false	false
true	true	true

■ *FOR EXAMPLE:*

```
boolean x = true;
boolean y = false;
boolean z = x && y;
```

In the preceding example, **z** would be **false** because **X && Y** is **false**.

■ *FOR EXAMPLE:*

This is a more realistic example:

```
if ((temperature > 80) && (humidity > 90))
{
    System.out.println("It's not just the heat, it's
the humidity!");
}
```

What we've done here is put two conditions in our *if* statement. In order for the annoying cliché to be printed, both the temperature **and the** humidity need to be high. Nothing is printed if either value is too low. The best way to remember the rule for AND is that "everything must be true" for the result to be true.

THE OR OPERATOR

The second operator we will cover is the OR operator. In Java, this looks like this:

```
X || Y
```

This is read as "X OR Y" where X and Y are boolean values. **x || y** is **true** if either **x** *or* **y** are **true**. Table 5.2 describes the OR operator:

Table 5.2 ■ The OR Operator

X	Y	X || Y
false	false	false
false	true	true
true	false	true
true	true	true

■ *FOR EXAMPLE:*

```
boolean x = true;
boolean y = false;
boolean z = x || y;
```

In the preceding example, **z** would be **true** because **x || y** is **true**.

■ *FOR EXAMPLE:*

Here is a better example:

```
if ((miles > 3000) || (months > 3))
{
    System.out.println("Your car warranty has expired!");
}
```

Again, we've put two conditions in our *if* statement. In this case, if either the car has more than 3000 miles *or* the car is over 3 months old, then the warranty is expired. The best way to remember the rule for OR is that "at least one thing must be true" for the result to be true.

THE NOT OPERATOR

The NOT operator is a very simple operator. It just means "the opposite value." In Java, it looks like this:

```
!X
```

This is read "not X," where X is a boolean value. **!X** is **true** if **X** is **false**. Likewise, **!X** is **false** if **X** is **true**. Remember the early 1990s when everyone, including old ladies in beer commercials, would say "Hey, you're really a good guitar player! Not!" Little did they know it, but they were using boolean operators to achieve their sarcasm. Table 5.3 describes the NOT operator:

Table 5.3 ■ The NOT Operator

X	!X
false	true
true	false

■ *FOR EXAMPLE:*

```
boolean x = true;
boolean y = !x;
```

In the preceding example, **y** is **false** because **!x** is **false**.

■ *FOR EXAMPLE:*

```
String password;
// Later
if (!password.equals("open sesame"))
{
    System.out.println("Sorry, incorrect password.");
}
```

In the preceding example, we want to print the message when the password *doesn't* match "open sesame." Without the NOT operator, the code would print the message *only* if the password matched. We need the opposite behavior so we use the NOT operator to reverse the boolean value that the **equals()** operator returns.

THE XOR OPERATOR

The last operator is called "exclusive or," which is abbreviated XOR (and pronounced "ex or"). In Java, it looks like this:

```
A ^ B
```

This is read as "A XOR B" where A and B are boolean values. **A** ^ **B** is **true** only if either **A** *or* **B** are **true**, but not if both **A** and **B** are **true**. Table 5.4 describes the XOR operator:

Table 5.4 ■ The XOR Operator

A	B	A ^ B
false	false	false
false	true	true
true	false	true
true	true	false

■ FOR EXAMPLE:

```
boolean x = true;
boolean y = false;
boolean z = x ^ y;
```

In this example **z** would have the value of **true** because **x** ^ **y** is **true**.

■ FOR EXAMPLE:

Here is a better example:

```
boolean haveCake;
boolean wantToEatCake;
// Later
if (haveCake ^ wantToEatCake)
    System.out.println("You're OK!");
else
    system.out.println("You can't have your cake and
eat it too!");
```

OK, so this example is a little silly, but the point is to show that it is only OK to have one condition be true, but not both. You can have a cake, or you can want to eat a cake, but you can't do both. XOR is the only operator that will return false if both operands are true. Neither AND nor OR will do this.

The best way to remember the rule for XOR is that "both values must be different" for the result to be true. Otherwise, the result is false.

LAB 5.1 EXERCISES

Exercises 5.1.1 through 5.1.4 are virtually identical to each other. All of the code examples are the same with the exception of the operator. Your job is to identify how the different operators change the behavior of the flow control statements.

5.1.1 THE AND OPERATOR

Use the following code for the next two questions:

```
boolean b1;
boolean b2;
if (b1 && b2)
    System.out.println("Yes");
else
    System.out.println("No");
```

a) What is the output if **b1** is **true** and **b2** is **false?**

_____

_____

b) What is the output if **b1** is **true** and **b2** is **true?**

_____

_____

Use the following code for next two questions:

```
int x = 0;
int y = 10;
```

```
while ((x < 5) && (y > 5))
{
    System.out.println("x = " + x);
    System.out.println("y = " + y);
    x++;
    y = y - 5;
}
```

c) How many times will this loop run?

_____

_____

d) Why does the while loop stop?

_____

_____

5.1.2 THE OR OPERATOR

Use the following code for the next two questions:

```
boolean b1;
boolean b2;
if (b1 || b2)
    System.out.println("Yes");
else
    System.out.println("No");
```

a) What is the output if **b1** is **true** and **b2** is **false**?

_____

_____

b) What is the output if **b1** is **true** and **b2** is **true**?

_____

_____

Use the following code for next two questions:

```
int x = 0;
int y = 10;
while ((x < 5) || (y > 5))
{
    System.out.println("x = " + x);
    System.out.println("y = " + y);
    x++;
    y = y - 5;
}
```

c) How many times will this loop run?

_____

_____

d) Why does the while loop stop?

_____

_____

5.1.3 THE NOT OPERATOR

Use the following code for the next two questions:

```
boolean b1;
boolean b2;
if (!(b1 || b2))
    System.out.println("Yes");
else
    System.out.println("No");
```

a) What is the output if **b1** is **true** and **b2** is **false**?

_____

_____

b) What is the output if **b1** is **true** and **b2** is **true**?

_____

_____

Use the following code for next two questions:

```
int x = 0;
int y = 10;
while (!(x < 5) || !(y > 5))
{
    System.out.println("x = " + x);
    System.out.println("y = " + y);
    x++;
    y = y - 5;
}
```

c) How many times will this loop run?

_____

_____

d) Why does the while loop stop?

_____

_____

5.1.4 THE XOR OPERATOR

Use the following code for the next two questions:

```
boolean b1;
boolean b2;
if (b1 ^ b2)
    System.out.println("Yes");
else
    System.out.println("No");
```

a) What is the output if **b1** is `true` and **b2** is `false`?

b) What is the output if **b1** is `true` and **b2** is `true`?

Use the following code for next two questions (Note, it's a little different from the previous examples):

```
int x = 0;
int y = 10;
while ((x < 5) ^ (y < 5))
{
    System.out.println("x = " + x);
    System.out.println("y = " + y);
    x++;
    y = y - 5;
}
```

c) How many times will this loop run?

d) Why does the while loop stop?

LAB 5.1 EXERCISE ANSWERS

5.1.1 ANSWERS

Use the following code for the next two questions:

```
boolean b1;
boolean b2;
if (b1 && b2)
    System.out.println("Yes");
else
    System.out.println("No");
```

a) What is the output if **b1** is **true** and **b2** is **false**?

Answer: The output is as follows because true and false is false.

No

b) What is the output if **b1** is **true** and **b2** is **true**?

Answer: The output is as follows because true and true is true.

Yes

Use the following code for next two questions:

c) How many times will this loop run?

Answer: One time. Keep reading if you don't know why.

d) Why does the while loop stop?

Answer: After the first time through the loop, y has the value of 5. The test (y > 5) is false, so the final test is false and the loop exits.

Here is a table showing each iteration through the loop:

x	y	x < 5	y > 5	(x<5) && (y>5)
0	10	true	true	true
1	5	true	false	false

5.1.2 ANSWERS

Use the following code for the next two questions:

```
boolean b1;
boolean b2;
if (b1 || b2)
     System.out.println("Yes");
else
     System.out.println("No");
```

a) What is the output if **b1** is **true** and **b2** is **false**?

Answer: The output is as follows because true or false is true.

Yes

b) What is the output if **b1** is **true** and **b2** is **true**?

Answer: The output is as follows because true or true is true.

Yes

Use the following code for the next two questions:

c) How many times will this loop run?

Answer: Five times.

d) Why does the while loop stop?

Answer: Because x is 5 (which is not less than 5) and y is −15 (which is not greater than 5). Both tests are false, so "false or false" is false.

Here is a table showing each iteration through the loop:

x	y	x < 5	y > 5	(x<5) || (y>5)
0	10	true	true	true
1	5	true	false	true
2	0	true	false	true
3	-5	true	false	true
4	-10	true	false	true
5	-15	false	false	false

5.1.3 ANSWERS

Use the following code for the next two questions:

```
boolean b1;
boolean b2;
if (!(b1 || b2))
    System.out.println("Yes");
else
    System.out.println("No");
```

a) What is the output if **b1** is **true** and **b2** is **false**?

Answer: The output is as follows:

No

true or false is true. Not true is false, so the else-clause is executed.

b) What is the output if **b1** is **true** and **b2** is **true**?

Answer: The output is as follows:

No

true or true is true. Not true is false, so the else *clause is executed.*

Use the following code for the next two questions:

c) How many times will this loop run?

Answer: Zero times!

d) Why does the while loop stop?

Answer: At the start, x is 0 and y is 10. (0 < 5) is true, so !(0 < 5) is false.

Then we have (10 > 5) which is true, but !(10 > 5) is false. We end up with false or false, which is false.

Here is a table showing each iteration through the loop:

x	y	!(x < 5)	!(y > 5)	!(x<5) || !(y>5)
0	10	false	false	false

5.1.4 ANSWERS

Use the following code for the next two questions:

```
boolean b1;
boolean b2;
if (b1 ^ b2)
    System.out.println("Yes");
else
    System.out.println("No");
```

a) What is the output if **b1** is **true** and **b2** is **false**?

Answer: The output is as follows because true xor false is true.

Yes

b) What is the output if **b1** is **true** and **b2** is **true**?

Answer: The output is as follows because true xor true is false.

No

Use the following code for the next two questions:

c) How many times will this loop run?

Answer: Two times.

d) Why does the while loop stop?

Answer: After the second time through the loop, x is 2 and y is 0. (x < 5) is true and (y < 5) is also true. true xor true is false, so the loop exits.

Here is a table showing each iteration through the loop:

x	y	x < 5	y < 5	(x<5) ^ (y<5)
0	10	true	false	true
1	5	true	false	true
2	0	true	true	false

LAB 5.1 SELF-REVIEW QUESTIONS

In order to test your progress, you should be able to answer the following questions.

1) What is the Java symbol for the AND operator?
   a) _____ and
   b) _____ &
   c) _____ &&
   d) _____ ||

2) What does the following code mean:

   ```
   B = !A
   ```

   a) _____ B equals OR A
   b) _____ B equals NOT A
   c) _____ B equals XOR A
   d) _____ The programmer is Canadian, eh?

3) What is **true** AND **true**?
   a) _____true
   b) _____false
   c) _____maybe

4) Which operator is used in the following expression:

   ```
   X ^ Y
   ```

   a) _____ AND
   b) _____ OR
   c) _____ NOT
   d) _____ XOR

5) Given the following table of values and results, what is the operator, **OP,** used on variables **X** and **Y?**

X	Y	X OP Y
false	false	false
false	true	true
true	false	true
true	true	true

a) _____ **AND**
b) _____ **OR**
c) _____ **NOT**
d) _____ **XOR**

6) How would you write the expression from question 5?

a) _____ **X && Y**
b) _____ **X !! Y**
c) _____ **X || Y**
d) _____ **X ^ Y**

Quiz answers appear in Appendix A, Section 5.1.

L A B   5 . 2

BOOLEAN EXPRESSIONS

LAB OBJECTIVES

After this lab, you will be able to:

• Construct Boolean Expressions

In Lab 5.1, we discussed the basic boolean operators. The real art of programming is combining these operators together to create meaningful boolean expressions. In the same way that mathematical operators, like *plus* and *multiply,* can be combined into mathematical equations (like $2 * 4 + 5 * 7$), so too can you combine the OR, AND, NOT, and XOR operators together into boolean expressions. Just like "normal" math, boolean math is a skill that is better learned *by doing* rather than *by reading.* We will practice this skill more thoroughly in the exercises later, but we must cover some basic concepts first.

BOOLEAN EXPRESSION CONCEPTS

The concepts for writing boolean expressions are exactly the same for writing mathematical ones.

• There is a left-to-right precedence in evaluating an expression.
• Use parentheses to change the precedence and order of evaluation.
• Construct your expression to simulate a real-life situation.

PRECEDENCE

First of all, "precedence" means "the order in which things are done." If an equation has more than one operator, which one is evaluated first? The answer is "The one with the higher precedence." For boolean operators, each operator is evaluated left to right. Consider the following expression:

```
false && false || true
```

This expression is evaluated in two steps:

- **false && false** (which is false)
- **false || true** (which is true)

Therefore, the result is **true.**

■ *FOR EXAMPLE:*

We can verify the result with the following code:

```
System.out.println(false && false || true);
```

The output is as follows:

```
true
```

If this expression had been evaluated right-to-left, then the result would have been **false.** The next example will demonstrate this.

USING PARENTHESES

If we want to change the order in which operators are evaluated, we use parentheses, just like a mathematical equation. Expressions inside parentheses are evaluated first, starting with the innermost set of parentheses.

■ *FOR EXAMPLE:*

Let's use the previous example, but add a set of parentheses:

```
System.out.println(false && (false || true));
```

The output is as follows:

```
false
```

By using the parentheses, we have changed the order in which the expression is evaluated. Now the sequence of events is:

- **`false && (something in parentheses)`** (result unknown)
- **`false || true`** (which is true)
- **`false && true`** (which is false)

While the expressions look similar, by adding the parentheses, we have changed the result by changing the order of events. We still go left-to-right, but now we get to the parentheses, so we must evaluate the expression inside the parentheses before continuing.

CONSTRUCTING EXPRESSIONS

So far, we have seen what boolean expressions can do, but not how to use them. Building a boolean expression is part skill, but also part art. There is usually more than one way of doing something, some ways more elegant than others. The heart of a computer program is its boolean expressions because they dictate the behavior of a program.

The first thing to consider when writing an expression is to know exactly what you are trying to accomplish. That may sound obvious, but programmers do sometimes lose sight of their overall goal and focus too closely on the code. If you can state your goal plainly, clearly, and in simple words, then writing a boolean expression to match that goal becomes much easier. Let's take a look at an example.

■ *FOR EXAMPLE:*

This example will construct a boolean expression for a given problem. We have broken the process into a sequence of steps that you can use for most problems:

1. First, we need a goal. For this example, we will write code to tell us if it OK to mow the lawn or not.
2. Next, we need to define the conditions of the goal. For this example, the conditions are that we only mow on weekends, and we only mow between the hours of 10 A.M. and 4 P.M.
3. Next, we need to look at what information we are given. For our example, we will have the following variables:

```
String today;    // The day of the week. e.g. "Monday"
int timeHour;    // The hour of the time in
                 // 24 hour format.
```

Note, **`timeHour`** only represents the *hour* of the current time. So, it were 3:50 A.M., **`timeHour`** would have a value of 3.

4. Next, we try to state the goal and conditions in terms of the input. Here goes: "Mow the lawn if today is Saturday or Sunday and the time is between 10:00 and 16:00 (4 P.M.)."

5. Next, we break down the conditions into smaller pieces that we can define in terms of the input we were given. The following code does just this:

```
boolean isSaturday = today.equals("Saturday");
boolean isSunday = today.equals("Sunday");
boolean afterTen = timeHour >= 10;
boolean beforeFour = timeHour < 16;     // 16 is 4pm
```

The reason we use *greater-equals* for **afterTen** is that any time in the 10 o'clock range is valid: 10:00, 10:01 and 10:59 are all valid. Conversely, none of the 4 o'clock times is valid, so we use the *less-than* operator. Otherwise, times like 16:15 would be considered valid.

6. Finally, we combine these pieces together with boolean operators to create the boolean expression.

```
if ((isSaturday || isSunday) && (afterTen && beforeFour))
    System.out.println("Mow the lawn.");
else
    System.out.println("Do not mow the lawn!");
```

The first thing to notice is that we use the OR operator for the (**isSaturday || isSunday**) test. You should also note that our statement from step 4 also used the word "or" to describe the conditions for the day. You will find this is usually the case when you state your conditions. If you find yourself *saying* "or," then you will probably *use* an OR operator. The same goes for saying and using "and" and "not."

Another thing to notice is that we put parentheses around the OR statement. This is important because without them, the meaning of the boolean expression would be different. That is, we wouldn't get the results that we wanted.

Now that we have our expression, it is important to test it. It is very easy and likely that you will make a mistake during this process. None of the steps listed in this example has exact and easy-to-follow instructions. It is quite possible to misinterpret the conditions or to have a flaw in your boolean logic. Mistakes like these are called "bugs" and every programmer makes them. You've probably heard the term "bug" before, so perhaps now you have a better understanding of where bugs can come from. Don't get discouraged if your code doesn't work the first time. Debugging your code is a normal part of writing a program.

The best way to look for bugs is to test your code. For this example, plug in some values for **today** and **timeHour** and see what the results are. Look back at the original problem statement: We said it was OK to mow the lawn on weekends between 10 A.M. and 4 P.M. The idea is to test values that are *in* and *out* of the "OK" range for both **today** and **timeHour**. If you find a value that is unexpected or incorrect, then you need to go back and look at your code.

Table 5.5 shows the results for this program for a few test values of **today** and **timeHour**.

Based on these sample test values, it appears the program works. Hooray for us! We will explore a more thorough testing method in the Lab Exercises.

Table 5.5 ■ Sample Test Values and Results

today	timeHour	OK to mow lawn?
Monday	2	Do not mow the lawn!
Sunday	11	Mow the lawn.
Sunday	18	Do not mow the lawn!
Wednesday	12	Do not mow the lawn!
Saturday	12	Mow the lawn.
Saturday	1	Do not mow the lawn!
Friday	9	Mow the lawn.
Sunday	14	Do not mow the lawn!

LAB 5.2 EXERCISES

5.2.1 CONSTRUCTING BOOLEAN EXPRESSIONS

Use the following code for next two questions:

```
boolean b1, b2, b3;
// Later
if (b1 && (b2 || b3))
    System.out.println("Yes");
else
    System.out.println("No");
```

a) Complete the following table for the given values:

bl	b2	b3	Output
false	false	false	
false	false	true	
false	true	false	
false	true	true	
true	false	false	
true	false	true	
true	true	false	
true	true	true	

b) If **b1** is **false,** do the values of **b2** and **b3** matter?

_____

_____

For the following three questions, we will be writing code to handle the following situation:

A college university needs to screen all of its incoming students for potential scholarship recipients. A student may receive a scholarship if they meet any of the following requirements:

1. The student is an athlete.
2. The student scored more than 1400 on their SAT.
3. The student's family makes less than $30,000 a year.

You will need to write an algorithm to test each student to see if they can potentially receive a scholarship. The following three questions will break up the process into separate steps:

c) What input will you need for this program? Define these inputs as variables.

_____

_____

d) State the problem in plain words using these variables.

_____

_____

e) Construct a boolean expression that prints the word "Scholarship" if the student can receive a scholarship.

_____

_____

We will test your solution to question e later, but first let us revisit the mow-the-lawn example from the lab and Table 5.5.

f) Table 5.5 contains a few test values, but does not test every possible value. Write code around the `if` statement that will test all possible values. The original code follows, along with some hints on what to do.

```
// Define variables. Perhaps define one more to help
// generate the days of the week.
String today;   // The day of the week. e.g. "Monday"
```

```
int timeHour;    // The hour of the time in 24 hour
                 // format.
// Place your code here. Hint: nested for loops.
boolean isSaturday = today.equals("Saturday");
boolean isSunday = today.equals("Sunday");
boolean afterTen = timeHour >= 10;
boolean beforeFour = timeHour < 16;    // 16 is 4pm
if ((isSaturday || isSunday) && (afterTen && beforeFour))
    System.out.println("Mow the lawn.");
else
    System.out.println("Do not mow the lawn!");
// Place more code here
```

LAB 5.2 EXERCISE ANSWERS

5.2.1 ANSWERS

Use the following code for next two questions:

```
boolean b1, b2, b3;
// Later
if (b1 && (b2 || b3))
    System.out.println("Yes");
else
    System.out.println("No");
```

a) Complete the following table for the given values:

Answer: The following table has been completed.

b1	b2	b3	Output
false	false	false	No
false	false	true	No
false	true	false	No
false	true	true	No
true	false	false	No
true	false	true	Yes
true	true	false	Yes
true	true	true	Yes

The important thing to learn here is **(b2 || B3)** is evaluated separately because of the parentheses.

b) If **b1** is **false,** do the values of **b2** and **b3** matter?

Answer: No, their values do not matter. false AND anything is false.

The Whole Truth About Boolean Expressions

Java tries to be smart about evaluating expressions. Since "**false** AND anything" is **false,** Java won't bother to evaluate the "anything" part if the first part is **false.** Likewise, "**true** OR anything" is always **true,** so again, the "anything" part is never evaluated since it doesn't need to be.

You will need to write an algorithm to test each student to see if they can potentially receive a scholarship. The following three questions will break up the process into separate steps:

c) What input will you need for this program? Define these inputs as variables.

Answer: The following is one possible answer:

```
boolean isAthlete;
int SAT;
int familyIncome
```

It's important to understand what you are working with, so well-named variables can help keep their meaning clear.

d) State the problem in plain words using these variables.

Answer: A student may receive a scholarship if he/she is an athlete or their SAT score is greater than 1400, or their family income is less than $30,000.

**LAB
5.2**

e) Construct a boolean expression that prints the word "Scholarship" if the student can receive a scholarship.

Answer: The following code will do what we want for this example:

```
if (isAthlete || (SAT > 1400) || (familyIncome < 30000))
{
    System.out.println("Scholarship");
}
```

While we could have used additional boolean variables like the lab's mow-the-lawn example did, we do not have to. It is just fine to put the boolean tests directly into the boolean expression.

We will test your solution to question e later, but first let us revisit the mow-the-lawn example from the Lab and Table 5.5.

f) Table 5.5 contains a few test values, but does not test every possible value. Write code around the **if** statement that will test all possible values. The original code follows, along with some hints on what to do.

Answer: The following is the complete code of a working example:

```
// Define variables. Perhaps define one more to help
String days[] = {"Sunday", "Monday", "Tuesday",
"Wednesday", "Thursday", "Friday", "Saturday"};
String today;   // The day of the week. e.g. "Monday"
int timeHour;   // The hour of the time in 24 hour
                // format.
// Place your code here. Hint: nested for loops.
for (int i=0; i<days.length; i++)
{
    today = days[i];
    for (timeHour=0; timeHour<24; timeHour++)
    {
      System.out.print("today is " + today);
      System.out.print(", time is " + timeHour);
      System.out.print(":00. ");
      boolean isSaturday = today.equals("Saturday");
```

```
            boolean isSunday = today.equals("Sunday");
            boolean afterTen = timeHour >= 10;
            boolean beforeFour = timeHour < 16;
        if ((isSaturday || isSunday)
            && (afterTen && beforeFour))
            System.out.println("Mow the lawn.");
        else
            System.out.println("Do not mow the lawn!");
        }
    }
```

To test every possible value, we need to try every possible value in the expression. The easiest way to do this is to loop through all of the possible values, and the best way to do this is with a *for* loop. Since we have two variables, we need two *for* loops. The **timeHour** values are easy to loop through since they are just integers from 0 to 23. However, the **today** value is different because it is a **String**. A common way of approaching this problem is to create an array of the **String** data, and then loop though the array using an **int** index. In the preceding solution, we define the array **days** that contains all of the days of the week. We then loop through the **days** array using the **int** index variable **i** in the *for* loop. Every cycle through the loop changes the value of **today** to be one of the days of the week.

The original code did not change, we just placed it inside two *for* loops. We also added some **print()** commands to print the values of **today** and **timeHour**. The values of **today** and **timeHour** are different each time we go through the loop so it is helpful to know which values we are testing. The output of this code is 168 lines long (7 days * 24 hours/day = 168 hours of the day to test). We won't print all of the output (save a few trees) but the following is just part of the output:

```
...
today is Saturday, time is 8:00. Do not mow the lawn!
today is Saturday, time is 9:00. Do not mow the lawn!
today is Saturday, time is 10:00. Mow the lawn.
today is Saturday, time is 11:00. Mow the lawn.
today is Saturday, time is 12:00. Mow the lawn.
today is Saturday, time is 13:00. Mow the lawn.
today is Saturday, time is 14:00. Mow the lawn.
today is Saturday, time is 15:00. Mow the lawn.
today is Saturday, time is 16:00. Do not mow the lawn!
today is Saturday, time is 17:00. Do not mow the lawn!
...
```

As you can see, the output changes at the threshold values of 10 and 16. Programs like these are called "Test Harnesses" because they test the functionality of a program, or part of a program.

Lab 5.2 Self-Review Questions

In order to test your progress, you should be able to answer the following questions.

1) What is the meaning of the word "precedence"?
   a) _____ **An expression that evaluates as "false"**
   b) _____ **An expression that evaluates as "true"**
   c) _____ **The order in which operators are evaluated**
   d) _____ **Evidence found in a Presidential crime**

2) What are the legal operators that can be used in a boolean expression?
   a) _____ **AND, OR, NOT**
   b) _____ **plus, minus, multiply**
   c) _____ **all of the above**
   d) _____ **none of the above**

3) What is the result of the following expression?

   ```
   true || true && true && false
   ```

   a) _____true
   b) _____false

4) What is the result of the following expression?

   ```
   true || (true && true && false)
   ```

   a) _____true
   b) _____false

5) What is the result of the following expression?

   ```
   X && !X
   ```

   a) _____true
   b) _____false
   c) _____Can't be determined

6) What is the result of the following expression?

```
x || !x
```

a) _____true
b) _____false
c) _____Can't be determined

7) What is the result of the following expression?

```
x ^ !x
```

a) _____true
b) _____false
c) _____Can't be determined

8) When you finish writing a boolean expression, what else should you do?

a) _____ **Celebrate!**
b) _____ **Test the code**
c) _____ **Try some sample values to see if the results are valid**
d) _____ **All of the above**

Quiz answers appear in Appendix A, Section 5.2.

CHAPTER 5

TEST YOUR THINKING

If Java is your first computer language, then this chapter might have been more difficult for you because it has less to do with Java and more to do with programming concepts in general. The heart of any computer program, regardless of the computer language, is the boolean logic controlling the flow control. Computers are very fast and very diligent, but they are also very stupid and have absolutely no common sense. Computers will do whatever you tell them to do, exactly, and to a fault. As a programmer, you need to be able to give very exact and specific instructions to the computer because it doesn't know any better. Good flow control is the key to getting the computer to do what you want. Everything else in this book, and most other computer books, is just "How do you do *this* in Java?" We will be showing you how to do many things in this book, but being able to tell the computer *when* and *why* to do these things is what separates a good programmer from a not-so-good programmer.

1) Consider your answer to Lab Exercise 5.2.1, question e. Write code to test the accuracy of your programming logic. Use the same concept used in Lab Exercise 5.2.1, question f, to test your code from question e. Since there are an infinite combinations for a student's situation, set some reasonable limits to the SAT and income boundary values. Additionally, you can adjust your loop to increment the test score by 10 or 100 each time through the loop.

It is a well-known fact that we have a leap year every four years on years that are evenly divisible by four. The years 1980, 1984, 1988, 1992, and 1996 have all been leap years. What is not so well known is that every 100 years we do not have a leap year. The year 1900 was not a leap year. Will the year 2000 be a leap year? The answer is "yes" because there is a third rule that says that every 400 years, the 100-year rule does not apply, and we do have a leap year. So, the years 2100, 2200 and 2300 will not be leap years, but the year 2400 will be. If you think these rules are confusing, don't blame us! This is all quite true!

2) Write code to test to see if a given year is a leap year. You might find it useful to use the *modulo* (%) function to determine if a year is a leap year.

CHAPTER 6

THE GRAPHICAL USER INTERFACE

Computers would be much more efficient if they didn't have to deal with people.

Kevin Chu

CHAPTER OBJECTIVES

In this chapter, you will learn about:

Perhaps a few years back, it would have been necessary for a book of this sort to spend time explaining the benefits of a *graphical user interface* (GUI). The GUI has become so prevalent nowadays that many computer users have never experienced accessing a computer purely through a *command-line interface* (CLI), and computers ranging from desktop PCs all the way up to supercomputers run operating systems with graphical interfaces. Not surprisingly, Java has both primitive graphics abilities as well as rich tool kits that provide extensive GUI functionality. Chances are good that you decided to learn Java because of the ease with which GUIs can be created. This chapter will prove that to you.

L A B   6 . 1

GUI BASICS

LAB OBJECTIVES

After this lab, you will be able to:

- Understand the Basic GUI Building Blocks
- Locate the GUI Tool Kits

Instead of rehashing the benefits of a GUI, let's jump right in and take a look at the building blocks of Java GUIs. Simply speaking, Java GUIs are comprised of *components* and *containers*.

COMPONENTS

Components are items with which you interact—when you press a button, move a scrollbar, or type into a text field, you are interacting with a component. Other common names for components are *widgets* and *controls*. It is from the components that a GUI derives its functionality. Common components include:

- Buttons
- Scrollbars
- Text entry fields

However, a GUI cannot be comprised solely of components; like the utensils in your kitchen, components require some type of holder to contain them.

CONTAINERS

Containers are simply that—they hold components. Your kitchen utensils are contained within a drawer, artwork is contained within a picture frame, and Java components are contained within Java containers. Containers also may contain other containers, which may contain other containers, *ad infinitum*. Examples of containers include:

- The splash-screen of a program
- The top-level "window" of a program
- A pop-up dialog box

A GUI is nothing more than a collection of containers and components that have been arranged in a pre-determined fashion.

Figure 6.1 shows a few GUI components.

■ *FOR EXAMPLE:*

A simple GUI might consist solely of a single container and a single component. Compile and run the following example of such a GUI. You need not concern yourself too much with the classes that are being used—these will be covered in the following labs.

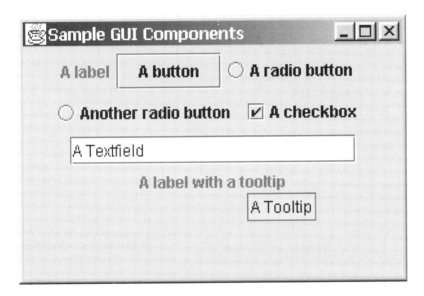

Figure 6.1 ■ A few GUI components

```
import javax.swing.*;
import java.awt.event.*;

public class SimpleGUI
{
    public SimpleGUI()
    {
        JFrame frame = new JFrame("Simple GUI Container");
        JLabel label = new JLabel("Simple GUI Component");
        label.setHorizontalAlignment(SwingConstants.CENTER);
        frame.getContentPane().add(label);
        frame.setSize(300,200);
        frame.setVisible(true);

        // Ignore the following for now.
        // It simply causes
        // the program to end when
        // the window is closed.
        frame.addWindowListener(new WindowAdapter()
        {
            public void windowClosing(WindowEvent evt)
            {
                System.exit(0);
            }
        });
    }
    public static void main(String[] argv)
    {
        SimpleGUI simple = new SimpleGUI();
    }
}
```

Though a simple GUI in terms of design, the preceding code illustrates the concept of containers and components. Even the most advanced Java GUIs you encounter will follow the same structure. Figure 6.2 illustrates the container and component relationship within this simple GUI.

The important steps in the creation of *SimpleGUI* can be summarized as follows:

1. Create a top-level container (a **JFrame** object).
2. Create a component (a **JLabel** object).
3. Add the component to the container with the container's **add** method.

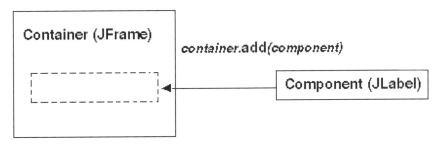

Figure 6.2 ■ Container/component hierarchy of SimpleGUI

4. Set the size of the top-level container.
5. Display the top-level container.

Quick, easy, and painless—welcome to the joys of GUI development with Java!

CHOOSE YOUR WEAPONS

Before you embark on the journey of GUI creation, you must arm yourself with the tools needed to perform your tasks. From the previous example, you may already have a good idea of where the appropriate classes can be found. They deserve a brief introduction in any case.

Let's begin by identifying the two toolkits at your disposal—the Abstract Windowing Toolkit (AWT) and the Java Foundation Classes (JFC or, more commonly, Swing). You may wish to fire-up your favorite Web browser and point it towards the Java API documentation.

The AWT is the original GUI toolkit from way back in the days of Java 1.0.x, and resides within the **java.awt.*** package hierarchy. Though only a few years old at best, it is eons-old in *internet-time*. Much of the AWT functionality has been replaced and greatly enhanced by Swing, so very little of the AWT is actually used directly by programmers any longer. However, the AWT still maintains core functionality, and you will probably use at least the following classes during the construction of a typical GUI:

*   **java.awt.Color**   - Basic color definitions
*   **java.awt.Font**   - Basic font definitions
*   **java.awt.Cursor**   - Cursor manipulation

In addition, the AWT provides classes for layout management and event handling—topics that will be covered in subsequent chapters.

**LAB
6.1**

The latest and greatest toolkit on the block is Swing. This toolkit offers enhanced performance and a wider variety of fully-featured components and containers for GUI development. You'll find the Swing classes located within the **javax.swing.*** package hierarchy. In general, all Swing classes that begin with *J* represent objects you can use within a GUI; the other classes are *utility* classes or interfaces that perform underlying tasks for the JVM. Because of the advantages of Swing, we will not cover GUI development using the old AWT containers and components; you'll thank us for it.

What this all boils down to is that the following import statements cover roughly 99 percent of the classes you will use for constructing basic GUIs:

```
import java.awt.*;
import javax.swing.*;
```

So, now that you are familiar with the location of your toolkits, let's get our hands dirty!

LAB 6.1 EXERCISES

6.1.1 UNDERSTAND THE BASIC GUI BUILDING BLOCKS

a) Provide four examples of a Java container.

_____

_____

b) Provide eight examples of a Java component.

_____

_____

Use the following application code to answer the remaining questions:

```
import javax.swing.*;
import java.awt.*;
import java.awt.event.*;

public class MoreComplexGUI
{
  public MoreComplexGUI()
  {
```

```
            JDialog dialog = new JDialog();
            JPanel panel = new JPanel();
            JLabel label1 = new JLabel("Hello");
            JLabel label2 = new JLabel("Everybody");

            panel.add(label1);
            panel.add(label2);
            dialog.getContentPane().add(panel);
            dialog.setTitle("Another Exciting Example");
            dialog.setSize(300,200);
            dialog.setVisible(true);

            // exit the application cleanly
            dialog.addWindowListener(new WindowAdapter()
            {
                public void windowClosing(WindowEvent evt)
                {
                    System.exit(0);
                }
            });
    }
    public static void main(String[] argv)
    {
            MoreComplexGUI mcg = new MoreComplexGUI();
    }
}
```

c) Identify the container(s) present in **MoreComplexGUI**.

_____

_____

d) Identify the component(s) present in **MoreComplexGUI**.

_____

_____

6.1.2 LOCATE THE GUI TOOL KITS

a) Describe how the Swing and AWT toolkits differ.

_____

_____

b) Identify any three Swing components in the Java API documentation. What Swing superclass do they all have in common?

_____

_____

c) Modify the `MoreComplexGUI` example to use a `JWindow` as the top-level container, rather than a `JDialog,` and run the example.

_____

_____

d) How do the `JFrame, JDialog,` and `JWindow` top-level containers differ; and what is this `getContentPane` method, anyhow?

_____

_____

LAB 6.1 EXERCISE ANSWERS

6.1.1 ANSWERS

a) Provide four examples of a Java container.

Answer: A container could be any object within a GUI that holds other objects (including other containers).

It is not possible to mention here all the container classes provided by Java, and I think you'd probably prefer slamming your finger in a car door to reading through such an exhaustive list. As we mentioned previously, examples of common containers include:

- The top-level frame of an application
- The splash screen of an application
- A pop-up dialog
- Any area that can be panned with a scrollbar

Specifically, this lab briefly introduced the **JFrame**, **JDialog**, and **JPanel** containers. There are many, many more containers provided by Java and you can even create your own. In the following labs, we will take a closer look at the specific container classes used within this chapter, as well as others.

b) Provide eight examples of a Java component.

Answer: The Java API documentation defines a component as "an object having a graphical representation that can be displayed on the screen and that can interact with the user." This pretty much sums it up.

If you encountered difficulties with naming eight components, think about all the GUIs with which you have interacted—you may be surprised at the number of components you have pushed, slid, dragged, or toggled. To name just a few components:

- the ubiquitous "button"
- radio button
- checkbox
- slider
- scrollbar
- menu
- drop-down list
- text-input field

The list goes on and on. Within this lab, the **JLabel** component was introduced very briefly. In following labs, we will take a closer look at the **JLabel** and many of these other components and examine how they can be used to provide GUI functionality.

c) Identify the container(s) present in **MoreComplexGUI.**

Answer: The following container classes were used within the **MoreComplexGUI** *example:* **JDialog** *and* **JPanel***. The result of this applet is shown in Figure 6.3.*

The **MoreComplexGUI** example used a top-level container class called **JDialog** within which the other container, **JPanel**, was placed. If you encountered difficulties in determining which classes were components,

Figure 6.3 ■ MoreComplexGUI example

just remember that components are added to containers—look for the classes that have their **add** methods called. Don't worry if you did not identify both of these containers; we will be investigating many containers throughout this chapter.

d) Identify the component(s) present in **MoreComplexGUI.**

Answer: The component **JLabel** *was used within the MoreComplexGUI example.*

The example used two **JLabel** instances to display text. If you were unable to determine that the label instances were components, recall the definition of a component from the answer to question b within this exercise:

". . . an object having a graphical representation that can be displayed on the screen and that can interact with the user."

Strictly speaking, the labels did not interact with the user, but they could have been programmed to do so; in the interest of simplicity, no user interactions were programmed. A good rule of thumb is "if you can see it within the GUI, it is most likely a component."

6.1.2 ANSWERS

a) Describe how the Swing and AWT toolkits differ.

Answer: The quick answer is that Swing provides much greater functionality than AWT and has much better performance. While AWT still provides the underpinnings for Swing, the AWT components and containers have been left in Java 2 primarily for backwards-compatibility.

The Whole Truth About AWT

It is still possible to develop complete GUIs using AWT components and containers, but this is highly discouraged and will not be covered in this book.

The lackluster performance and extensibility of the AWT is caused by the way it handles GUI components; to preserve the look-and-feel of the platform on which the Java application or applet is run, the designers of the AWT used what is known as *native peers*. Basically, every time an AWT component is to be created within a GUI, the JVM asks the computer's native windowing system to create the component. If you want a button, the JVM would ask your windowing system to provide a button; if you want a menu, the JVM would ask your windowing system to provide a menu—this is not a very flexible approach to cross-platform functionality. Because of the native peers, AWT is referred to as a *heavyweight* toolkit.

Swing does not depend upon native peers, and as such is known as a *lightweight* toolkit. It is written entirely in Java, allowing Swing to provide functionality that is independent from the platform on which it is running. Once you have become familiar with Swing basics, you will discover a wealth of classes that allow you to manipulate your GUIs in very powerful ways that are unavailable to AWT programmers.

Unless you have very specific requirements to use AWT, don't. Mixing heavyweight and lightweight components can be tricky—most every seasoned Java GUI programmer will recommend against it, and you will rarely see the results you are expecting.

b) Identify any three Swing components in the Java API documentation. What Swing superclass do they all have in common?

Answer: It does not matter which three Swing components you chose; they all have **JComponent** *as a common superclass. Why is this important, you ask? It is* *important because every Swing component inherits the methods from this class. Learning a few of the important methods in* **JComponent** *will quickly provide you with insight into how you can customize any Swing component.*

Let's take a look at some of the most commonly used methods of **JComponent**. This list is by no means complete, but these few methods provide quite a bit of customization for all components.

Table 6.1 ■ Commonly-used Methods of JComponent Classes

Method name	Method description
`setBackground(Color bg)`	This method sets the background color of the component. However, Swing components are not *opaque* by default— if you want the background color of the component to show as specified, you will also need to call the **setOpaque** method described later.
`setForeground(Color fg)`	Similar to the previous method, this sets the foreground color. Most often, the foreground color affects the color of text within the component.
`setEnabled(boolean enabled)`	This method enables or disables the component. Disabled components become non-interactive—buttons cannot be pressed, text fields do not accept input, etc. In addition, disabled components usually turn greyscale to indicate that they are not enabled.
`setOpaque(boolean isOpaque)`	If you want a component to be opaque, meaning that the background of the container underneath does not show through, you can set that property with this method. By default, **JComponent** component subclasses are not opaque. This method could be used in conjunction with **setBackground** to change the background color of a component.
`setToolTipText(String text)`	Tool tips are little windows containing descriptive text which are popped-up

when your mouse lingers over a component. This is very typical of toolbars,
which display icons for the individual
tools and rely upon tool tips for textual
descriptions.

`setVisible(boolean aFlag)`	If you want to make a visible compo-nent invisible, you can use this method.

These are but a few of the many, many methods available to all Swing
components. Feel free to experiment with these methods in conjunction
with any of the following examples. Master these methods, and you'll be
bending the GUI to your will in no time.

c) Modify the *MoreComplexGUI* example to use a **JWindow** as the top-level container, rather than a **JDialog**.

Answer: The conversion should be quite straightforward—replace the instantiation of
JDialog *with* **JWindow***. If you really want to learn good habits and maintain
friendships with other programmers who might look at your code, you should also
change the variable name from* **dialog** *to something more diagnostic—like* **window.**
Pretty simple, huh?

The top-level Swing container classes are remarkably similar and inter-
changeable. The three most commonly used top-level container classes
have already been introduced to you; they are **JFrame**, **Jwindow**, and
JDialog. Though they are considered top-level containers, you can use
as many of them as necessary within an application.

d) How do the **JFrame**, **JDialog**, and **JWindow** top-level containers differ;
and what is this **getContentPane** method, anyhow?

*Answer: The basic difference between the top-level container classes is the manner in
which the user is allowed to manipulate the containers. All of these Swing top-level
containers contain within them a* **content-pane***. This is simply another container into
which components are placed, instead of placing components directly into the top-level
container itself.*

First things first—why so many top-level containers? Consider the ubiquitous word processing program (which shall remain nameless) that has
become a staple application throughout businesses everywhere.

When it first starts, a *splash-screen* is displayed. This screen is simply an advertisement of sorts, a diversion while the program loads into memory. You cannot close it, minimize it, or even move its location. This is the functionality provided by **JWindow.**

After the application has consumed vast amounts of system memory, it launches. The application window with which you interact can be moved, resized, minimized or closed. This is the quintessential top-level container for applications, and the **JFrame** class provides this functionality.

After you have spent hours writing a chapter about GUIs for a Java programming book and neglected to save your work (students writing term papers know exactly where we are going with this example), the program invariably crashes. What ends up on your screen is a small box known as a *dialog,* which serves the purpose of telling you what you already know—the program has died, you've lost all your work, and there is absolutely nothing you can do about it. This top-level container can be moved, sometimes resized, but cannot be minimized. This is the functionality provided by **JDialog**—to pop-up dialogs for immediate attention of the user. Of course, your programs will be much more robust than that word processor, right?

Now, about that *content-pane;* every Swing top-level container is guaranteed to have another container within. This container is known as the content-pane, and it is into this container that you place all child containers and components. The reasoning behind this is a bit advanced, but suffice it to say that such a setup provides great flexibility for more advanced GUIs.

The method **getContentPane** returns a reference to that container. In the previous examples, the following syntax was used to add a component to the content-pane:

```
dialog.getContentPane().add(panel);
```

If you are dealing quite often with the content-pane, it is wasteful to call getContentPane over and over. In such cases, a better approach would be to create a reference to this content-pane and then add all containers and components to this reference. This can be done with the following code snippet:

```
JFrame frame = new JFrame("My Title");
JPanel contentPanel = (JPanel)frame.getContentPane();
```

Now you can manipulate or add components to the content-pane as often as you'd like without calling **getContentPane** again and again:

```
// set the background color
contentPanel.setBackground(Color.red);
// add a button to the content panel
JButton button = new JButton("Press Me");
contentPanel.add(button);
```

LAB 6.1 SELF-REVIEW QUESTIONS

In order to test your progress, you should be able to answer the following questions.

1) Which of the following are the two general categories of objects used to create GUIs?
   a) _____ Frames and panels
   b) _____ Components and controls
   c) _____ Containers and components
   d) _____ Widgets and windows
   e) _____ Gin and tequila

2) Which one of the following is NOT a component?
   a) _____ a button
   b) _____ a text-input field
   c) _____ a dialog box

3) Which one of the following is NOT a container?
   a) _____ a label
   b) _____ a frame
   c) _____ a panel

4) Which of the following statements is correct?
   a) _____ Containers may be added to other containers.
   b) _____ Components may be added to other components

5) Which one of the following top-level containers cannot be moved by the user?
   a) _____ JFrame
   b) _____ JDialog
   c) _____ JWindow

6) Which one of the following top-level containers can be moved, but not minimized by the user?
   a) _____ JFrame
   b) _____ JDialog
   c) _____ JWindow

7) Which one of the following top-level containers can be moved, resized, minimized and closed by the user?
   a) _____ JFrame
   b) _____ JDialog
   c) _____ JWindow

8) Which of the following containers does not have a content-pane?
   a) _____ JFrame
   b) _____ JApplet
   c) _____ JWindow
   d) _____ JPanel

   Quiz answers appear in Appendix A, Section 6.1.

L A B   6 . 2

APPLICATION VERSUS APPLET GUIs

LAB OBJECTIVES

After this lab, you will be able to:

- Construct a Simple Application GUI
- Construct a Simple Applet GUI

The previous lab contained many examples of application GUIs. In this lab, we will investigate the differences between applications and applets from the perspective of GUI programming.

As an application developer, there is a trade-off between the flexibility of creating your own GUIs from the ground-up and the time it takes to develop the infrastructure. For simple tasks, creating an applet may be far more convenient than developing an application. Though applets do not provide the extreme flexibility of an application, both a top-level container and a basic infrastructure are provided. As well, applets are delivered via a Web browser—this makes distribution of your applet trivial.

■ FOR EXAMPLE:

Let's compare a simple application and a simple GUI. Both will perform the task of displaying a colored background with some text. First, the application:

```
import javax.swing.*;
import java.awt.event.*;
import java.awt.*;

public class ComparisonApp
{
```

```
public ComparisonApp()
{
        JFrame frame = new JFrame("Comparison Application");
        JLabel label = new JLabel("Some arbitrary text");
        label.setHorizontalAlignment(SwingConstants.CENTER);

        frame.getContentPane().add(label);
        frame.getContentPane().setBackground(Color.red);
        frame.setSize(300,200);
        frame.setVisible(true);

        // you can ignore the following for now— it causes
        // the application to exit when the frame is closed
        frame.addWindowListener(new WindowAdapter()
        {
                public void windowClosing(WindowEvent evt)
                {
                        System.exit(0);
                }
        });
}
public static void main(String[] argv)
{
        ComparisonApp app = new ComparisonApp();
}
}
```

Now, for comparison let's take a look at an applet which has identical (albeit relatively useless) functionality:

```
import javax.swing.*;
import java.awt.*;
public class ComparisonApplet extends JApplet
{
  public void init()
  {
        JLabel label = new JLabel("Some arbitrary text");
        label.setHorizontalAlignment(SwingConstants.CENTER);
        getContentPane().setBackground(Color.red);
        getContentPane().add(label);
  }
}
```

You can run this applet with the following HTML:

```
<HTML>
<APPLET CODE="ComparisonApplet.class" WIDTH=300 HEIGHT=200>
If you can read this, your browser does not support Java!
</APPLET>
</HTML>
```

Comparing the two, it is easy to tell that applet programming can be much faster than application programming. The applet achieved the same level of functionality as the application, but did it with less than half the code. No code had to be written to create a top-level container, nor did code have to be written to handle the initialization or closure of the GUI.

From a GUI perspective, the applet is nothing more than a modified type of **JPanel** container. The Web browser or appletviewer simply takes an applet and places it within its existing frame with a predetermined size at a predetermined location. This is why applets are not standalone executables like normal applications—an applet depends upon resources provided by the program in which it is displayed.

As well as providing a basis upon which a GUI can be formed, applets also provide a control structure much simplified over a normal application. As you recall from previous chapters, calling the main method of a class starts a normal application. Because applets run under the control of a Web browser or appletviewer, applet initialization, startup, and shutdown are handled in a more controlled manner. Command line arguments are passed to applets via the HTML pages from which the applets run. Creating an applet can be as simple as defining actions for a few applet methods that are called by the Web browser or appletviewer at various times during the life of the applet.

Because applets relieve the programmer from many tasks associated with GUI creation and system interaction, a novice Java programmer is able to learn quickly and see results immediately when programming applets.

LAB 6.2 EXERCISES

6.2.1 CONSTRUCT A SIMPLE APPLICATION GUI

a) Modify the `ComparisonApp` class shown previously so that the background color is blue and assign the text label a tool tip that reads "This is my first tool tip!"

_____

_____

b) Create your own application that displays a green `JDialog` that contains the text "Your program has just crashed. Tough luck!"

_____

_____

6.2.2 CONSTRUCT A SIMPLE APPLET GUI

Use your knowledge of applets along with the Java API documentation as a reference to answer the following questions:

a) Java applications are started by calling the **main** method of a class. How are Java applets started?

_____

_____

b) Java applications are passed runtime arguments via the **main** method of a class. How are arguments passed to Java applets?

_____

_____

c) GUIs created by an application must provide their own top-level containers. What provides the top-level containers for an applet?

d) Using the `ComparisonApplet` shown previously as a reference, under what conditions is the `init` method called? What about the methods `start, stop,` and `destroy?`

e) Create your own applet that displays a green background and contains a text label that reads "It ain't easy being green."

LAB 6.2 EXERCISE ANSWERS

6.2.1 ANSWERS

a) Modify the *ComparisonApp* class shown previously so that the background color is blue and assign the text label a tool tip that reads "This is my first tool tip!"

Answer: Only two modifications need be made to this application—the color assignment needs to be changed, and a line needs to be added to specify the tool tip text. Here's how it is done:

Changing the color of the background is very straightforward. The line

```
frame.getContentPane().setBackground(Color.red);
```

should be changed so that the color specified is blue:

```
frame.getContentPane().setBackground(Color.blue);
```

As you recall from the previous lab, a tool tip can be set with the **setToolTipText** method. All Swing components derive this method from **JComponent,** so all you need to do is add the following line somewhere within the constructor method:

```
label.setToolTipText("This is my first tool tip");
```

When your mouse pointer lingers over this label, you should see the tool tip appear.

b) Create your own application that displays a green JDialog that contains the text "Your program has just crashed. Tough luck!"

Answer: Your mileage may vary from the application that is presented here, but it is only important that the specified functionality is included.

```
import javax.swing.*;
import java.awt.*;
import java.awt.event.*; // for WindowEvent class

public class CrashDialog
{
    public CrashDialog()
    {
            JDialog dialog = new JDialog();
            dialog.setTitle("Aieee!!");
            JLabel label = new JLabel(
            "Your program has just crashed. Tough luck!");
            label.setHorizontalAlignment(SwingConstants.CENTER);
            dialog.getContentPane().add(label);
            dialog.setSize(300,100);
            dialog.setVisible(true);

            // ignore this for now— it simple exits the
            // application when the dialog is closed
            dialog.addWindowListener(new WindowAdapter()
            {
                    public void windowClosing(WindowEvent evt)
                    {
                            System.exit(0);
                    }
            });
    }
    public static void main(String[] argv)
    {
            CrashDialog cdialog = new CrashDialog();
    }
}
```

Your application should be somewhat similar, though the proper window closing routine and the centering of the label text are optional. Both subjects will be covered in later labs.

6.2.2 ANSWERS

a) Java applications are started by calling the *main* method of a class. How are Java applets started?

*Answer: Java applets are started when the Web browser or appletviewer applications call methods defined within the **JApplet** class. To initially load an applet, the browser will call the **init** method of the applet. Once the applet is loaded and ready to run, the browser will call the **start** method of the applet.*

Applets depend upon the application within which they are displayed to provide the mechanism for loading and starting the applet. Consider an applet embedded within a Web page—the browser is in charge of loading and starting that applet whenever you navigate to that page; in fact, there is quite a bit of housekeeping performed by the browser so that applets perform properly. Whenever a browser loads an HTML page that contains an applet, the **init** method of the applet is called. This method usually contains code necessary to setup the applet GUI and perform initialization of any data needed by the applet. Once the applet is loaded, the browser calls the **start** method of the applet. This method can be used to begin animations, start music or begin processing of data. Alternatively, the **start** method can be written to do nothing. It is not always necessary to perform a task within this method.

b) Java applications are passed runtime arguments via the *main* method of a class. How are arguments passed to Java applets?

*Answer: Applets receive all arguments from the HTML page from which they are loaded. This is accomplished via the **PARAM** HTML tag.*

Unlike applications, which take runtime arguments from the command line, applets must receive all parameters from the HTML file from which the applet was launched. The basic HTML syntax for embedding an applet uses the **APPLET** tag. The **HEIGHT** and **WIDTH** arguments to the tag are required. If you wanted to embed an applet named **MyApplet** with a height and width of 200 pixels, the HTML fragment would look like the following:

```
<APPLET CODE="MyApplet.class" WIDTH=200 HEIGHT=200>
If you can read this, Java is NOT enabled on your
browser!
</APPLET>
```

As shown, any text between the opening and closing **APPLET** tags will be displayed only if the browser does not support Java.

To specify parameters to this applet, you would use the **PARAM** tag. To specify a parameter named "color" which has a value of "blue" the HTML would be as follows:

```
<APPLET CODE="MyApplet.class" WIDTH=200 HEIGHT=200>
<PARAM NAME="color" VALUE="blue">
If you can read this, Java is NOT enabled on your
browser!
</APPLET>
```

You can specify any number of **PARAM** tags within the **APPLET** block. Your applet can then query these parameters by name using the **getParameter** method. If the previous HTML was used to embed **MyApplet**, the following **init** method could be used to query for the value of the color parameter and print it to the Java console:

```
public void init()
{
    // query HTML for value of "color" parameter
    String colorParam = getParameter("color");
    System.out.println("color parameter equals " + color);
}
```

Typically, the **init** method is responsible for querying parameter values needed by the applet. Parameters are an excellent way to modify the behavior or appearance of your applet without writing different versions of the applet. By simply modifying (or dynamically generating) HTML tags, you can feed your applet all kinds of useful information.

c) GUIs created by an application must provide their own top-level containers. What provides the top-level containers for an applet?

Answer: The browser or appletviewer applications provide the top-level containers for the display of an applet.

As mentioned previously, when programming with applets you are provided a top-level frame by your browser or appletviewer. The applet itself is a type of container known as a **Panel** that contains a content-pane into which you can immediately place other containers or components. Because a basic container is provided, GUI development within applets is a quicker process than GUI development within applications.

d) Using the **ComparisonApplet** shown previously as a reference, under what conditions is the **init** method called? What about the methods **start**, **stop**, and **destroy?**

Answer: The Web browser maintains strict control over the runtime of an applet by calling several methods at explicitly-defined times during operation. In this manner, the browser is able to control the entire life cycle of an applet and provide the programmer with a basic flow of control that is guaranteed.

All applets derive from the common class **java.awt.Applet,** and Swing applets are nothing more than a subclass of an AWT applet. As such, there are methods defined within this class that are called by the browser to control the applet as it runs. Of these methods, the most important methods are as follows:

```
public void init()
```

This method is called whenever an applet is initially loaded by the browser. This method is typically used by applet programmers to read parameters, setup the GUI and perform any other initializations required to ready the applet for action. This method is usually used instead of defining a constructor—the browser does not pass any parameters to the constructor of an applet, so it is not very useful to define a constructor at all.

```
public void start()
```

This method is called following **init** and whenever an applet becomes visible within the browser. Usually, animation or audio clips are started within this method, if applicable.

```
public void stop()
```

This is called when the applet is no longer visible within the browser, such as when the applet is scrolled out of the visible area of the current HTML page, or when the user navigates to a different URL. This method is usually responsible for stopping animation or audio clips that were started by the **start** method.

```
public void destroy()
```

This method is called before the applet is unloaded from the browser. After this method completes, the applet is dead. This method is used to release any resources (besides memory) being used by the applet. Though beyond the scope of this book, such resources could include database connections, file handles or other limited resources provided by the operating system. Often, an applet does not make use of any such resources so this method need not be overridden.

This is by no means an exhaustive list of methods defined for an applet. You are encouraged to take a look at the Java API documentation for other methods available to applet programmers; however, creating an applet can be as simple as overriding one or more of the above methods as necessary to your task.

Though you are providing the bodies of these methods when writing an applet, you generally will not be calling the above methods yourself at any time—the browser will call all these methods when appropriate.

e) Create your own applet which displays a green background and contains a text label which reads "It ain't easy being green."

Answer: Your class definition may be different from that which is shown below. It is only important that the same functionality is achieved. Here is our class (note that the centering of the text was strictly optional):

```
import javax.swing.*;
import java.awt.*;
public class GreenApplet extends JApplet
{
    public void init()
    {
            JLabel label = new JLabel(
                "It ain't easy being green.");
            label.setHorizontalAlignment(SwingConstants.CENTER);
            JPanel contentPanel = (JPanel)getContentPane();
            contentPanel.setBackground(Color.green);
            contentPanel.add(label);
    }
}
```

LAB 6.2 SELF-REVIEW QUESTIONS

In order to test your progress, you should be able to answer the following questions.

1) From the GUI construction perspective, an applet is simply which of the following?
   a) _____ Frame
   b) _____ Window
   c) _____ Panel
   d) _____ Application

2) Applet initialization is performed by which one of the following methods?
   a) _____ init
   b) _____ start
   c) _____ stop
   d) _____ destroy

3) When an applet is scrolled off screen or the browser navigates away, which one of the following methods is called by the browser?
   a) _____ init
   b) _____ start
   c) _____ stop
   d) _____ destroy

4) Parameters are passed to applets via which of the following?
   a) _____ the command line
   b) _____ HTML tags
   c) _____ You can't fool me—applets don't take parameters!

5) Applets need **a main()** method.
   a) _____ True
   b) _____ False

Quiz answers appear in Appendix A, Section 6.2.

LAB 6.2

L A B   6 . 3

THE USE OF LABELS

LAB OBJECTIVES

After this lab, you will be able to:

- Manipulate Labels
- Add Labels to a GUI

Let's begin with the simplest of the Swing components, the label. As one might guess by the name, a label is a holder of text. It is not an interactive component, so the most *action* you could expect to receive from a label is a tool tip.

The Swing label class is **JLabel**; and as one would expect of Swing components, it lives within the **javax.swing** package hierarchy. You have already seen numerous examples of the **JLabel** class in action, so let's take a look at some of the few constructors available for the standard label.

```
public JLabel(String text)
```

This constructor takes only one parameter, a **String** containing the text to be displayed within the **JLabel**, and the default alignment of the text is left-justified. You have seen examples of the use of this constructor in the previous labs. Creating a label with this constructor is quite straightforward.

```
public JLabel(String text, int horizontalAlignment)
```

This constructor takes the same **String** parameter as above, but takes an **int** value as well, which determines the horizontal alignment of the displayed text. Valid horizontal alignment values are defined in the **SwingConstants** class, which contains a number of constant values used within many of the Swing components. The most common horizontal alignment values are:

```
SwingConstants.LEFT      (this is the default for a JLabel)
SwingConstants.CENTER
SwingConstants.RIGHT
```

Alternatively, the horizontal alignment can be modified at any time with the **setHorizontalAlignment** method. This method has the following signature:

```
public void setHorizontalAlignment(int alignment)
```

As one might expect, the **alignment** parameter accepts the same values as the constructor with the **horizontalAlignment** parameter.

In addition to the horizontal alignment, you are also able to modify the vertical alignment. The signature of this method is:

```
public void setVerticalAlignment(int alignment)
```

The valid values for vertical alignment are:

```
SwingConstants.TOP
SwingConstants.CENTER    (this is default for a JLabel)
SwingConstants.BOTTOM
```

■ *FOR EXAMPLE:*

A code fragment that instantiates a **JLabel** and sets a few alignment properties would look like the following:

```
JLabel rightLabel = new JLabel("I lean to the right");
rightLabel.setHorizontalAlignment(SwingConstants.RIGHT);
rightLabel.setVerticalAlignment(SwingConstants.RIGHT);
```

LAB 6.3 EXERCISES

6.3.1 *MANIPULATE LABELS*

a) Provide the code necessary to set the background color of a **JLabel** to red.

_____

_____

b) Provide the code necessary to set a tool tip for a `JLabel`.

_____

_____

c) Which method would return a `String` that contains the current text within the `JLabel`?

_____

_____

6.3.2 ADD LABELS TO A *GUI*

Use the following applet `init` method to answer these questions:

```
public void init()
{
    JPanel content = (JPanel)getContentPane();
    // ignore this for now—it simply modifies
    // the layout management of the content-pane
    content.setLayout(new GridLayout(3,1));

    JLabel defaultLabel = new JLabel("Default (Left)");
    JLabel centerLabel = new JLabel("Centered");
    JLabel rightLabel  = new JLabel("Right");
}
```

a) What code would be necessary to horizontally-align the `center-Label` and `rightLabel` as appropriate to their names?

_____

_____

b) Set the background color of all three labels so that they are unique. What code was required to do this?

_____

_____

c) The `JLabel` class contains a method named `setIcon`. What is the purpose of this method?

_____

_____

LAB 6.3 EXERCISES

6.3.1 ANSWERS

a) Provide the code necessary to set the background color of a `JLabel` to red.

Answer: Though not covered in the introduction to this lab, you should recall that `JLabel` *is a subclass of* `JComponent`. *The* `JComponent` *class defines the method* `setBackground` *that can be used to set the background color of the* `JLabel`.

The code required to set the background of a `JLabel` to the color red is as follows. If you recall, Swing components are not opaque by default, so the background color will not be displayed until they are set opaque.

```
label.setBackground(Color.red);
label.setOpaque(true);
```

If you neglected to set the label opaque, you undoubtedly noticed that the label did not display a red background. This is a common mistake, so keep it in mind. The usual course of action is to set *the background color of the container in which the label it to be placed*—in this way, the transparent label does not affect the background color of the container. We are simply working the other direction with this exercise.

b) Provide the code necessary to set a tool tip for a `JLabel`.

Answer: Once again, you must dredge up memories from the previous labs to answer this question. Setting the tool tip text is quite straightforward:

```
label.setToolTipText("Hello, I am a label");
```

c) Which method would return a `String` that contains the current text within the `JLabel`?

Answer: The method `getText` *will return a* `String` *that contains the current text within the* `JLabel`. *The use of this method is illustrated here:*

```
JLabel label = new JLabel("This is my text");
String theText = label.getText();
// theText now contains "This is my text"
```

In addition to querying the label for the current text, you can also set the text of the label at any time within your program with the **setText** method. For example, the following fragment of code instantiates a label and then sets the text to a new value:

```
JLabel label = new JLabel("Some text here");
label.setText("Some NEW text here");
```

**LAB
6.3**

6.3.2 ANSWERS

a) What code would be necessary to horizontally-align the **centerLabel** and **rightLabel** as appropriate to their names?

Answer: The labels can be aligned appropriately with the **setHorizontalAlignment** *method as follows:*

```
centerLabel.setHorizontalAlignment(SwingConstants.CENTER);
rightLabel.setHorizontalAlignment(SwingConstants.RIGHT);
```

b) Set the background color of all three labels so that they are unique. What code was required to do this?

Answer: Though the colors you chose may differ than those here, the process is the same nonetheless. Did you run your code? If so, did you get the results you expected? Do remember that the **setOpaque** *method must be called to ensure that the background colors of the label appear.*

```
defaultLabel.setOpaque(true);
defaultLabel.setBackground(Color.red);
centerLabel.setOpaque(true);
centerLabel.setBackground(Color.green);
rightLabel.setOpaque(true);
rightLabel.setBackground(Color.blue);
```

As mentioned in the previous exercises, if the labels are not set opaque the background color will not appear. You can test this by setting the color of the content-pane and then toggling the opacity of the labels. Neat, huh?

c) The **JLabel** class contains a method named **setIcon**. What is the purpose of this method?

Answer: **JLabel** *objects are not limited to containing text. In fact, a very powerful feature of the* **JLabel** *is that it can contain an icon in addition to, or instead of, text.*

The use of images will be covered in a later chapter, at which time you will be given the opportunity to make use of images within **JLabel** objects. Right now, it is only important that you realize the **JLabel** has this functionality.

Lab 6.3 Self-Review Questions

In order to test your progress, you should be able to answer the following questions.

1) The **JLabel** class is able to represent which of the following content?
   a) _____ text
   b) _____ images
   c) _____ both text and images

2) Which of the following parameters to the **setVerticalAlignment** method is invalid?
   a) _____ SwingConstants.CENTER
   b) _____ SwingConstants.TOP
   c) _____ SwingConstants.DEFAULT
   d) _____ SwingConstants.BOTTOM

3) After you have instantiated a **JLabel,** the text cannot be modified.
   a) _____ True
   b) _____ False

4) Default horizontal alignment of text within a JLabel is
   a) _____ Right-justfied
   b) _____ Left-justified
   c) _____ Centered

5) What method is used to change the color of a JLabel?
   a) _____ setColor
   b) _____ changeColor
   c) _____ useColor
   d) _____ setBackground

Quiz answers appear in Appendix A, Section 6.3.

L A B 6 . 4

THE USE OF BUTTONS

LAB OBJECTIVES

After this lab, you will be able to:

- Manipulate Buttons
- Add Buttons to a GUI

A GUI without buttons is like springtime without flowers. This lab will introduce a number of different button types that you can use within your GUIs to solicit user interaction. All of the buttons introduced within this lab are subclasses of **javax.swing.AbstractButton,** an abstract class (so you can't create an instance of **AbstractButton**), which defines the base functionality for all standard button types. All of these button types are capable of displaying text, icons, or both; however, dealing with icons is a topic saved for a following chapter.

■ *FOR EXAMPLE:*

Let's start right off with the standard button, appropriately named **JButton.** The following code fragment simply creates a button and a panel, and adds the button to the panel.

```
JButton okButton = new JButton("OK");
JPanel panel = new JPanel();
panel.add(okButton);
```

The use of **JButton** is quite straightforward—the constructor takes a **String** parameter that contains the text to be displayed within the button, and it is added to a container in a manner no different than you have already seen countless times.

TOGGLE BUTTONS

In addition to the **JButton,** Swing provides several other *toggle buttons.* Unlike a conventional button, toggle buttons remain in the state they entered when pressed—if the button was not selected, a button press will cause the button to remain selected until pressed again. The most common types of toggle buttons are *checkboxes* and *radio buttons.*

Checkboxes are most often used to solicit *yes/no* or *on/off* configuration information from the user. This is a common component on many Web browsers, where annoying dialogs are often popped-up on the screen that contain a "do not show this warning again" checkbox, and configuration options can be selected or deselected via checkboxes. The Swing checkbox class is **JCheckBox,** and a common constructor for the class is defined as:

```
JCheckBox(String text, boolean selected)
```

Where **text** is the text you wish displayed alongside the checkbox and **selected** indicates whether the checkbox is selected by default. Another common constructor is similar, but omits the **selected** parameter—this creates a checkbox that is not selected by default. In all cases, the specified text will be displayed to the right of the checkbox.

Radio buttons are used to present mutually exclusive options to a user. If a GUI is designed to display several options from which only one may be selected at any given time, radio buttons should be used. The Swing radio button class is **JRadioButton,** and the common constructors for the class are identical to those shown previously for the checkbox class.

■ *FOR EXAMPLE:*

The following applet makes use of both the **JButton** and **JCheckbox.** When the checkbox is selected, the button will beep when pressed. Don't concern yourself too much with either the positioning of the buttons (layout management), or the event handling (making something happen when you press the button). These topics will be covered in the following chapters.

```
import javax.swing.*;
import java.awt.*;
import java.awt.event.*;
public class ButtonApplet extends JApplet
{
    JButton button;
```

```
JCheckBox checkbox;

public void init()
{
        JPanel contentPane = (JPanel)getContentPane();
        contentPane.setLayout(new FlowLayout());

        button = new JButton("OK");
        checkbox = new JCheckBox(
            "Beep when button is pressed", true);
        contentPane.add(checkbox);
        contentPane.add(button);

        // don't worry too much about this for now—
        // it sets up a handler for button press events.
        button.addActionListener(new ActionListener()
        {
                public void actionPerformed(ActionEvent evt)
                {
                        doMyButtonAction();
                }
        });
}

// Perform an action when the button is pressed,
// but only if the checkbox is selected
public void doMyButtonAction()
{
        if(checkbox.isSelected())
        {
                Toolkit.getDefaultToolkit().beep();
        }
}
}
```

Figure 6.4 shows the result of ButtonApplet.

LAB 6.4 EXERCISES

6.4.1 MANIPULATE BUTTONS

Use the applet **ButtonApplet**, provided within the lab, to answer the following questions:

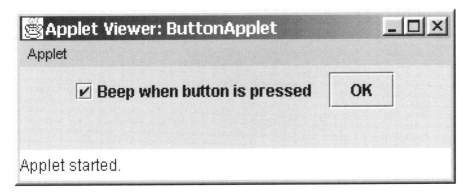

Figure 6.4 ■ The ButtonApplet

a) Write the code required to change the text color of the **JButton** to green.

_____

_____

b) Modify the **doMyButtonAction** method so that pressing the **JButton** will enable or disable the **JCheckBox.**

_____

_____

c) Modify the applet so the **JButton** text contains the number zero, and each time it is pressed it increments the number by one. Maintain the current beeping functionality.

_____

_____

6.4.2 ADD BUTTONS TO A *GUI*

Use the applet **ButtonApplet** provided within the lab to answer the following questions:

a) Convert the applet so that three **JRadioButton** objects are used instead of the single checkbox. Name the radio buttons "Green", "Blue", and "Red". Modify **doMyButtonAction** so that the button text changes the appropriate color when the button is pressed.

b) After making the modifications in the previous question, did you obtain the results you were expecting?

LAB 6.4 EXERCISE ANSWERS

6.4.1 ANSWERS

a) Write the code required to change the text color of the **JButton** to green.

*Answer: Modifying the text color of a **JButton** is no different from modifying the text color of a **JLabel**, or any other **JComponent** for that matter.*

Because the **JButton** class is a subclass of **JComponent,** we can change the text color of the **JButton** with the **setForeground** method. The following code would do the trick:

```
button.setForeground(Color.green);
```

b) Modify the **doMyButtonAction** method so that pressing the **JButton** will enable or disable the **JCheckBox**.

*Answer: The button event handling has already been provided (don't worry, we will discuss this in Chapter 8) so most of the work has been done. All that needs to be done is call **setEnabled** on the button as appropriate.*

As you may recall from the first lab of this chapter, all Swing components inherit the method **setEnabled**, which enables or disables a component. In addition to **setEnabled**, all Swing components inherit the method **isEnabled**, which returns a boolean value indicating the current enabled state of the component. With these two methods, the

doMyButtonAction method can be modified to enable and disable the checkbox as follows:

```
public void doMyButtonAction()
{
    checkbox.setEnabled(!checkbox.isEnabled());
}
```

Your modification may have been done differently, most likely with an **if** statement that checks the enabled state of the checkbox and then calls **setEnabled** as appropriate. That is fine—this version is simply a bit more concise.

c) Modify the applet so the **JButton** text contains the number zero, and each time it is pressed it increments the number by one. Maintain the current beeping functionality.

LAB 6.4

Answer: The text of a **JButton** *can be modified with the* **setText** *method, so the modifications required are nothing more than incrementing an integer value and setting the text of the button to that value.*

Your answer probably differs slightly from that shown here. It is only important that you receive the same results, and that you have learned the **setText** method can be used to set the text of the **JButton.** One of many possible solutions is shown following, with the modified lines in **bold** type:

```
import javax.swing.*;
import java.awt.*;
import java.awt.event.*;

public class ButtonsApplet extends JApplet
{
    JButton button;
    JCheckBox checkbox;
    int pressCounter = 0;

    public void init()
    {
        JPanel contentPane = (JPanel)getContentPane();
        contentPane.setLayout(new FlowLayout());

        button = new JButton(String.valueOf(pressCounter));
        checkbox = new JCheckBox(
```

```
                              "Beep when button is pressed", true);

                contentPane.add(checkbox);
                contentPane.add(button);

                // don't worry too much about this for now—
                // it sets up a handler for button press events.
                button.addActionListener(new ActionListener()
                {
                        public void actionPerformed(ActionEvent evt)
                        {
                                doMyButtonAction();
                        }
                });
        }

        // Perform an action when the button is pressed,
        // but only if the checkbox is selected
        public void doMyButtonAction()
        {
                button.setText(String.valueOf(++pressCounter));
                if(checkbox.isSelected())
                {
                        Toolkit.getDefaultToolkit().beep();
                }
        }
}
```

The only tricky part of this exercise is the conversion of an integer value into a **String** object, so that it could be used with the **setText** method. Do not worry if you had difficulties determining how to make the conversion—a large part of the learning process is investigating how others perform tasks and incorporating these into your own bag-of-tricks.

6.4.2 ANSWERS

a) Convert the applet so that three **JRadioButton** objects are used instead of the single checkbox. Name the radio buttons "Green", "Blue", and "Red". Modify **doMyButtonAction** so that the button text changes the appropriate color when the button is pressed.

Answer: Adding the following code will create and add the three radio buttons. Your answer may vary. For brevity's sake, not all of the code is shown. If you want to see the complete code, see the next answer.

LAB
6.4

```
    …
    JRadioButton greenButton, blueButton, redButton;
    public void init()
    {
    …
        greenButton = new JRadioButton("Green");
        blueButton = new JRadioButton("Blue");
        redButton = new JRadioButton("Red");

        contentPane.add(greenButton);
        contentPane.add(blueButton);
        contentPane.add(redButton);
    …
    }
    …
    public void doMyButtonAction()
    {
            if(greenButton.isSelected())
            {
                button.setForeground(Color.green);
            }
            else if(blueButton.isSelected())
            {
                button.setForeground(Color.blue);
            }
            else if(redButton.isSelected())
            {
                button.setForeground(Color.red);
            }
    }
    …
```

Figure 6.5 shows the three radio buttons.

Your answer probably differs from what is shown. It is only important that you were able to instantiate the radio buttons and add them correctly to the applet.

If you encountered difficulties replacing the checkbox with radio buttons, progress to the next answer where an example is shown. If you successfully replaced the checkbox with radio buttons, you are probably wondering why things did not work as you had intended—move along to the next answer for clarification.

b) After making the modifications in the previous question, did you obtain the results you were expecting?

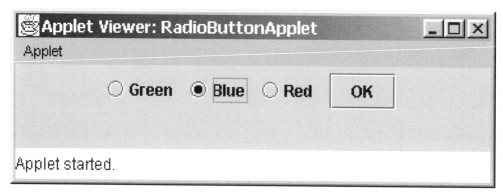

Figure 6.5 ■ The RadioButtonApplet

Answer: After making the modifications, you probably realized that the applet was not performing as you would expect—the radio buttons did not act in a mutually exclusive manner. As you might have guessed, there is more to the use of radio buttons than was previously covered.

The astute reader now asks the question, "Why don't the radio buttons respond in a mutually exclusive manner?" Indeed, it is possible to select more than one button at a time with the current GUI.

To achieve the desired functionality, the GUI must know which buttons comprise a group of mutually exclusive buttons; this is done with the **ButtonGroup** class. Think of a **ButtonGroup** as an invisible container—it is never displayed within the GUI, and exists only to aggregate buttons that must be mutually exclusive. By adding toggle buttons to a **Button-Group,** you ensure that selecting one button causes all the others of the group to be deselected.

Similar to a Swing container, the **ButtonGroup** can be instantiated with an empty constructor, and members can be inserted into the group with the **add** method.

A **ButtonGroup** *represents an aggregation of toggle buttons, but is not itself a visible container.*

If you add toggle buttons to a **ButtonGroup** *but neglect to add them to a visible container object as well, the buttons will not be visible within your GUI.*

One possible solution follows. This solution contains the necessary code for creation of a **ButtonGroup** object and to add the radio buttons to this

ButtonGroup. The code in **boldface** is responsible for creating the **ButtonGroup** and adding the radio buttons.

```java
import javax.swing.*;
import java.awt.*;
import java.awt.event.*;


public class ButtonsApplet extends JApplet
{
    JButton button;
    ButtonGroup group;
    JRadioButton greenButton, blueButton, redButton;

    public void init()
    {
        JPanel contentPane = (JPanel)getContentPane();
        contentPane.setLayout(new FlowLayout());

        button = new JButton("OK");
        greenButton = new JRadioButton("Green");
        blueButton = new JRadioButton("Blue");
        redButton = new JRadioButton("Red");

        contentPane.add(greenButton);
        contentPane.add(blueButton);
        contentPane.add(redButton);
        contentPane.add(button);

        // Create a ButtonGroup and add the radio buttons—
        // this allows the buttons to be mutually exclusive
        group = new ButtonGroup();
        group.add(greenButton);
        group.add(blueButton);
        group.add(redButton);

        // don't worry too much about this for now—
        // it sets up a handler for button press events.
        button.addActionListener(new ActionListener()
        {
            public void actionPerformed(ActionEvent evt)
            {
                doMyButtonAction();
            }
        });
    }
```

```
// Perform an action when the button is pressed,
// but only if the checkbox is selected
public void doMyButtonAction()
{
        if(greenButton.isSelected())
        {
                button.setForeground(Color.green);
        }
            else if(blueButton.isSelected())
        {
                button.setForeground(Color.blue);
        }
        else if(redButton.isSelected())
        {
                button.setForeground(Color.red);
        }
}
}
```

LAB 6.4 SELF-REVIEW QUESTIONS

In order to test your progress, you should be able to answer the following questions.

1) What is the base class from which all Swing button objects are derived?
   a) _____ JButton
   b) _____ ButtonGroup
   c) _____ AbstractButton

2) Which of the following components should be used for soliciting yes/no or on/off input?
   a) _____ JButton
   b) _____ JRadioButton
   c) _____ JCheckBox

3) Which of the following components should be used for soliciting mutually exclusive input?
   a) _____ JButton
   b) _____ JRadioButton
   c) _____ JCheckBox

4) Adding buttons to a **ButtonGroup** container ensures that the buttons will be visible within the GUI.
   a) _____ True
   b) _____ False

5) Text associated with a **JCheckBox** is positioned to which side of the box?

a) _____ top

b) _____ bottom

c) _____ left

d) _____ right

Quiz answers appear in Appendix A, Section 6.4.

L A B   6 . 5

THE USE OF TEXT COMPONENTS

LAB OBJECTIVES

After this lab, you will be able to:

- Use the JTextfield and JPasswordField Components
- Use the JTextPane Component

Buttons and labels provide great flexibility in the design of GUIs, but quite often the GUI must solicit the user for text input. Passwords, login IDs, URLs—these are just a few parameters that require free-form text input from users. Of course, Swing has many components for text input and we will take a look at a few of the most common of these components in this lab, all of which are subclasses of `javax.swing.text.JTextComponent`.

THE TEXTFIELD COMPONENTS

For soliciting single-line text input, Swing provides the **JTextField** and **JPasswordField** components. Often-used constructors for the **JText-Field** class are as follows:

```
JTextField(int columns)
JTextField(String text)
JTextField(String text, int columns)
```

The **columns** parameter specifies the size of the text field. Specifically, it specifies how many standard characters can fit within the visible area of the text field. For variable-width fonts, the columns are sized as per the width of a lowercase *m* in the currently selected font—did you really need to know this? Probably not.

The **text** parameter specifies the default text to be displayed within the component. If you feel the burning desire to have your textfield display a default value, you could do so with the **text** parameter.

The **JPasswordField** is a subclass of **JTextField** and has identical constructors.

■ FOR EXAMPLE:

The following applet demonstrates how a **JTextField** is instantiated and displayed. This should be old-hat to you by now. . . .

```
import javax.swing.*;
import java.awt.*;

public class TextApplet extends JApplet
{
    JPanel contentPanel;
    JLabel label;
    JTextField textField;

    public void init()
    {
        contentPanel = (JPanel)getContentPane();
        contentPanel.setLayout(new FlowLayout());
        label = new JLabel("Input text here: ");
        textField = new JTextField("A default
        value", 20);
        contentPanel.add(label);
        contentPanel.add(textField);
    }
}
```

As you can see, this process is very similar to all the other components we have investigated in this chapter. As a Swing component, you also have a variety of methods available to modify the appearance and functionality of this textfield.

THE TEXTAREA COMPONENT

Sometimes a single line of text is just not enough either for input or for the display of text. For such circumstances, Swing provides a larger, multiline text input and display area called a **JTextArea.**

Similar to the **JTextField** and **JPasswordField,** common constructors for **JTextArea** are as follows:

```
JTextArea(int rows, int columns)
JTextArea(String text)
JTextArea(String text, int rows, int columns)
```

The **rows** and **columns** parameters specify the size of the text area. The **text** parameter specifies default text to be displayed within the text area. Naturally, you also access to all the wonderful **JComponent** methods that can be used to modify the appearance and functionality of the text area.

LAB 6.5 EXERCISES

6.5.1 USE THE *J*TEXTFIELD AND *J*PASSWORDFIELD COMPONENTS

Use the following applet to answer these questions:

```
import javax.swing.*;
import java.awt.event.*;
import java.awt.*;

public class TextFieldApplet extends JApplet
{
  JPanel contentPanel;
  JLabel label;
  JTextField textField;
  JButton button;

  public void init()
  {
        contentPanel = (JPanel)getContentPane();
        contentPanel.setLayout(new FlowLayout());
        label = new JLabel("Input text here: ");
        textField = new JTextField("A default value", 20);
        button = new JButton("OK");
```

```
        // You know the drill-- action handling will
        // be covered in a following chapter
        button.addActionListener(new ActionListener()
        {
                public void actionPerformed(ActionEvent evt)
                {
                        doMyButtonAction();
                }
            });

        contentPanel.add(label);
        contentPanel.add(textField);
        contentPanel.add(button);
    }

  public void doMyButtonAction()
  {
        showStatus(textField.getText());
  }
}
```

a) What method is being called to retrieve the text from the **JTextField?** What method should be called if the text field was modified to be a **JPasswordField?**

_____

_____

b) Modify the applet so that pressing the *OK* button will set the text within the field to a default value. What modifications were required?

_____

_____

c) Apparently, centered text is all the rage in Europe and product marketing has decreed that all text fields must follow the new trend. What modifications are required to center-justify the text within the text field?

_____

_____

6.5.2 USE THE JTEXTAREA COMPONENT

Use the following applet to answer these questions:

```java
import javax.swing.*;
import java.awt.event.*;
import java.awt.*;

public class TextAreaApplet extends JApplet
{
    JPanel contentPanel;
    JTextArea textArea;
    JButton button;

    public void init()
    {
            contentPanel = (JPanel)getContentPane();
            contentPanel.setLayout(new FlowLayout());
            textArea = new JTextArea("A default value", 20, 40);
            textArea.setLineWrap(true);
            button = new JButton("Clear");

            // You know the drill— action handling will
            // be covered in a following chapter
            button.addActionListener(new ActionListener()
            {
                    public void actionPerformed(ActionEvent evt)
                    {
                            doMyButtonAction();
                    }
            });

            contentPanel.add(textArea);
            contentPanel.add(button);
    }
    public void doMyButtonAction()
    {
            // does nothing
    }
}
```

a) Modify `TextAreaApplet` so that pressing the button will clear all text from the `JTextArea`. What modifications were necessary?

_____

_____

b) The director of public relations has taken a lot of criticism from users of this applet because the text area does not perform line-wrapping. What modifications could you make to implement this feature?

_____

_____

LAB 6.5 EXERCISE ANSWERS

6.5.1   ANSWERS

a) What method is being called to retrieve the text from the `JTextField`? What method should be called if the text field was modified to be a `JPasswordField`?

Answer: The method **getText** *is being called to retrieve the text from the text field. The password field, however, has a different method for obtaining the text.*

The **getText** method is inherited from **JTextComponent,** the superclass of **JTextField**. It returns a **String** containing the text shown in the text field.

JPasswordField does things a bit differently, however. The method used to retrieve the text from a password field is **getPassword.** For the sake of security, though this is really nothing more than an inconvenience, **getPassword** returns a **char** array. Converting the **char** array to a **String** object is quite straightforward, and can be done on one line as follows:

```
String thePassword = new String(passwordField.getPassword());
```

Because the **String** object has a constructor that takes a **char** array, you can simply feed the returned **char** array into a **String** constructor. Ostensibly, all this extra work is done to enhance security; but because Java stores array elements within consecutive memory addresses, it really is just a pain in the rear. Such is life.

b) Modify the applet so that pressing the *OK* button will set the text within the label to a default value. What modifications were required?

*Answer: Just as with the **JLabel** and **JButton** components, you can use the **setText** method to display an arbitrary **String** within the component.*

Déjà vu? Yes, it seems that most of these components have a **setText** method that allows you to set a **String** to be displayed. In this example, you can modify **doMyButtonAction** so that it sets a default **String** value each time it is pressed. Your solution may differ, so it is only important that the same functionality is achieved. One possible solution is as follows:

```
public void doMyButtonAction()
{
    textField.setText("Just some arbitrary text");
}
```

If you have not already noticed, mastery of a few basic component methods will take you very far along the road to GUI programming nirvana. We can only point you in the right direction. . . .

c) Apparently, centered text is all the rage in Europe, and product marketing has decreed that all text fields must follow the new trend. What modifications are required to center-justify the text within the text field?

*Answer: Just as you were able to set the horizontal alignment within the **JLabel**, you can do the same with **JTextField** and **JPasswordField**.*

The method that can be used to set the horizontal alignment of text within the **JTextField** or **JPasswordField** is **setHorizontalAlignment,** and is defined as follows:

```
public void setHorizontalAlignment(int alignment)
```

where alignment is an **int** value which specifies the alignment type. As with **JLabel,** you can use the values defined within the **SwingConstants** class, or you can use the values defined locally within **JTextField.** These values are:

```
SwingConstants.CENTER or JTextField.CENTER
SwingConstants.LEFT   or JTextField.LEFT
SwingConstants.RIGHT  or JTextField.RIGHT
```

So the only modification required to **TextFieldApplet** would be the addition of the following line after the instantiation of the **JTextField:**

```
textField.setHorizontalAlignment(SwingConstants.CENTER);
```

or, if you would rather use the locally defined variables (it really makes no difference, though it is nice to standardize) the modification would be:

```
textField.setHorizontalTextAlignment(JTextField.CENTER);
```

6.5.2 ANSWERS

a)   Modify **TextAreaApplet** so that pressing the button will clear all text from the **JTextArea.** What modifications were necessary?

Answer: **JTextArea** *inherits the* **setText** *method from its superclass* **JTextComponent.** *This method can be used to easily clear the text from the text area.*

The method **doMyButtonAction** should be modified to call **setText** on the text area with either a **null** value or an empty **String.** This will clear the text area when the button is pressed. Your method may differ slightly, but the addition of either one of the following lines to **doMyButtonAction** would do the trick:

```
textArea.setText(null);
```

or

```
textArea.setText("");
```

By assigning the contents of the text area to null or an empty String, you clear the entire text area. There are other ways to do this as well, but this is the most basic (and easiest) method.

b)   The director of public relations has taken a lot of criticism from users of this applet because the text area does not perform line-wrapping. What modifications could you make to implement this feature?

Answer: As luck would have it, there is a method you can call to set line-wrapping on a **JTextArea.** *The method is named, quite appropriately,* **setLineWrap** *and takes a boolean value indicating whether or not text should wrap.*

The signature of the **setLineWrap** method is as follows:

```
public void setLineWrap(boolean wrap)
```

The parameter **wrap** indicates whether or not text should wrap from one line to the next. Because text does not wrap in our example applet, we can gather that line-wrapping is not enabled by default. To enable line-wrapping, you should simply call this method following instantiation of the **JTextArea:**

```
textArea.setLineWrap(true);
```

Great—now the text area performs line-wrapping. However, words are still split between lines. Though the director of public relations did not specify that he wanted words wrapped as well, let's do that for him.

Once line-wrap has been enabled, you can enable word-wrapping with the method **setWrapStyleWord.** The signature of this strangely named method is as follows:

```
public void setWrapStyleWord(boolean word)
```

The parameter word indicates whether or not word-wrapping should occur, so to implement word-wrapping as well in the applet, we should add the following line after we enable line-wrapping:

```
textArea.setWrapStyleWord(true);
```

Viola—we now have both line and word wrapping enabled. The director would be proud!

LAB 6.5 SELF-REVIEW QUESTIONS

In order to test your progress, you should be able to answer the following questions.

1) Which of the following is the base class from which all Swing text input components derive?
   a) _____ JTextField
   b) _____ JTextArea
   c) _____ JTextComponent

2) Which of the following components should be used for soliciting information from the user that is not to be echoed back to the GUI in readable format?
   a) _____ JTextField
   b) _____ JPasswordField
   c) _____ JTextArea

3) It is possible to set the horizontal text alignment of a JTextField and JPassword-Field.

a) _____ True

b) _____ False

4) The JTextArea supports line-wrapping, but word-wrapping is not supported.

a) _____ True

b) _____ False

5) The text within a JTextArea can be cleared by calling its clearText method.

a) _____ True

b) _____ False

Quiz answers appear in Appendix A, Section 6.5.

LAB
6.5

CHAPTER 6

TEST YOUR THINKING

The graphical input to your program can be a very important part of the overall program. If a program is hard to use, people won't want to use it. Always remember that the U in GUI stands for *User*. You don't yet have all of the tools needed to make a complete GUI (those chapters are coming up), but understanding the basic building blocks of a GUI is a key part of building the entire user interface.

1) Write code to create Figure 6.1, the sample GUI components.

C H A P T E R   7

LAYOUT MANAGERS

All you need is the desire to make beautiful things happen on canvas.

Bob Ross, artist

Artists have the ability to transfer a picture from their minds onto a canvas. When building a graphical interface, you must similarly transfer an image in your mind into code. Your paintbrush is the *layout manager,* a tool that allows you to position and size graphical components to create the interface of your design.

In Java, there are several *Container* classes, such as **Panel**, **Frame**, and **Applet**. Every *Container* also has a *LayoutManager* associated with it. A layout manager does not actually contain any components; rather, it is an object, which works with a container, and whose job it is to *manage* the *layout* of the container's contents. A layout manager can control the *size, shape,* and *positions* of each component. Java smartly separates the *layout* behavior from the *container* so that every container can have any kind of layout. While dozens of different layout managers are available, we will cover what we feel are the three most useful. First, we will discuss two of the three layout managers, the **BorderLayout**, and the **GridLayout**. Then we will show you how you can combine layout managers together so that you can mix and match different layout behaviors. Lastly, we will explore the third layout manager, the **GridBagLayout**, and its multitude of uses.

L A B   7 . 1

THE BORDERLAYOUT

> ## LAB OBJECTIVES
>
> After this lab, you will be able to:
>
> • Use the BorderLayout Manager

The best example of layout manager behavior is to look at your Web browser (it doesn't matter which browser you are using because they all have similar characteristics). Your browser has a row of buttons (*Back, Forward, Reload, Home*), a text area where you can type in a URL, and the main Web page window. The relative positioning of these components is controlled by something very much like a layout manager. If you resize your browser window, some of the components (like the main window) may *stretch* or *shrink*, but some (like the buttons) may also become *hidden* or *exposed*. These are the functions of a layout manager.

You have already used one layout manager, the **FlowLayout**. This is the default layout manager for most containers. Its job is very simple; it does nothing! The **FlowLayout** is the organizational equivalent of a *pile*. That is, no organization. The authors considered having a **FlowLayout** lab, but we feared it might induce a coma, so we'll just mention it here. Just know that it exists.

THE BORDER LAYOUT

The **BorderLayout** is a nice, general-purpose layout manager. It is simple to use, yet quite flexible in its abilities. The **BorderLayout** divides an area into five regions, into which you can place different components. The first four regions, called *North*, *South*, *East* and *West*, border the fifth region, called *Center*. When you add a component to a container, you must specify in which region to add it.

Figure 7.1 shows the five regions of a **BorderLayout**.

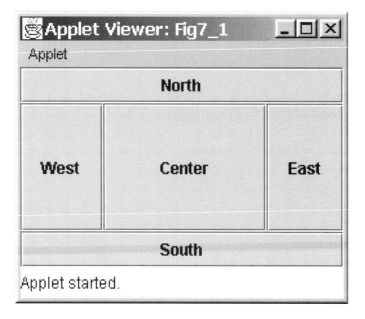

Figure 7.1 ■ The BorderLayout with all regions filled

Let's look at the code that created Figure 7.1.

■ FOR EXAMPLE:

Here is the full code that produced Figure 7.1:

```
import java.awt.*;
import javax.swing.*;
import java.applet.Applet;

public class Fig7_1
    extends Applet
{
    public void init()
    {
        setLayout(new BorderLayout());
        add(new JButton("North"), BorderLayout.NORTH);
        add(new JButton("South"), BorderLayout.SOUTH);
        add(new JButton("East"), BorderLayout.EAST);
        add(new JButton("West"), BorderLayout.WEST);
        add(new JButton("Center"),BorderLayout.CENTER);
        resize(250, 150);
    }
}
```

This particular code example is an **Applet**, *however, the exact same layout manager code (inside the* **init()** *block) could be used with a* **Panel**, **Frame**, *or* **JFrame** *inside their constructor blocks. As always, all future examples will only show the init() block code.*

The first thing we did is replace the old **FlowLayout** with a new **Border-Layout** object using the **setLayout()** method. We then added some **JButton** objects using a different form of the **add()** method. The values **BorderLayout.NORTH** and **BorderLayout.EAST** are called *constraints* and they tell the **BorderLayout** where to place each component.

Look back at Figure 7.1. Notice how each **JButton** is stretched and shaped to fill the window? The **BorderLayout** always fills its region and does so by stretching its components. Also notice how the *North* and *South* regions extend to the left and right edges, but the *East* and *West* regions do not extend to the top or the bottom. We will explore why this is significant in the exercises.

The API definition for this form of the **add()** method is as follows:

```
public Component add(Component comp, Object constraints)
```

■ FOR EXAMPLE:

Let's look at another example of the **BorderLayout**. This time we will not fill in all of the border regions. We will use the previous example but take out the *East* and *South* components. Our code now looks like the following:

```
setLayout(new BorderLayout());
add(new JButton("North"), BorderLayout.NORTH);
add(new JButton("West"), BorderLayout.WEST);
add(new JButton("Center"), BorderLayout.CENTER);
resize(250, 150);
```

The result of this code is Figure 7.2.

Notice how the entire region is still rectangular. There are no "holes" from not having a *South* or *East* component. The *Center* and *West* components have been stretched to fill the remaining space.

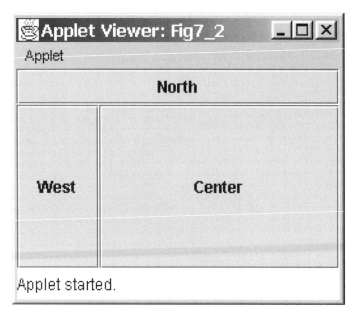

Figure 7.2 ■ **The BorderLayout with only North, West, and Center**

■ *FOR EXAMPLE:*

Let's look at one final example of the **BorderLayout**, this time a practical use! In this example, we are going to create a small form that someone could fill out. There is a title, a label, and an area to type in.

```
setLayout(new BorderLayout());
JLabel title = new JLabel("You are at the Border!",
    JLabel.CENTER);
add(title, BorderLayout.NORTH);
JLabel label = new JLabel("Passport #",
JLabel.RIGHT);
add(label, BorderLayout.WEST);
JTextField text = new JTextField("1234567890");
add(text, BorderLayout.CENTER);
resize(250, 50);
```

The result of this code is Figure 7.3.

Figure 7.3 actually looks like something you might see in a real program or Web page. Welcome to the world of GUI design! Hopefully, this lab's

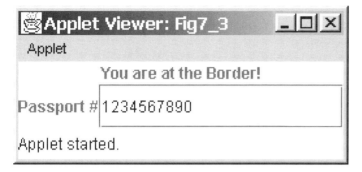

Figure 7.3 ■ **A practical use for the BorderLayout**

exercises will be more exciting and rewarding (unlike that yawner, *Boolean Logic*) because you get to create some cool-looking graphic interfaces.

LAB 7.1 EXERCISES

7.1.1 THE BORDERLAYOUT MANAGER

Some of the questions in these Exercises require you to resize the applet. If you are using the appletviewer program, then this is not a problem, as you can just drag the window to resize it. However, if you are running your applet from a Web browser, you need to change the height and width parameters in the HTML file. Personally, the authors recommend using the appletviewer.

a) Enter the code that generated Figure 7.1 and run it. Now resize it so that it is *wider*. Which regions also get wider?

_____

_____

b) Using the same window from question a, resize the window so that it is *taller*. Which regions get taller?

_____

_____

c) Write code to create the layout as in Figure 7.4.

_____

_____

d) Create a Frame or Applet that contains buttons in all of the regions except the Center region. What happens now?

_____

_____

LAB 7.1 EXERCISE ANSWERS

7.1.1 ANSWERS

a) Enter the code that generated Figure 7.1 and run it. Now resize it so that it is *wider*. Which regions also get wider?

Answer: The North, South, and Center regions get wider.

The point of this question is to show that the *East* and *West* regions will only be as wide as they need to be to fit their components. They will, however, stretch vertically to fill the window.

b) Using the same window from question a, resize the window so that it is *taller*. Which regions get taller?

Answer: The Center, West and East regions get taller.

Similarly to question a, the point of question b is to show that the *North* and *South* regions will only be as tall as they need to be to fit their components. They will, however, stretch horizontally to fill the window.

c) Write code to create the layout as in Figure 7.4.

Answer: The following code was used to create Figure 7.4.

```
JFrame f = new JFrame("Exercise 7.1.1 c");
Container c = f.getContentPane();
c.add(new JButton("Press Me!"), BorderLayout.CENTER);
c.add(new Scrollbar(), BorderLayout.EAST);
c.add(new JTextField("JTextField"),
BorderLayout.SOUTH);
f.resize(200, 150);
f.show();
```

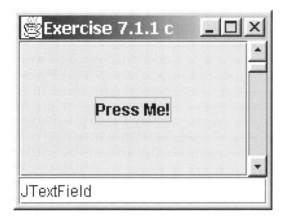

Figure 7.4 ■ Build this layout

This code uses a **JFrame** just to show the fact that a **Frame** and **JFrame** already have a **BorderLayout** as the default layout manager. Thus, we don't have to set the layout of the **JFrame** (or **Frame**). Likewise, we wanted to show that when you use the **JFrame** or **JApplet** classes, you must add components to the *content pane*, not the object itself. Likewise, you must use the content pane's **setLayout()** method.

Regardless of how you wrote your program, the important part is the layout. The three *add* lines in the middle of the code are the important lines. Also, we hope you were able to recognize the three different components placed in the frame (JButton, JtextField, and Scrollbar).

d) Create a Frame or Applet that contains buttons in the all of the regions except the Center region. What happens now?

Answer: There is a hole remaining in the Center area.

Depending on your windowing system, the hole is probably just a gray space. None of the other regions will stretch to fill this space. It is assumed that the *Center* region is the "main" region and that *something* will be there.

LAB 7.1 SELF-REVIEW QUESTIONS

In order to test your progress, you should be able to answer the following questions.

1) Which of the follow attributes does a layout manager not control?
   a) _____ length
   b) _____ position
   c) _____ visibility
   d) _____ width
   e) _____ color

2) Which constraint puts a component on the bottom?
   a) _____ LayoutManager.BOTTOM
   b) _____ BorderLayout.SOUTH
   c) _____ BorderLayout.BOTTOM
   d) _____ LayoutManager.SOUTH

3) Which package must you import to use a BorderLayout?
   a) _____ java.lang.*
   b) _____ javax.swing.*
   c) _____ java.awt.*
   d) _____ java.layout.*
   e) _____ None, it's there by default

4) Which regions will stretch horizontally? Check all that apply.
   a) _____ NORTH
   b) _____ SOUTH
   c) _____ CENTER
   d) _____ EAST
   e) _____ WEST

5) Which regions will stretch vertically? Check all that apply.
   a) _____ NORTH
   b) _____ SOUTH
   c) _____ CENTER
   d) _____ EAST
   e) _____ WEST

6) If a container has components in the *South*, *West*, and *Center* regions, the *West* component will touch the bottom of the window.
   a) _____ True
   b) _____ False

7) Which region puts a component in the upper-left corner?

a) _____ **NE**

b) _____ **NORTHEAST**

c) _____ **NORTH + EAST**

d) _____ **LayoutManager.NORTHEAST**

e) _____ **None of the above**

Quiz answers appear in Appendix A, Section 7.1.

L A B   7 . 2

THE GRIDLAYOUT

LAB OBJECTIVES

After this lab, you will be able to:

* Use the GridLayout Manager

The **GridLayout** is another simple but effective layout manager. True to its name, the **GridLayout** places all components into a grid. Everything is laid out in neat rows and columns and every component is the same size. Think of the **GridLayout** as the "Official Layout Manager" of the Utopian Society.

THE BASIC GRIDLAYOUT

Figure 7.5 shows a sample **GridLayout**. It is a 3 × 3 grid with a **JButton** in each compartment.

Notice that each component in the grid is the same size. If you resize the entire window, then each component will be resized so that all components are the same size.

■ *FOR EXAMPLE:*

The extremely simple code that produced Figure 7.5 follows.

```
String labels[] = {"One", "Two", "Three", "Four",
    "Five", "Six", "Seven", "Eight", "Nine"};
setLayout(new GridLayout(3, 3));
for (int i=0; i<labels.length; i++)
    add(new JButton(labels[i]));
resize(240, 180);
```

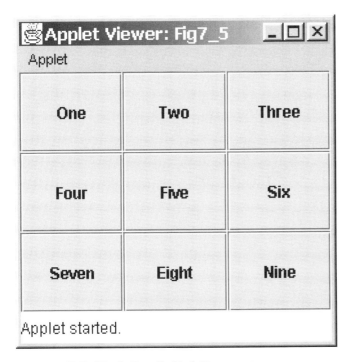

Figure 7.5 ■ A 3 × 3 GridLayout

When you construct the new **GridLayout,** you must pass in the number of *rows* and *columns* in the grid. In this example, there are three of each. As Figure 7.5 shows, components are added starting in the upper-left corner and each row is filled in before moving down to the next row. Thus, the order in which components are added to the container determines their position.

ADJUSTING THE GAP BETWEEN COMPONENTS

You've probably been asking yourself, "Can I adjust the gap spacing between each component?" Well, you'll be pleased to know the answer is "Yes!" By passing in additional values to the **GridLayout** constructor, we can set both the *horizontal* and *vertical* gap values. Both *hgap* and *vgap,* as they are called, are the number of pixels between each component. Now, let's all try to remain calm and look at an example.

■ *FOR EXAMPLE:*

To create Figure 7.6, we made one small change to the previous example, as follows:

```
setLayout(new GridLayout(3, 3, 10, 10));
```

The difference is that we added the hgap and vgap values to the constructor. Figure 7.6 shows the result of the change.

As you can see, the entire window is still the same size, but each component is slightly smaller to make room for the gaps.

Here is a summary of the API definitions for the **GridLayout** constructor, its methods, and the **add()** method to use with the **GridLayout**:

```
public GridLayout(int rows, int cols)
public GridLayout(int rows, int cols, int hgap, int vgap)
public Component add(Component comp)
```

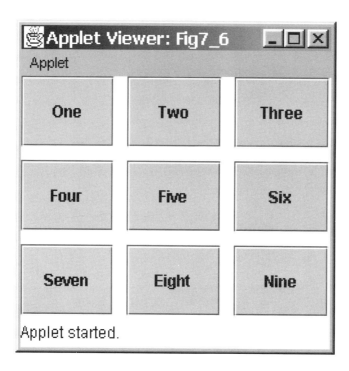

Figure 7.6 ■ The same 3 × 3 GridLayout with gap spacing values of 10

LAB 7.2 EXERCISES

7.2.1 THE GRIDLAYOUT MANAGER

a) How would you construct a GridLayout to hold 12 components and have a gap spacing of 5 pixels? Use a 4×3 grid.

_____

_____

b) Use a `GridLayout` to create a touch-tone phone pad.

_____

_____

c) Create a 4×4 GridLayout, but only add 10 items to the container. What happens?

_____

_____

d) Create a 1×2 (or 2×1) `GridLayout` and add `JTextField` and a `JScrollbar` to the container. Do you think this is a good idea?

_____

_____

LAB 7.2 EXERCISE ANSWERS

7.2.1 ANSWERS

a) How would you construct a GridLayout to hold 12 components and have a gap spacing of 5 pixels? Use a 4 x 3 grid.

Answer: The following code will work:

```
new GridLayout(4, 3, 5, 5)
```

b) Use a `GridLayout` to create a touch-tone phone pad.

Answer: The following code will work:

```
new GridLayout(4, 3, 5, 5)
String labels[] = {"1", "2", "3", "4", "5", "6",
    "7", "8", "9", "*", "0", "#"};
setLayout(new GridLayout(4, 3, 5, 5));
for (int i=0; i<labels.length; i++)
    add(new JButton(labels[i]));
resize(150, 100);
```

The preceding code will generate the layout as in Figure 7.7.

Remember, add the buttons in the correct order so that they are correctly positioned.

c) Create a 4 × 4 GridLayout, but only add 10 items to the container.
    What happens?

Answer: Bad things.

Well, at least unexpected things. You might expect to see a 4 × 4 grid with only 10 items in it. However, you don't. Instead, you get something as in Figure 7.8; clearly, this is not what you wanted or expected.

The truth is that the results are undefined. You might get something you want, and you might not. While there may be some rhyme or reason to this behavior, the lesson to learn here is: *always fill your GridLayouts!* If you need to have a "blank" spot, you can add an empty label, like this:

```
add(new Label(""));
```

Figure 7.7 ■ A simulation of a touch-tone phone

Figure 7.8 ■ An unfilled 4 × 4 GridLayout. Not exactly what you would expect

This will create an empty spot in the grid, yet still fill the grid. We will also revisit this concept with the **GridBagLayout** manager later in this chapter.

d) Create a 1 x 2 **GridLayout** and add **JTextField** and a **JScrollbar** to the container. Do you think this is a good idea?

Answer: Probably not a good idea for a mixture of these particular components.

Text fields are horizontal objects and vertical scrollbars are, well, vertical! When you force them to be the same size by using a **GridLayout,** it doesn't look too good. We will see ways of getting around issues like this later in the chapter.

LAB 7.2 SELF-REVIEW QUESTIONS

In order to test your progress, you should be able to answer the following questions.

Use the following code for Questions 1 though 4

```
new GridLayout(6, 3, 5, 4)
```

1) How many rows are there in the **GridLayout**?
   a) _____ 6
   b) _____ 3
   c) _____ 18
   d) _____ 4
   e) _____ **Can't tell**

2) How many columns are there in the **GridLayout**?
a) _____ 6
b) _____ 3
c) _____ 18
d) _____ 4
e) _____ **Can't tell**

3) What is the vertical gap space in the **GridLayout**?
a) _____ 6
b) _____ 3
c) _____ 18
d) _____ 4
e) _____ **Can't tell**

4) How many components are in the **GridLayout**?
a) _____ 6
b) _____ 3
c) _____ 18
d) _____ 4
e) _____ **Can't tell**

5) The first component goes into which grid?
a) _____ **Upper-left**
b) _____ **Lower-left**
c) _____ **Upper-right**
d) _____ **Lower-right**
e) _____ **Center**

6) All components managed by a **GridLayout** are the same size.
a) _____ **True**
b) _____ **False**

Quiz answers appear in Appendix A, Section 7.2.

L A B 7 . 3

COMBINING LAYOUT MANAGERS

LAB OBJECTIVES

After this lab, you will be able to:

• Combine Multiple Layout Managers

So far, neither of the two layout managers we've explored could do everything that we need them do. Both the **GridLayout** and the **BorderLayout** had their strengths and their weaknesses. There are actually dozens of layout managers available, but none of them is the *one perfect layout manager*. What can we do about it? Well, in Java, containers can contain other containers, and each container can have a different layout manager. By combining the layout managers together, we can get a combination of layout behaviors.

GUI layout can sometimes be more about creativity than programming. In this lab, we will show you a few common tricks, and then your creativity can take over.

PUTTING CONTAINERS INSIDE CONTAINERS

Let's see an example of using two containers and two layout managers. The most commonly used containers are the **Panel** and **JPanel**. Figure 7.9 shows how we create a new **JPanel** and then add it to a **Border-Layout**.

The **JPanel** contains three **JButtons** and uses a **GridLayout** to keep the buttons in a 1 × 3 formation. The Applet frame uses a **BorderLayout** and by placing the **JPanel** in the *SOUTH* region, we place all of the **JButtons** in the *SOUTH*, too.

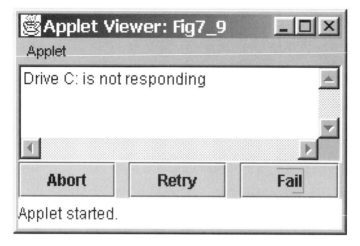

Figure 7.9 ■ A GridLayout inside a BorderLayout

■ *FOR EXAMPLE:*

Here is the code that produced Figure 7.9:

```
setLayout(new BorderLayout());
JPanel panel = new JPanel();
String message = "Drive C: is not responding";
add(new TextArea(message), BorderLayout.CENTER);
panel.setLayout(new GridLayout(1, 3, 10, 5));
panel.add(new JButton("Abort"));
panel.add(new JButton("Retry"));
panel.add(new JButton("Fail"));
add(panel, BorderLayout.SOUTH);
resize(250, 100);
```

You can see that we added the **JPanel** in the exact same way that we have added a **JButton** before. In fact, there is no difference. You can add a panel any place where you could add a button or a label. It is quite common to have many layers of *nested* containers to achieve a desired layout.

When designing your program's graphical look, sometimes it's best to just draw it on paper first, and then use the *divide and conquer* approach to figure out how to implement it. Look for components that can be grouped together, and then put them into a container together with the proper layout manager. Now you can consider that whole group of objects as just one object. Suddenly your problem is a little simpler. Now repeat this process until you reach the outer container and you're done!

LAB
7.3

WINDOW RESIZING

One of the most important attributes of a layout manager is how it re-shapes the components when the main window is resized. Your layout might look okay when you first create it, but when you resize the window, things suddenly don't look so hot. Here are some tricks to help preserve your layouts after a resize.

KEEPING THINGS SKINNY OR FLAT

You have already seen an example of a scrollbar being reshaped *fat and wide*, and of a text field being reshaped *tall and skinny*. These are two examples of undesirable layout behavior. We need to keep the tall things tall and the flat things flat. The easiest way to achieve all of these goals is to use the *North* and *South* regions of a **BorderLayout** for flat objects, and the *West* and *East* regions for tall objects. Reserve the *Center* region for objects (or other containers) that can be resized to any shape.

KEEPING THINGS THE SAME SIZE

You might also want to keep a group of objects the same size relative to each other, or maintain their relative position to each other (*Bob* is always to the left of *Sam*). For simple cases, the **GridLayout** is a good choice to solve both of these problems. Once you have added your components to the container, you no longer have to worry about them.

LAB 7.3 EXERCISES

7.3.1 COMBINING MULTIPLE LAYOUT MANAGERS

a) Create an interface that matches the Calendar program shown in Figure 7.10. Note that not all of the keys are the same size.

Examine the following code for the next question:

```
setLayout(new BorderLayout());
resize(350, 100);
Panel top = new Panel();
```

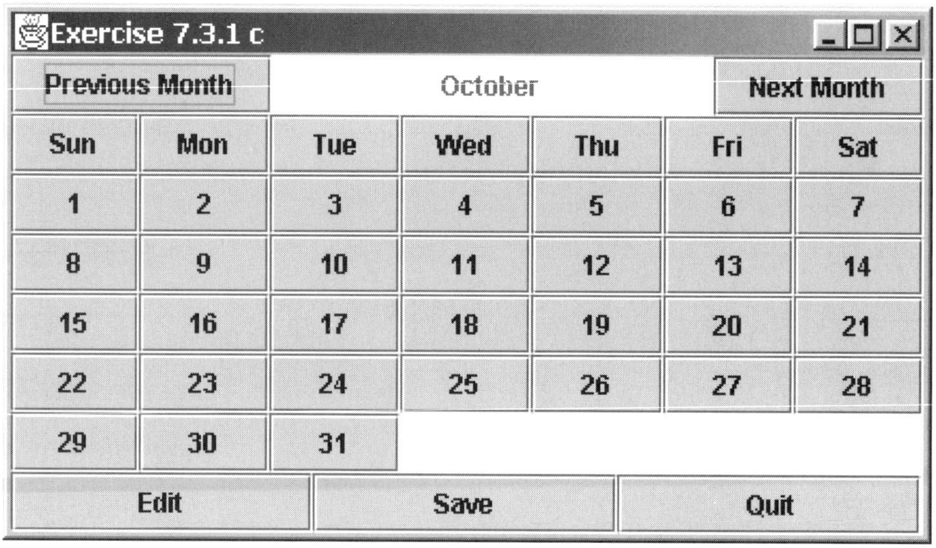

Figure 7.10 ■ A simulation of a calendar display

```
top.setLayout(new GridLayout(1, 3));
Panel bottom = new Panel();
bottom.setLayout(new GridLayout(1, 3));
add(top, BorderLayout.NORTH);
for (int i=1; i<=3; i++)
{
   top.add(new JButton("Button " + i));
   bottom.add(new JButton("Button " + i));
}
add(bottom, BorderLayout.SOUTH);
```

The preceding code makes two panels, each with three buttons. The difference between the **top** and **bottom** panels is that **top** is added to the Applet first, and then **top**'s buttons are added. Conversely, **bottom** has its buttons added first, and then **bottom** is added to the Applet.

b) Do you think this will make a difference in the final output?

_____

_____

c) Look at the numeric keypad of your computer. Can you design a layout that replicates the keypad using just the **GridLayout** and

`BorderLayout`? Hint: Don't spend too much time on this since we are going to show you a better way later.

LAB 7.3 EXERCISE ANSWERS

7.3.1 ANSWERS

a)   Create an interface that matches the Calendar program shown in Figure 7.10. Note that not all of the keys are the same size.

Answer: The following code created Figure 7.10:

```
import java.awt.*;
import javax.swing.*;
public class Fig7_10
    extends Panel
{
    /**
     * Constructor.
     */
    public Fig7_10 () {
        super();
        setLayout(new BorderLayout());
        // Create new panels
        Panel top = new Panel();
        Panel middle = new Panel();
        Panel bottom = new Panel();
        // Set layouts of panels
        top.setLayout(new BorderLayout());
        middle.setLayout(new GridLayout(6, 7));
        bottom.setLayout(new GridLayout(1, 3));
        // Add calendar components
        // Top
        top.add(new JButton("Previous Month"),
            BorderLayout.WEST);
        JLabel month = new JLabel("October",
            JLabel.CENTER);
        top.add(month, BorderLayout.CENTER);
        top.add(new JButton("Next Month"),
            BorderLayout.EAST);
```

```
            add(top, BorderLayout.NORTH);
            // Middle
            // Add days names
            String days[] = {"Sun", "Mon", "Tue", "Wed",
                    "Thu", "Fri", "Sat"};
            for (int i=0; i<days.length; i++)
                    middle.add(new JButton(days[i]));
            // Add days
            for (int day=1; day<=31; day++)
            {
                    Integer Day = new Integer(day);
                    middle.add(new JButton(Day.toString()));
            }
            add(middle, BorderLayout.CENTER);
            // Bottom
            bottom.add(new JButton("Edit"));
            bottom.add(new JButton("Save"));
            bottom.add(new JButton("Quit"));
            add(bottom, BorderLayout.SOUTH);
    }

    public static void main(String args[])
    {
            Frame f = new Frame("Exercise 7.3.1 c");
            Fig7_10 figure = new Fig7_10();
            f.add(figure, BorderLayout.CENTER);
            f.pack();
            f.show();
    }
}
```

We gave you the whole program this time so you can see what everything does. Make sure that you understand which *who* is being placed inside *whom*. If you run this program (it is a program, not an Applet), you'll be able to resize the window and watch all of the components resize, too.

Some important things to notice: You don't have to use all of the regions of a **BorderLayout**. We've said this before, but it's worth saying again. The **top** panel uses just three of the regions (West, Center, and East) and the outer panel only uses North, Center, and South.

b) Do you think this will make a difference in the final output?

Answer: It will not make a difference in the final output.

Figure 7.11 shows the result of the code for this question.

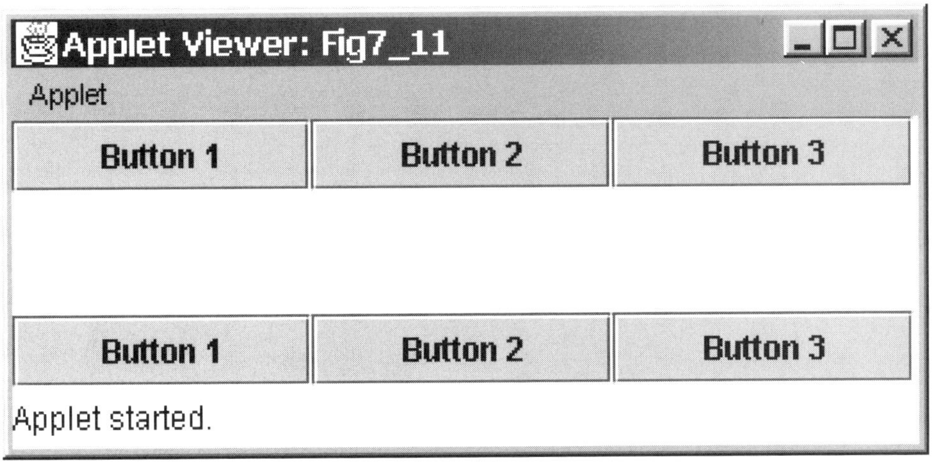

Figure 7.11 ■ The result of the code for question b

Layout managers will update themselves every time a component is added or removed from the container. Thus, it is not necessary to fill a container before adding it to a second container.

c) Look at the numeric keypad of your computer. Can you design a layout that replicates the keypad?

Answer: While you can get close, it's very difficult to replicate a keypad exactly. The following code will make a reasonable approximation of a numeric keypad. It looks better when sized small—and if you stand across the room!

```
import java.awt.*;
import javax.swing.*;
public class Numpad
    extends Frame
{
    JButton buttons[] = new JButton[17];
    static int LOCK = 10;
    static int MULTIPLY = 11;
    static int DIVIDE = 12;
    static int MINUS = 13;
    static int PLUS = 14;
    static int ENTER = 15;
    static int DOT = 16;

    public Numpad2(String label)
    {
        super(label);
```

```
                    createButtons();
                    Panel topPanel = new Panel();
                    Panel oneToNine = new Panel();
                    Panel zeroDot = new Panel();
                    Panel numbers = new Panel();
                    Panel plusEnter = new Panel();
                    topPanel.setLayout(new GridLayout(1, 4));
                    topPanel.add(buttons[LOCK]);
                    topPanel.add(buttons[MULTIPLY]);
                    topPanel.add(buttons[DIVIDE]);
                    topPanel.add(buttons[MINUS]);
                    add(topPanel, BorderLayout.NORTH);
                    oneToNine.setLayout(new GridLayout(3, 3));
                    oneToNine.add(buttons[7]);
                    oneToNine.add(buttons[8]);
                    oneToNine.add(buttons[9]);
                    oneToNine.add(buttons[4]);
                    oneToNine.add(buttons[5]);
                    oneToNine.add(buttons[6]);
                    oneToNine.add(buttons[1]);
                    oneToNine.add(buttons[2]);
                    oneToNine.add(buttons[3]);
                    zeroDot.setLayout(new BorderLayout());
                    zeroDot.add(buttons[0], BorderLayout.CENTER);
                    zeroDot.add(buttons[DOT], BorderLayout.EAST);
                    numbers.setLayout(new BorderLayout());
                    numbers.add(oneToNine, BorderLayout.CENTER);
                    numbers.add(zeroDot, BorderLayout.SOUTH);
                    add(numbers, BorderLayout.CENTER);
                    plusEnter.setLayout(new GridLayout(2, 1));
                    plusEnter.add(buttons[PLUS]);
                    plusEnter.add(buttons[ENTER]);
                    add(plusEnter, BorderLayout.EAST);
             }
             public static void main(String args[])
             {
                    Numpad pad = new Numpad("Numpad");
                    pad.pack();
                    pad.show();
             }
      }
```

While this example isn't perfect, it is a good example of the *Divide and Conquer* approach to programming. We have taken the whole problem and subdivided it into smaller issues by placing panels inside of other panels. Each individual panel manages its own *real estate* and doesn't have to worry about the other panels. Of course, the downside of this is that the individual panels don't coordinate with the other panels. If you run and resize this program, you'll see that some of the keys, like *dot*, don't stay in formation.

The point of this question was to show how you can organize your layouts by grouping together smaller layouts. At the same time, we also showed you some of the limitations of the Grid/Border combination. Understanding these limitations will make you appreciate the **GridBagLayout** in the next Lab.

LAB 7.3 SELF-REVIEW QUESTIONS

In order to test your progress, you should be able to answer the following questions.

1) It is not possible to nest one container inside another.
   a) _____ True
   b) _____ False

2) There is a maximum depth to nesting containers.
   a) _____ True
   b) _____ False

3) You can only nest containers with the same layout manager.
   a) _____ True
   b) _____ False

4) A container is treated just like any other component by its parent container.
   a) _____ True
   b) _____ False

5) You must fill a container first before nesting it in another container.
   a) _____ True
   b) _____ False

6) The outer container must always be a BorderLayout.
   a) _____ True
   b) _____ False

Quiz answers appear in Appendix A, Section 7.3.

L A B 7 . 4

THE GRIDBAGLAYOUT

> ## LAB OBJECTIVES
>
> After this lab, you will be able to:
>
> - Use the GridBagContraints Class
> - Use the GridBagLayout Manager

The **GridBagLayout** is one of the most powerful and versatile layout managers. It is also one of the most intimidating to learn. We say this not to scare you but to prepare you. The **GridbagLayout** may be a little challenging at first, but once you master it, you can do almost anything. In all honesty, the **GridBagLayout** is not that complicated, so don't let yourself get discouraged easily.

As we said, the **GridBagLayout** is very versatile, especially when dealing with large numbers of components. If you only have a few components, then the **BorderLayout** and **GridLayout** managers are probably sufficient. However, if you have lots of components to lay out, and they must interact with each other, then the **GridBagLayout** may be the best choice to use.

The **GridBagLayout** works like the **GridLayout**, in that there is a *grid* upon which the components are placed. However, with the **GridBagLayout**, components can fill more than one grid *cell*. The grid cells themselves don't even have to be the same size. This means that all of the components do not have to be the same size and shape, as with the **GridLayout**. Also, the positioning of a component can be relative to another component, or fixed point. You can say things like "put Button1 under Button2" or "always keep Button3 in the lower-left corner." Finally, you never have to specify the actual size of the grid; the **GridBagLayout** will figure this out for you.

■ *FOR EXAMPLE:*

Figure 7.12 shows an example layout created using a **GridBagLayout**.

Figure 7.12 uses a 3 × 3 grid, but note how some of the buttons span more than one *cell*, either horizontally or vertically. This would not be possible using anything but a **GridBagLayout**. While you might be able to create something that looked similar, resizing the window might disrupt the balance of the components and lose the grid alignment. With the **GridBagLayout,** the relative sizes, shapes, and positions of the components are preserved.

GRIDBAG CONSTRAINTS

To achieve its miraculous results, the **GridBagLayout** uses a class called **GridBagConstraints**. *Constraints* are rules that are applied to each component and dictate how that component should be laid out. You have already seen simple examples of a *constraint* with the **BorderLayout**; **BorderLayout.NORTH** and **BorderLayout.EAST** are constraints. The **GridBagLayout** takes this concept further and allows you to specify several different *constraining attributes*.

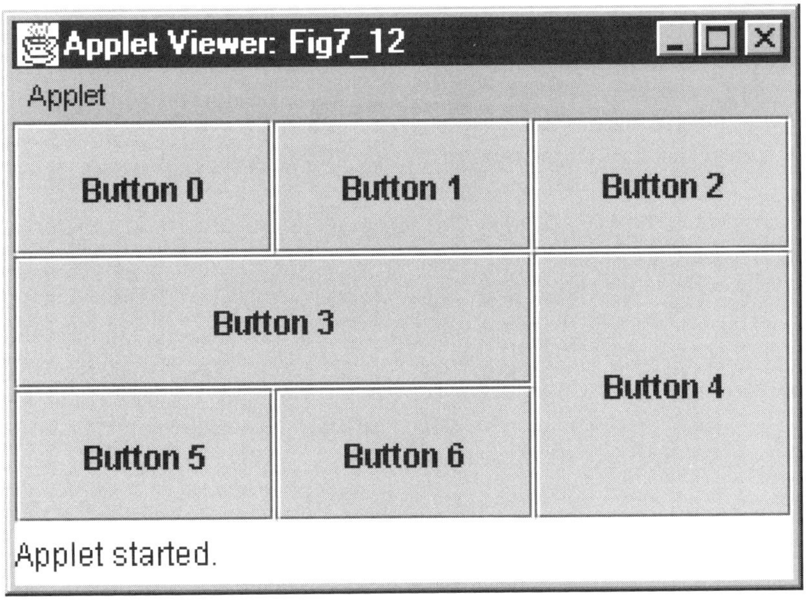

Figure 7.12 ■ Example layout using a GridBagLayout

■ *FOR EXAMPLE:*

A **GridBagConstraints** object contains several fields, each of which is a *constraining attribute*. The following code shows how the **GridBagLayout** uses a **GridBagConstraints** object:

```
setLayout(new GridBagLayout());
GridBagConstraints gbc = new GridBagConstraints();
gbc.fill = GridBagConstraints.BOTH;
gbc.weightx = 1;
gbc.weighty = 1;
add(new JButton("Constrain Me!"), gbc);
```

Notice that we used the two-argument form of the **add()** method, just like we did with the **BorderLayout**. This links the component (the button) with the set of constraints (**gbc**) just like the **BorderLayout** linked the component with a named region (like North or Center). The fields **fill**, **weightx**, and **weighty** are three examples of the *constraining attributes* that can be modified. The **GridBagLayout** will then use these attribute values to properly display the component.

Also notice that **gbc.fill** is set to **GridBagConstraints.BOTH**. This value, like **BorderLayout.SOUTH**, is a special value defined in the class **GridBagConstraints**. Table 7.1 lists some of the **GridBagConstraints** fields and values. Note: All field *names* and *values* in the table should be prepended with **"GridBagConstraints."** For example, **"RELATIVE"** should really be **"GridBagConstraints.RELATIVE"**.

For a complete list of constraints, see the API definitions for **GridBagLayout** and **GridBagConstraints**.

Not all constraints work with each other, so be mindful of which values you are setting, as you may "cancel" something else. Also, some of the constraints work together, meaning that you to need set two attributes to see any change in layout behavior. For example, **fill** won't do anything by itself; you also need to set one of the **weight** values as well. Likewise, **gridwidth** won't take effect until there is a second row. It's idiosyncrasies like these that cause a lot of swearing and head banging when first learning about the **GridBagLayout**.

USING THE GRIDBAGLAYOUT

Just like the government, the best way to understand the **GridBagLayout** is to see it in action. You can read all about the theory of how something works, but until you see how things really work, you'll never really

Table 7.1 ■ GridBag Constraint Fields

Constraint	Default	Description
gridx gridy	RELATIVE	The component's grid coordinates. Location (0, 0) is the upper-left corner. The default value means the component should be placed to the right of (gridx), or below (gridy), the previously added component. Otherwise, you can specify exactly which grid a component should occupy. Setting just gridx to 0 will trigger a new row.
gridwidth gridheight	1	The number of cells the component should span, either horizontally or vertically. By default, this is 1. There are also two special values: REMAINDER for the last item in a row or column, and RELATIVE for the second-to-last item.
fill	NONE	The grid cell may be larger than the component in that cell. By default, a component will not expand to fill any extra space in its cell. However, you can specify values of HORIZONTAL, VERTICAL, or BOTH to have the component expand within the cell horizontally, vertically, or in both directions.
anchor	CENTER	Sets the anchor point for the component to "hold on to" when the window is resized. Other possible values are NORTH, SOUTH, EAST, WEST, NORTHEAST, SOUTHEAST, NORTHWEST, and SOUTHWEST. These apply to the grid's cell, not the whole window.
weightx weighty	0	Sets the weight, or proportional spacing, for the row or column. Weights of 0 will cause the components to not spread out evenly over the window. Instead, the components will cluster together in the center. Components with non-zero weights will be spaced in proportion to their weight values.

LAB
7.4

understand. Your first few attempts at creating a layout with a **GridBagLayout** may result in some trial and error (maybe a lot of error), so remember to stay calm and consider these attempts as *learning experiences*!

■ FOR EXAMPLE:

Let's revisit Figure 7.12 and look at the code that produced it. The following code was written for an Applet, but would also work in any class that extended a container, such as **Panel** or **Frame**.

```
setLayout(new GridBagLayout());
JButton buttons[] = new JButton[7];
for (int i=0; i<buttons.length; i++)
    buttons[i] = new JButton("Button " + i);
GridBagConstraints gbc = new GridBagConstraints();
// First row.
// Add first row of buttons, all evenly spaced
// and expanded both horizonally and vertically.
gbc.fill = GridBagConstraints.BOTH; // Fill all
                                    // space.
gbc.weightx = 1; // Spread out horizontally.
gbc.weighty = 1; // Spread out vertically.
add(buttons[0], gbc);
add(buttons[1], gbc);
gbc.gridwidth = GridBagConstraints.REMAINDER; // End row!
add(buttons[2], gbc);
// Second row
// One double-width button, and one double-height
button
gbc.gridwidth = 2; // Double width
add(buttons[3], gbc);
gbc.gridwidth = 1; // Reset to single width
gbc.gridheight = 2; // Double height
add(buttons[4], gbc);
// Third row.
// Two single-width buttons (and bottom of Button4).
gbc.gridx = 0; // Start new row
gbc.gridheight = 1; // Reset to single height
add(buttons[5], gbc);
gbc.gridx = 1; // Place in column 1
add(buttons[6], gbc);
```

Make sure that you read the comments in the preceding code, as they describe what is being done and when. Note that in this example we are reusing the same set of **GridBagConstraints** (**gbc**) for each component. This is not required, although sometimes it is more practical. You could just as easily create a new **GridBagConstraints** for every component.

Don't worry if this seems a little overwhelming at first, we will be taking a step-by-step approach in the exercises to hopefully make things clearer.

LAB 7.4 EXERCISES

7.4.1 USE THE GRIDBAGCONSTRAINTS CLASS

a) Does the **GridBagConstraints** class actually do anything? Why or why not?

b) What are the values of **GridBagConstraints.RELATIVE** and **GridBagConstraints.REMAINDER**? Do you see the reason for using the class variables instead of the actual values?

7.4.2 USE THE GRIDBAGLAYOUT MANAGER

The following questions will use and modify the following code, henceforth referred to as the *base code*:

```
public void init()
{
    setLayout(new GridBagLayout());
    GridBagConstraints gbc = new GridBagConstraints();
    // Start
    add(new JButton("Button 1"), gbc);
    add(new JButton("Button 2"), gbc);
    setSize(300, 200);
}
```

Add the base code to an **Applet** viewed with the appletviewer (you need to be able to resize quickly to really understand).

Since the questions do build on each other, the authors recommend that you check your answers after each question and make sure that your code is working.

a) Run the base code. Where are the two buttons placed and how large are they? Do they move when you resize the window?

_____

_____

Make the following changes to the base code:

**LAB
7.4**

```
// Start
gbc.fill = GridBagConstraints.HORIZONTAL;
gbc.weightx = 1;
add(new JButton("Button 1"), gbc);
gbc.weightx = 3;
add(new JButton("Button 2"), gbc);
```

b) Where are the buttons, and what happens when you resize the window?

_____

_____

Using the same code from question b, comment out the **fill** line so it looks like the following, and rerun the program.

```
// c.fill = GridBagConstraints.HORIZONTAL;
```

c) What effect did commenting out that line have?

_____

_____

We will now add a second row of buttons. Modify the base code so that it looks like the following code.

```
// Start
gbc.fill = GridBagConstraints.HORIZONTAL;
gbc.weightx = 1;
```

```
add(new JButton("Button 1"), gbc);
gbc.weightx = 3;
gbc.gridwidth = GridBagConstraints.REMAINDER;
add(new JButton("Button 2"), gbc);
gbc.weightx = 10;
gbc.gridwidth = 1;
add(new JButton("Button 3"), gbc);
gbc.weightx = 1;
gbc.gridwidth = GridBagConstraints.REMAINDER;
add(new JButton("Button 4"), gbc);
setSize(300, 200);
```

d) Why is Button I now wider than Button 2? It wasn't before!

Add the following code to the code from question d. Place it right after the "Button 4" code.

```
gbc.gridwidth = 2;
add(new JButton("Button 5"), gbc);
```

e) What happens with Button 5?

f) Write code to produce the layout in Figure 7.13.

g) Write code to produce the layout in Figure 7.14. Hint: *Ahoy, Matey!*

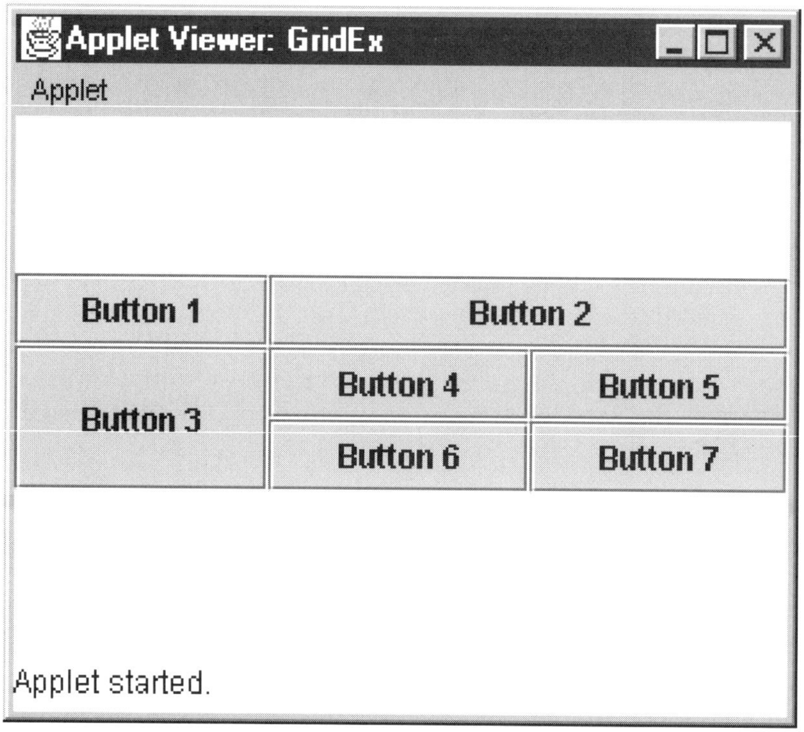

Figure 7.13 ■ Challenge #1

LAB 7.4 EXERCISE ANSWERS

7.4.1 ANSWERS

a) Does the **GridBagConstraints** class actually do anything? Why or why not?

Answer: No, but it is important.

The **GridBagConstraints** class contains many *fields*, but no *methods*. That is, it has data, but no functions, not even *accessor* or *mutator* methods for its data. Putting all of the data into one class makes the data convenient to handle and easy to pass in to the **add()** method. The **GridBagLayout** class then uses all of this data to layout its components.

b) What are the values of **GridBagConstraints.RELATIVE** and **GridBagConstraints.REMAINDER**? Do you see the reason for using the class variables instead of the actual values?

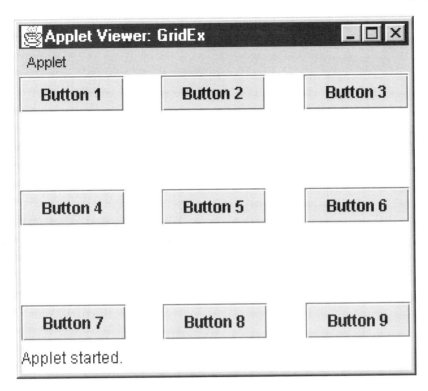

Figure 7.14 ■ Challenge #2

Answer: Use the following code to get the results:

```
System.out.println(GridBagConstraints.RELATIVE);
System.out.println(GridBagConstraints.REMAINDER);
```

The preceding code will generate the following output:

```
-1
0
```

While it would be possible to use just the values **-1** and **0,** it would be considered a very bad programming practice to do so. First of all, you, the programmer, as well as the programmer who wrote the **GridBagLayout**, would have to remember which value is **RELATIVE** and which value is **REMAINDER**. One of you is bound to make a mistake and introduce a bug somewhere. This practice of giving human-readable names to numbers (or other values) is quite common and encouraged. Imagine if you had to remember all *nine* of the **anchor** point values!

7.4.2 ANSWERS

a) Where are the two buttons placed and how large are they?

Answer: The buttons are grouped in the center and are their minimum size (not stretched at all), as shown in Figure 7.15. Resizing the window does not affect their sizes.

If the default values are used, then the **GridBagLayout** will group all of the components in the center, left to right, and not resize them at all. Any extra space in the main window just becomes a border around the cluster. It's almost as useless as the **FlowLayout**!

b) Where are the buttons, and what happens when you resize the window?

Answer: The buttons now span the width of the window as shown in Figure 7.16. Button 2 remains about three times wider than Button 1 even when the window is resized.

LAB
7.4

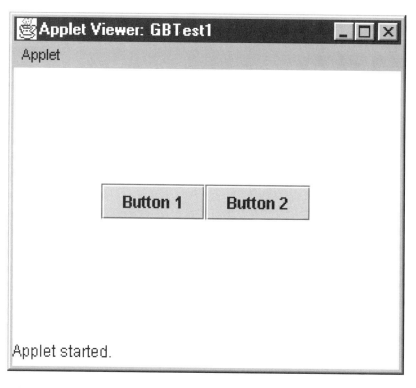

Figure 7.15 ■ Two buttons using the default GridBagConstraints values

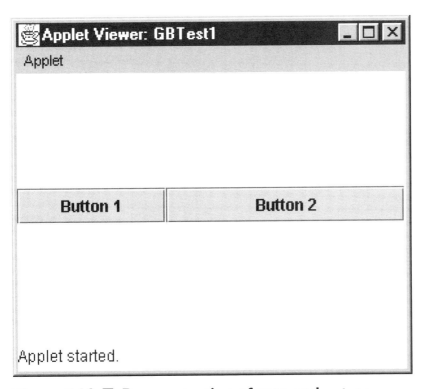

Figure 7.16 ■ **Demonstration of** `fill` **and** `weightx`

By setting the **weightx** values for the buttons to a 3:1 ratio, the widths of each button retains that same 3:1 ratio. We also set the value of **gbc.fill** to **GridBagConstraints.HORIZONTAL**. This causes the buttons to *fill* up all of the available *horizontal* space. The buttons do not fill any of the vertical space.

c) What effect did commenting out that line have?

Answer: The buttons no longer fill up the horizontal space, as shown in Figure 7.17.

The default value of **fill** is **GridBagConstraints.NONE**, which prevents the buttons from expanding in any direction. Because the **weightx** values are still set, the *cells* are still spaced proportionally, but the buttons are just not filling their cells.

If this is a little confusing, then just remember that **weightx** and **weighty** control the size of the grid *cell*, and **fill** controls whether the component fills the cell or not.

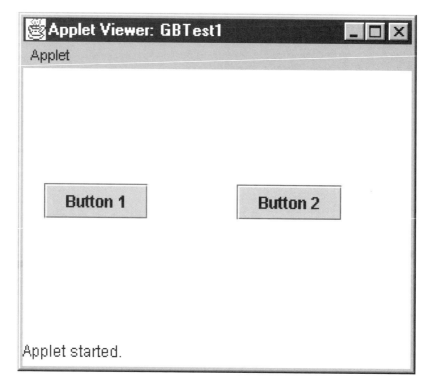

Figure 7.17 ■ **Same as Figure 7.16, but `fill` set to NONE (the default)**

d) Why is Button 1 now wider than Button 2?

*Answer: Button 1 is now in the same column as Button 3. Button 3 has a **weightx** equal to 10, so the whole column now has a **weightx** of 10. The new result is shown in Figure 7.18.*

There are two things to notice. The first is that the *weight* value of a column is equal to the highest **weightx** value in the entire column. The same is true for rows and **weighty** values with respect to vertical spacing.

The second thing to notice is that we created the second row by setting Button 2's **gridwidth** to **GridBagConstraints.REMAINDER**. Doing this triggered a new row. If you think about it, if that button uses the *remainder* of the row, then there can't be any more buttons, right? We did the same thing for Button 4, so it will also be the last component in its row. If we added another button (which we did in the next question) then it will start the third row.

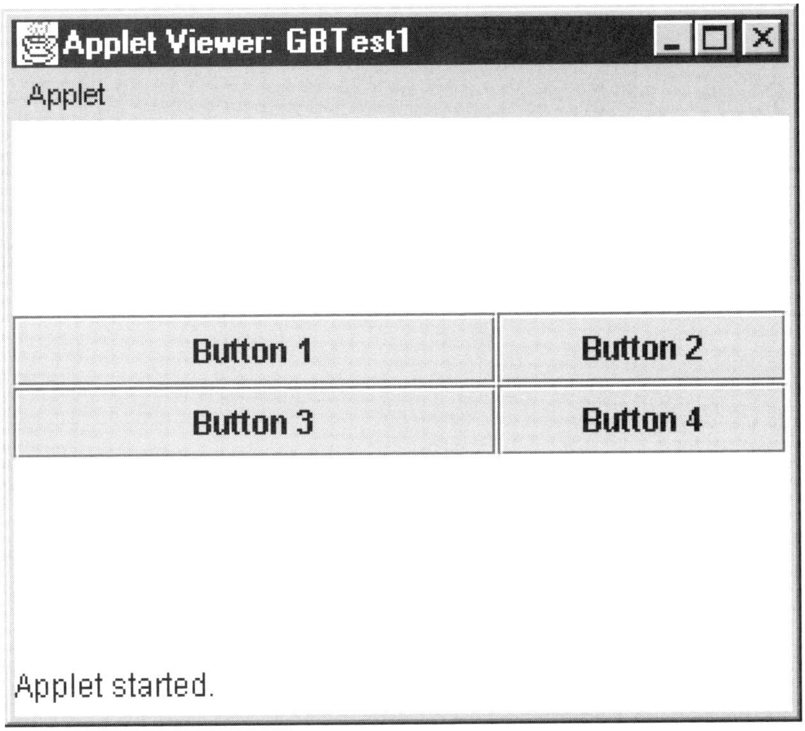

Figure 7.18 ■ The left column is wider because Button 3 has the largest `weightx`

e)   What happens with Button 5?

Answer: Button 5 spans two columns as show in Figure 7.19.

The **gridwidth** constraint sets the number of grid cells that a component will use. This is different from widening the cells like we've been doing up to this point. Note, however, that setting the **gridwidth** to 2 will not actually create two columns. There must be two columns created in some other manner.

As an "exercise left to the reader" (we've always wanted to say that), go back and comment out the "**fill**" line so that none of the components fill their cells. The results are pretty ugly, but they also show that **gridwidth** (and **gridheight**) need **fill** turned on in order to really work.

In case you got lost, the complete code up to this point follows.

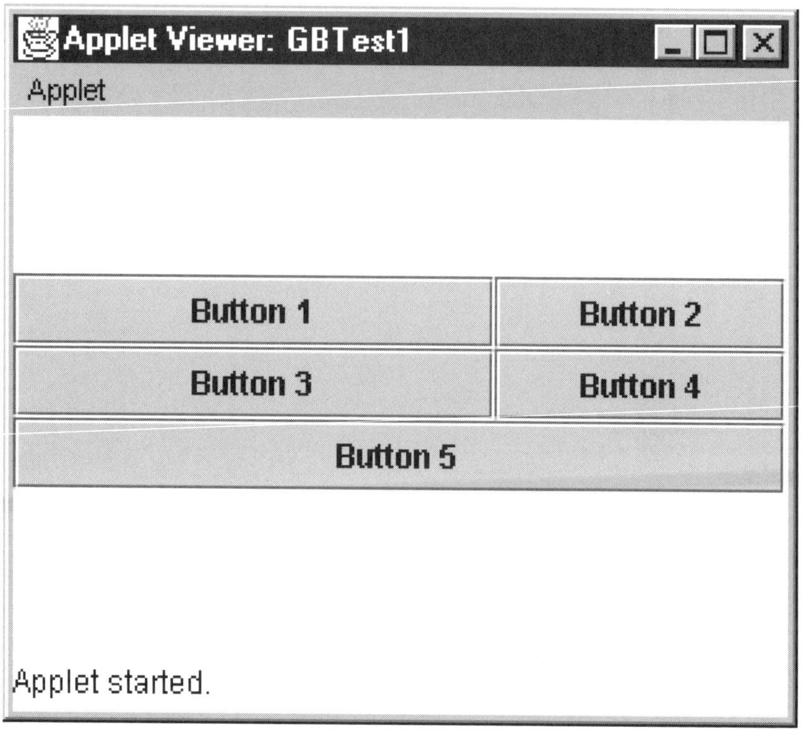

Figure 7.19 ■ Button 5 spans two grid cells

```
public void init()
{
    setLayout(new GridBagLayout());
    GridBagConstraints gbc = new GridBagConstraints();
    // Start
    gbc.fill = GridBagConstraints.HORIZONTAL;
    gbc.weightx = 1;
    add(new JButton("Button 1"), gbc);
    gbc.weightx = 3;
    gbc.gridwidth = GridBagConstraints.REMAINDER;
    add(new JButton("Button 2"), gbc);
    gbc.weightx = 10;
    gbc.gridwidth = 1;
    add(new JButton("Button 3"), gbc);
    gbc.weightx = 1;
    gbc.gridwidth = GridBagConstraints.REMAINDER;
    add(new JButton("Button 4"), gbc);
    gbc.gridwidth = 2;
    gbc.weightx = 100;
```

```
        add(new JButton("Button 5"), gbc);
        setSize(300, 200);
    }
```

f) Write code to produce the layout in Figure 7.13.

Answer: The following code produced Figure 7.13.

```
public void init()
{
    setLayout(new GridBagLayout());
    GridBagConstraints gbc = new GridBagConstraints();
    gbc.fill = GridBagConstraints.BOTH;
    gbc.weightx = 1;
    add(new JButton("Button 1"), gbc);
    gbc.gridwidth = GridBagConstraints.REMAINDER;
    add(new JButton("Button 2"), gbc);
    gbc.gridwidth = 1;
    gbc.gridheight = 2;
    add(new JButton("Button 3"), gbc);
    gbc.gridheight = 1;
    add(new JButton("Button 4"), gbc);
    gbc.gridwidth = GridBagConstraints.REMAINDER;
    add(new JButton("Button 5"), gbc);
    gbc.gridwidth = 1;
    add(new JButton("Button 6"), gbc);
    add(new JButton("Button 7"), gbc);
    setSize(300, 200);
}
```

Hopefully this wasn't too difficult. The one caveat is that you needed to set the **fill** value to **GridBagConstraints.BOTH** so that Button 3 would stretch vertically. You also needed to reset the **gridheight** back to 1 after adding Button 3, otherwise it seems to cancel out some how.

g) Write code to produce the layout in Figure 7.14. Hint: *Ahoy, Matey!*

Answer: The following code produced Figure 7.14.

```
public void init() {
    setLayout(new GridBagLayout());
    GridBagConstraints gbc = new GridBagConstraints();
    gbc.weightx = 1;
    gbc.weighty = 1;
    gbc.anchor = GridBagConstraints.NORTHWEST;
    add(new JButton("Button 1"), gbc);
```

```
gbc.anchor = GridBagConstraints.NORTH;
add(new JButton("Button 2"), gbc);
gbc.anchor = GridBagConstraints.NORTHEAST;
gbc.gridwidth = GridBagConstraints.REMAINDER;
add(new JButton("Button 3"), gbc);
gbc.gridwidth = 1;
gbc.anchor = GridBagConstraints.WEST;
add(new JButton("Button 4"), gbc);
gbc.anchor = GridBagConstraints.CENTER;
add(new JButton("Button 5"), gbc);
gbc.gridwidth = GridBagConstraints.REMAINDER;
gbc.anchor = GridBagConstraints.EAST;
add(new JButton("Button 6"), gbc);
gbc.anchor = GridBagConstraints.SOUTHWEST;
gbc.gridwidth = 1;
add(new JButton("Button 7"), gbc);
gbc.anchor = GridBagConstraints.SOUTH;
add(new JButton("Button 8"), gbc);
gbc.anchor = GridBagConstraints.SOUTHEAST;
add(new JButton("Button 9"), gbc);
setSize(300, 200);
}
```

The trick here was to use the **anchor** property (Ahoy!) to get each button to bind to one of the nine anchor points. The second *trick* was to keep the **fill** value at **NONE** (that is, don't set it). The default anchor point is the *Center*, as we have seen. When the cell is larger than the component you can choose where in the cell the component is placed. For this example, we anchored each component to one of the nine anchor points.

LAB 7.4 SELF-REVIEW QUESTIONS

In order to test your progress, you should be able to answer the following questions.

1)   The **GridBagLayout** uses which other class?
   a) _____ **GridBagProperties**
   b) _____ **GridBagConstraints**
   c) _____ **GridBagAttributes**
   d) _____ **GridBagParameters**
   e) _____ **WindBagPoliticians**

2) You must use a new **GridBagConstraints** for each component?
   a) _____ **True**
   b) _____ **False**

3) Which attribute can signal the end of a row?
   a) _____ **gridwidth**
   b) _____ **gridy**
   c) _____ **weightx**
   d) _____ **fill**
   e) _____ **anchor**

4) Which attribute sets the horizontal spacing?
   a) _____ **gridwidth**
   b) _____ **gridy**
   c) _____ **weightx**
   d) _____ **fill**
   e) _____ **anchor**

5) Which attribute causes a component to be resized?
   a) _____ **gridwidth**
   b) _____ **gridy**
   c) _____ **weightx**
   d) _____ **fill**
   e) _____ **anchor**

6) Which attribute controls a component's position with in a cell?
   a) _____ **gridwidth**
   b) _____ **gridy**
   c) _____ **weightx**
   d) _____ **fill**
   e) _____ **anchor**

7) Which attribute controls a component's position with in the grid?
   a) _____ **gridwidth**
   b) _____ **gridy**
   c) _____ **weightx**
   d) _____ **fill**
   e) _____ **anchor**

Quiz answers appear in Appendix A, Section 7.4.

C H A P T E R   7

TEST YOUR THINKING

In creating Figure 7.12, we reused the same set of **GridBagConstraints** for each button. We could just as easily have created a new **GridBagConstraints** object for each button, and then set each component's values separately.

1) What are the pros and cons of these two approaches?

2) Create a layout that draws a numeric keypad like the one found on a standard computer keyboard.

3) Simulate a **BorderLayout** using a **GridLayout**.

C H A P T E R   8

EVENTS

CHAPTER OBJECTIVES

In this chapter, you will learn about:

Now that you have learned how to construct graphical user interfaces, you are probably wondering how you get them to actually *do* something. From the previous chapters, you learned how to construct a GUI, but we purposefully did not cover user interaction; so aside from a few examples, you have been creating noninteractive graphical interfaces—buttons can be pushed, for example, but they do not do anything in response.

The key to being interactive is determining what the user is doing within your GUI, and then acting appropriately. Java uses *events* to signal that something has happened within your program; the programmer must write code to listen for these events and then take action as appropriate—this is known as *event handling*.

L A B   8 . 1

BASIC EVENT
HANDLING

LAB OBJECTIVES

After this lab, you will be able to:

- Listen for and Handle Events

Applications with a GUI put the user in charge. Unlike command-line programs, which typically force a user through a very strict set of procedures, GUIs allow the user to "call the shots" and navigate the application. For this reason, applications are considered *event-driven*; this means once the application has created its GUI, it simply waits around to be notified when a user moves or clicks the mouse, pushes a button or slides a scrollbar. User input drives the application from one task to the next, rather than having the application drive the user through certain predefined tasks.

Take, for example, that wonderful word-processing program you use on a fairly regular basis. The program is designed to create documents; although it puts many tools at your disposal, it does not know in advance which buttons you will press, text you will input, or menu items you will select. The application must sit around and wait for these things to happen, and then know what to do—this is all handled by the Java *event-delegation* model.

Every GUI component is able to report state changes, and allow other objects to register interest in these state-changes. Being a paragon of object-oriented design, Java state changes are encapsulated within an *event* object, which is a subclass of the **java.util.EventObject** class. Different subclasses of **EventObject** exist to represent different types of events and provide specific information regarding the event. These event subclasses exist within the `java.awt.event` and `javax.swing.event` packages.

When a state change occurs, such as when a button is pressed, the button will create a specific type of event object and *fire* the event to all interested *listener* classes. So, to be notified when a button is pressed, you need only inform the button that you are interested in its actions and provide a suitable *event handler* to process the incoming events.

The process of event handling can be broken down into a few simple steps:

- Determine which type of event will be fired by the component
- Provide a handler method for the specific event type
- Register with the component as a listener for that event type

■ FOR EXAMPLE:

Let's investigate each of these steps a bit further as we construct a GUI with a working button:

```
import javax.swing.*;
import java.awt.*;

public class BasicEventApplet extends JApplet
{
    JButton button = new JButton("I'm active!");
    JPanel contentPanel = (JPanel)this.getContentPane();
    public void init()
    {
        contentPanel.setLayout(new FlowLayout());
        contentPanel.add(button);
    }
}
```

So far, this is nothing new. Now let's hook up the button to actually do something.

DETERMINING THE EVENT TYPE

Probably the trickiest part of event handling is determining of what event types are fired by a particular component, and which specific events you are interested in processing. Keep in mind that almost every action the user takes, from moving the mouse inside a component to resizing a frame, causes events to be fired. Clearly, you will not be interested in handling all these events—many of these events are handled internally, and unless you have very specific requirements they can be safely ignored.

Unfortunately, determining which event objects are fired by a particular component is not an easy task. To speed up the process, Table 8.1 lists common GUI components and the types of events they fire, which will be of most use to the beginning programmer. This is by no means an exhaustive list of either components or events. Understanding events and the event-handling mechanism within Java is often difficult for beginning programmers, and this is meant solely to help you on your way.

Keep in mind that any events generated by a class are also generated by all subclasses as well—this means that **every** Swing component fires

**Table 8.1 ■ Overview of Useful Events Generated
by Common Components**

Component	Event Type	Event Description
JButton	ActionEvent	Generated when button is clicked
JCheckBox	ActionEvent	Generated when checkbox is clicked—either selected or deselected
JComponent	MouseEvent	Generated when mouse enters or exits a component, when the mouse button is clicked or released, and when the mouse is dragged (moved with button down)
	ComponentEvent	Generated when a component is resized, hidden or shown.
JTextField	ActionEvent	Generated when the user is finished entering text (when the enter key is pressed)
JToggleButton	ActionEvent	Generated when a toggle button (JCheckBox, JRadioButton, etc.) is selected
Window	WindowEvent	Generated when a window is opened, closed, about to be closed, activated, deactivated, iconified or deiconified.

MouseEvents and ComponentEvents, and **every JWindow, JDialog,** and **JFrame** generates WindowEvents.

We can tell from Table 8.1 that the button will fire an **ActionEvent** object when it is pressed. So, let's continue and see how we can handle the **ActionEvent**.

PROVIDE A HANDLER METHOD
FOR THE SPECIFIC EVENT TYPE

For every event type there exists a corresponding *listener* interface. Any object that wishes to be a listener for a particular event must first implement the interface for that event type. These interfaces contain *handler* methods that will be called when an event of a certain type is fired. The reason for this is clear—it serves as a pact between the listener and the event source that the listener will know how to handle the incoming events. If you want to play ball, you'd better know the rules.

Luckily, determining the interface to implement is not as much of a shot in the dark as determining the types of events that are fired by a component. For every event type, there is a corresponding interface named **XXXListener**, where **XXX** is the type of event this interface handles. These interfaces are located within the **java.awt.event** and **javax.swing.event** packages. In our example, we will want our class to implement the **ActionListener** interface because we are interested in ActionEvents.

Let's implement the **ActionListener** interface within our example applet. This interface is quite simple, as it only contains the following method that must be implemented:

```
public void actionPerformed(ActionEvent e)
```

Here's our example applet with a very basic handler implementation. All additions are in bold type.

```
import javax.swing.*;
import java.awt.*;
import java.awt.event.*;    // ActionListener & ActionEvent
public class BasicEventApplet extends JApplet
                        implements ActionListener
{
    JButton button = new JButton("I'm active!");
    JPanel contentPanel = (JPanel)this.getContentPane();
```

```
public void init()
{
    // arrange components
    contentPanel.setLayout(new FlowLayout());
    contentPanel.add(button);


}
// this satisfies the ActionListener interface
public void actionPerformed(ActionEvent e)
{
    // just beep, for now
    Toolkit.getDefaultToolkit().beep();
}
}
```

As you can see, there is not much to setting up a handler for an event type. Try running this applet and you will notice that it still does not work properly—there is just one step left to perform.

REGISTER WITH THE COMPONENT AS A LISTENER FOR THAT EVENT TYPE

To this point, our class contains a button that is generating ActionEvents when pressed, and we have set up a handler to process the ActionEvents fired by the button. We have not yet, however, told the button that we are interested in its ActionEvents.

All components that generate events provide methods that allow other objects to register as listeners for those events. The registration methods are named **addXXXListener**, where **XXX** is the type of event for which a listener is registered and the single argument to the method is a listener interface that corresponds to the type of event. The registration method for objects that fire ActionEvents is

```
public void addActionListener(ActionListener l)
```

To receive ActionEvents from the JButton in our applet, we need only call this method as follows:

```
button.addActionListener(this);
```

Recall that the keyword **this** refers to the current class, which is just fine because our class has already implemented the **ActionListener** interface. Here is the complete class, with the latest changes in bold type:

```
import javax.swing.*;
import java.awt.*;
import java.awt.event.*;
public class BasicEventApplet extends JApplet
                              implements ActionListener
{
    JButton button = new JButton("I'm active!");
    JPanel contentPanel = (JPanel)this.getContentPane();
    public void init()
    {
        // register this class as an
        // ActionEvent listener
        button.addActionListener(this);
        // arrange components
        contentPanel.setLayout(new FlowLayout());
        contentPanel.add(button);

    }
    // this satisfies the ActionListener interface
    public void actionPerformed(ActionEvent e)
    {
        // just beep, for now
        Toolkit.getDefaultToolkit().beep();
    }
}
```

Event handling will never be called an *easy* process, but once you have
done this a few times for yourself it will become second nature.

LAB 8.1 EXERCISES

8.1.1 LISTEN FOR AND HANDLE EVENTS

Use the following applet to answer questions a through c.

```
import javax.swing.*;
import java.awt.event.*;

public class StatusApplet    extends JApplet
                             implements ActionListener
{
    JButton button = new JButton("Set Status");
    JTextField tfield  = new JTextField(20);
```

```
JPanel panel = new JPanel();

public void init()
{
    panel.add(tfield);
    panel.add(button);
    this.getContentPane().add(panel);
}

// satisifies implementation of ActionListener
public void actionPerformed(ActionEvent evt)
{
    this.showStatus(tfield.getText().trim());
}
}
```

The Whole Truth

Unfortunately, determining which events are fired by a particular component is a nontrivial exercise. As an introductory text, it would be pointless to list all the events fired by each component because most of these events are handled internally and would not concern any but the most advanced Java programmers.

Now that you have a cursory understanding of the event handling process, however, you can begin to investigate events yourself. To determine which events are fired by a particular class, consult the Java API documentation for that class and search it and its parent classes for **addXXXListener** methods, where **XXX** represents an event type. The API documentation displays not only the methods belonging to a class, but also all methods inherited from parent classes, so this should be a fairly painless activity. The single argument to each **addXXXListener** method is an appropriate listener interface, and each listener interface defines handler methods for the particular event type. Each of these handler methods takes a single parameter—an event object. Once you have gained more experience with events, you will find that the **addXXXListener** method name is enough to tip you off to the underlying event that is fired. Happy hunting!

a) Run the applet. Why does the status line of the applet not get set appropriately when the button is pressed?

_____

_____

b) Modify **StatusApplet** so that the applet status is updated whenever either the button is pressed or the *enter* key is pressed when the text field has focus. What changes were necessary?

_____

_____

c) Further modify **StatusApplet** so that a second button exists that clears the status bar. What changes were necessary?

_____

_____

LAB 8.1 EXERCISE ANSWERS

8.1.1 ANSWERS

a) Run the applet. Why does the status line of the applet not get set appropriately when the button is pressed?

Answer: Three steps to event handling were introduced in this lab. One of these steps was not performed within the applet. Let's examine the steps once again and see what was left-out.

Let's review the three steps for event handling:

- Determine which type of event will be fired by the component

As we have already demonstrated within the lab, and as shown in Table 8.1, the **JButton** will fire an **ActionEvent** when it is pressed. So, the listener class must implement the **ActionListener** interface. The applet implements **ActionListener**, so this part is taken care of.

- Provide a handler method for the specific event type

Because the applet implements the **ActionListener** interface, it must contain an **actionPerformed** method or it will not compile—this is part of the "pact" between the event source and the event listener, which is enforced by the compiler. Because the class compiled, and because you can easily see the **actionPerformed** method within the class, this is not the problem either.

  • Register with the component as a listener for that event type

Where within the applet is the listener registered with the button? I think we have solved the great mystery—the listener class (in this case, the applet itself) never actually registered itself as a listener for the button's ActionEvents. Your remedy to this situation should have been to register the applet class as an ActionEvent listener with the button. Within the **init** method of the applet, you should have added the following line of code:

```
button.addActionListener(this);
```

Because the applet is also the listener, the keyword **this** is used.

b)   Modify **StatusApplet** so that the applet status is updated whenever either the button is pressed or the *enter* key is pressed when the text field has focus. What changes were necessary?

Answer: In addition to events from the button, the applet must also listen for events from the text field. You should have followed the three-step process for event handling to make sure proper events from the text field were received in addition to the events from the button.

Consulting Table 8.1, we can determine that the **JTextField** class will fire an **ActionEvent** when input has ended (when the *enter* key is pressed). Because the applet already implements the **ActionListener** interface, it is already suited to listen for **ActionEvents** fired by the text field. Because we already have defined an **actionPerformed** method, we already have an appropriate event handler; the same handler method will be called whenever the applet receives an **ActionEvent** from any class with which it has registered itself as a listener. Neither a new handler method nor a different class need be created to handle events from different objects.

Just as any number of identical event types can be processed by a handler method for that type, an event source can fire the same event to any number of registered listeners. This means that several listener ob-

jects can be notified when a certain event occurs. Though all listener objects are guaranteed to receive the fired event, the order in which they receive the event is undefined—meaning that the event could be dispatched in any order to the listeners.

Make judicious use of multiple listeners for the same event. Though it may be useful under certain circumstances, you cannot rely upon the order in which the listeners are notified. If you find yourself relying upon a certain order of notification, it would be better to structure your program so that one single handler receives the notification and then delegates the event to other interested objects itself.

Now that we have determined that all the appropriate event handling plumbing is in place, we simply need to register an **ActionListener** with the text field object. As with the button, we can register the applet to receive ActionEvents with the following line of code placed within the **init** method of the applet:

```
tfield.addActionListener(this);
```

The existing handler will be called whenever an **ActionEvent** is fired by either the button or the text field. Since the action performed should not differ between the two, our solution is complete.

c) Further modify StatusApplet so that a second button exists that clears the status bar. What changes were necessary?

Answer: Because one handler is perfectly capable of fielding events from multiple sources, we can use the same handler method already present in the applet to handle events from this new button as well. However, we need to discern not only that a button press occurred, but from which button the event was fired.

Listening for an ActionEvent is trivial—we are already listening for such events from both the status button and (as of our modifications in the previous answer) the text field. Now we must be able to determine the source of an event.

If you recall the introduction to this Lab, it was mentioned that all events were encapsulated within a subclass of **java.util.EventObject**. Taking a look within the Java API documentation, it is shown that the **EventObject** contains the following method to reveal the source of the event:

```
public Object getSource()
```

Because all Java events are subclasses of **EventObject**, every event carries around with it a reference to the class which fired the event. When a handler receives an event, it can call this method of the event and act accordingly. Assuming you added the new button correctly (and if you didn't, perhaps you should consider a different line of work), the following modified handler method will determine if the event was fired from the clear button (named **clearButton**). If so, it will clear the status area and exit instead of setting the status message.

```
public void actionPerformed(ActionEvent evt)
{
    if(evt.getSource().equals(clearButton))
    {
        // this event was from the clear button
        this.showStatus("");
        return;
    }
    // if not from the clear button, it's business as usual
     this.showStatus(tfield.getText().trim());
}
```

Would the above solution work if the **ActionEvent** handler existed in a different class than the GUI components? Probably not, unless you declare your GUI components to be public, and that is highly discouraged.

So, what can be done if the handler exists within a class that does not have access to the GUI components? Such could easily be the case if you decided to offload event handling to a separate class, or to an inner class.

As luck would have it, there is an answer. Components that fire Action-Events provide the following method to make an event unique:

```
public void setActionCommand(String command)
```

This command can be used to set a value that is sent along with the **ActionEvent** object. The event handler can then query for this value using the **ActionEvent** method

```
public String getActionCommand()
```

A more powerful use of this feature is to have a component modify its action command depending upon its state. In this manner, a single component can fire events to the same listener but have the listener take different actions depending upon the current action command. In our example, the **clearButton** action command can be set to clear the status area if text exists, or clear the text field if the status field is already empty. Try coding this yourself.

Here is the final rendition of **StatusApplet** using variable action commands. The various action commands are declared **final**, which is simply good programming practice.

```
import javax.swing.*;
import java.awt.event.*;

public class StatusApplet extends JApplet
    implements ActionListener
{
    final String CLEAR_STATUS = "clear_status";
    final String CLEAR_FIELD = "clear_field";

    JButton button = new JButton("Set Status");
    JButton clearButton = new JButton("Clear");
    JTextField tfield  = new JTextField(20);
    JPanel panel = new JPanel();

    public void init()
    {
        button.addActionListener(this);
        clearButton.addActionListener(this);
        clearButton.setActionCommand(CLEAR_STATUS);
        tfield.addActionListener(this);
        panel.add(tfield);
        panel.add(button);
        panel.add(clearButton);
        this.getContentPane().add(panel);
    }

    // satisifies implementation of ActionListener
    public void actionPerformed(ActionEvent evt)
    {
        String command = evt.getActionCommand();
        if(command.equals(CLEAR_STATUS))
        {
            this.showStatus("");
            clearButton.setActionCommand(CLEAR_FIELD);
            return;
        }
        else if(command.equals(CLEAR_FIELD))
```

```
        {
            tfield.setText("");
            return;
        }
        this.showStatus(tfield.getText().trim());
        clearButton.setActionCommand(CLEAR_STATUS);
    }
}
```

LAB 8.1 REVIEW QUESTIONS

In order to test your progress, you should be able to answer the following questions.

1) What is the base class from which all state event objects are derived?
    a) _____ java.awt.AWTEvent
    b) _____ javax.swing.event.AncestorEvent
    c) _____ java.awt.ContainerEvent
    d) _____ java.util.EventObject

2) If no listener is specified for a component's events, what happens?
    a) _____ The event is handled by a default event handler method
    b) _____ The event is ignored
    c) _____ The Java compiler will generate a fatal error
    d) _____ The program will exit immediately

3) If multiple listeners are registered for an event, in what order are the listeners notified of the event?
    a) _____ Listeners are notified in the order in which they registered
    b) _____ Listeners are notified in reverse registration order
    c) _____ Listeners are notified in an undetermined order
    d) _____ Only the last listener to register will receive notification

4) Objects can register themselves as listeners for their own events.
    a) _____ True
    b) _____ False

5) Any object may register as a listener for another object's events.
    a) _____ True
    b) _____ False

Quiz answers appear in Appendix A, Section 8.1.

LAB 8.2

DIFFERENT APPROACHES TO EVENT HANDLING

LAB OBJECTIVES

After this Lab, you will be able to:

- Handle Events Using Adapters and Inner Classes

Now that you have gotten your hands dirty with basic event handling, it is worthwhile to mention a few "shortcut" processes that allow you to handle events in a more concise manner. Oftentimes you may be interested in an event that is fired under a number of different conditions. Because it is fired under several different conditions, several handler methods are defined within the listener interface; although you are interested in only one of those conditions, the listener interface forces you to implement every defined handler method. Clearly, there must be a better way to handle such an event.

■ FOR EXAMPLE:

A little-known fact to neophyte Java GUI developers is that an application does not automatically exit when the top-level frame is closed from the window manager system menu (often, this is simply an "X" button in the upper right-hand corner of the window). Until explicitly told to exit, the program continues to run without a visible top-level frame. The following code illustrates this behavior; run this program from the command line and then close the window from the system menu. You'll notice that the program continues to spew messages to the command line even after the window is closed—the program is still running.

```
import javax.swing.*;
public class MarathonApp
{
    JLabel label = new JLabel(
        "It just keeps going, and going...");
    JFrame frame = new JFrame("MarathonApp Example");

    public MarathonApp ()
    {
        frame.getContentPane().add(label);
        frame.setSize(300,100);
        frame.setVisible(true);

        // ignore the following code-
        // it simply reminds the user we are running
        while(true)
        {
            try
            {
                Thread.sleep(1000);
                System.out.println("I'm still here!");
            }
            catch(InterruptedException ex)
            {
                // ignore
            }
        }
    }
    public static void main(String args[])
    {
        MarathonApp app = new MarathonApp();
    }
}
```

To exit cleanly when the frame is closed, you must register a listener with the **frame** object, and exit when you receive a **WindowClosing** event. Refer to Table 8.1, where this event was introduced. Unfortunately, the WindowListener interface contains seven handler methods that must be implemented. Even though we are only interested in the **windowClosing** handler, we must spend the time implementing six other methods simply so that we can ignore the events!

Implementing all seven handler methods within the listener interface is quite a waste. Even after removing our "reminder" code, the size of the class has grown and your fingers probably are beginning to resent performing such a fruitless task.

The modified class is as follows, with the "reminder" code removed and additional code shown in bold type:

```
import javax.swing.*;
import java.awt.event.*;

public class MarathonApp implements WindowListener
{
    JLabel label = new JLabel(
        "It just keeps going, and going...");
    JFrame frame = new JFrame("MarathonApp Example");

    public MarathonApp ()
    {
        frame.addWindowListener(this);
        frame.getContentPane().add(label);
        frame.setSize(300,100);
        frame.setVisible(true);
    }
    public static void main(String args[])
    {
        MarathonApp app = new MarathonApp();
    }
    // all this, just to satisfy the interface definition
    public void windowActivated(WindowEvent e)
    {
        // ignore window activated events
    }
    public void windowDeactivated(WindowEvent e)
    {
        // ignore window deactivated events
    }
    public void windowIconified(WindowEvent e)
    {
        // ignore window iconified events
    }
    public void windowDeiconified(WindowEvent e)
    {
        // ignore window deiconified events
    }
    public void windowOpened(WindowEvent e)
```

```
    {
        // ignore window opened event
    }
    public void windowClosed(WindowEvent e)
    {
        // ignore window closed event
    }
    public void windowClosing(WindowEvent e)
    {
        // aha- this I do care about!
        System.exit(0);
    }
}
```

Certainly this approach works, but it is time-consuming and wasteful. To reduce swearing amongst Java programmers (and believe me, it is becoming an increasing activity these days . . .) *event adapter* classes were created.

Event adapter classes are abstract classes that define empty methods for all the handler methods specified within a particular listener interface. Because the classes are abstract, you cannot instantiate them directly; instead, they must be subclassed. By creating a subclass of the adapter class, you can selectively override handler methods you require and simply ignore all the others.

Not every listener interface has a corresponding adapter class, though; for interfaces with only one or two methods specified, it is of very little benefit. For our above scenario, however, it is very beneficial. Similar to the listener interfaces, all the adapter classes live within the **java.awt.event** and **javax.swing.event** packages, and they are named **XXXAdapter**, where **XXX** is the event type for which they implement an interface.

One lingering issue remains. Because adapters are classes and not interfaces, any class you have defined which already extends another class cannot also extend an adapter class—this is not allowed within the Java language specification, and the compiler will complain bitterly. For example, if the class which creates your GUI is already a subclass of **JFrame**, you cannot also subclass an event adapter. When using interfaces, this is never a problem—a class can implement as many interfaces as it requires. So, what are our options for using adapter classes?

Three basic methods will be introduced:

- Create a separate class that extends the adapter class
- Create an inner-class that extends the adapter class
- Create an anonymous inner-class that extends the adapter class

Though the last two concepts have not been formally introduced, we will provide a very brief overview of their usage so that you can explore them at your own pace.

CREATING A SEPARATE CLASS

This method is quite basic—instead of handling the event within the class that created the GUI, delegate event handling to a specialized class. Because this is a specialized class for event handling, it can extend the appropriate adapter class and it leaves your application free to extend any other class as need be.

CREATE AN INNER-CLASS

An *inner-class* is a class that is defined within another class—a nested class definition. Similar to a member variable, an inner class is only visible within its scope, which is the block of code in which it is defined. As well, inner classes can only reference variables that exist within their scope and are declared **final**. Basically, this means that inner classes are very limited in how they are able to interact with their enclosing class. Inner classes are an advanced Java topic, so they will not be covered in detail; however, the following example should provide you with ample knowledge to continue your inner-class education.

Here is a modified version of **MarathonApp** that defines a subclass of **WindowAdapter** as an inner class. Modifications from the original application are shown in bold type:

```
import javax.swing.*;
import java.awt.event.*;

public class MarathonApp
{
    JLabel label = new JLabel(
        "It just keeps going, and going...");
    JFrame frame = new JFrame("MarathonApp Example");
    MyWindowAdapter mwa = new MyWindowAdapter();

    public MarathonApp ()
    {
        frame.addWindowListener(mwa);
        frame.getContentPane().add(label);
        frame.setSize(300,100);
        frame.setVisible(true);
    }
```

```
public static void main(String args[])
{
    MarathonApp app = new MarathonApp();
}


// inner-class which handles our window events
class MyWindowAdapter extends WindowAdapter
{
    public void windowClosing(WindowEvent e)
    {
        System.exit(0);
    }
}
}
```

The inner-class definition saves space and reduces the amount of programming that needs to be done in order to satisfy the listener interface. Inner-classes can be of great value to the Java programmer, and not simply for event handling. As you continue to develop your Java programming skills, you are encouraged to learn more about inner-classes and experiment with them. Consider this a very brief introduction that is intended only to introduce the concept.

CREATE AN ANONYMOUS INNER-CLASS THAT EXTENDS THE ADAPTER CLASS

Anonymous inner-classes take the concept of inner-classes one step further, and they are truly an advanced Java concept. If they were not so powerful for event handling, they most certainly would not be introduced outside of an advanced Java textbook.

Anonymous inner-classes are inner-classes created for one-time use within an application. A standard inner-class is defined in one statement and instantiated in another. Anonymous inner-classes have a syntax that allows both definition and instantiation to occur within the same statement. As you may have guessed, anonymous inner-classes are created without a name, so they cannot be referred to following creation and can only be instantiated once.

Aside from these differences, anonymous inner-classes perform similarly to inner-classes, and their use is largely attributed to preference or style considerations. Outside of event handling, they have little use. For our **MarathonApp** example, they solve the problem of creating a listener class in a quick manner.

Following is an implementation of the **MarathonApp** program, using an anonymous inner-class to handle the window events. Modifications from the original application are shown in bold type:

```
import javax.swing.*;
import java.awt.event.*;

public class MarathonApp
{
    JLabel label = new JLabel(
        "It just keeps going, and going...");
    JFrame frame = new JFrame("MarathonApp Example");

    public MarathonApp ()
    {
        frame.getContentPane().add(label);
        frame.setSize(300,100);
        frame.setVisible(true);
        frame.addWindowListener(
            new WindowAdapter()
            {
                public void windowClosing(WindowEvent e)
                {
                    System.exit(0);
                }
            }
        );
    }

    public static void main(String args[])
    {
        MarathonApp app = new MarathonApp();
    }
}
```

Don't be alarmed if the syntax of the anonymous inner-class scares you—it scares us too! Anonymous inner-classes are a very powerful mechanism to handle events, and mark the beginnings of your foray into the great world of advanced Java programming skills.

LAB 8.2 EXERCISES

8.2.1 HANDLE EVENTS USING ADAPTERS AND INNER CLASSES

Use the following applet to answer questions a through c.

```
import javax.swing.*;
import java.awt.*;

public class FocusApplet extends JApplet
{
    JPanel contentPanel = (JPanel)this.getContentPane();
    JPanel touchPanel = new JPanel();
    JLabel touchLabel = new JLabel("Active Region");

    public void init()
    {
        touchLabel.setHorizontalAlignment(
            SwingConstants.CENTER);
        touchPanel.setBackground(Color.white);
        touchPanel.add(touchLabel);
        contentPanel.setLayout(new GridLayout(2,0));
        contentPanel.add(touchPanel);
    }
}
```

a) Modify the applet so that the status area is updated every time the mouse enters or leaves the active region. Accomplish this using an inner-class that extends the appropriate adapter class.

_____

_____

b) Further modify the applet so that the *x* and *y* coordinates of the mouse pointer are displayed in the status area whenever the mouse is within the active region.

_____

_____

LAB 8.2 EXERCISE ANSWERS

8.2.1 ANSWERS

a) Modify the applet so that the status area is updated every time the mouse enters or leaves the active region. Accomplish this using an inner class that extends the appropriate adapter class.

*Answer: This question is intended to test both your understanding of the previous and the current lab. First you must determine which event is fired by the **JPanel** class, and then you must implement a handler which takes appropriate action.*

According to Table 8.1, you should be interested in registering a listener for MouseEvents. Because **JPanel** is a subclass of **JComponent,** it will fire a **MouseEvent** whenever the mouse enters, exits, is clicked, or is dragged within the panel.

Just to complicate matters, there are two mouse listener interfaces from which to choose—**MouseListener** and **MouseMotionListener**. By consulting the Java API documentation, it should be clear that **MouseListener** is the interface that handles events fired whenever a mouse enters or exits a component.

Because you were asked to use a subclass to handle the mouse events, and because you are only interested in two of the five methods defined within the **MouseListener** interface, the subclass should extend the **MouseAdapter** abstract class. If you did not subclass the adaper, too bad—more work for you!

Following is one solution to the problem. Your solution may not appear identical to that which is shown here. It is only important that your solution causes the desired outcome.

```
import javax.swing.*;
import java.awt.*;
import java.awt.event.*;

public class FocusApplet extends JApplet
{
    JPanel contentPanel = (JPanel)this.getContentPane();
    JPanel touchPanel = new JPanel();
    JLabel touchLabel = new JLabel("Active Region");
    MyMouseListener mml = new MyMouseListener();
```

```
public void init()
{
    touchLabel.setHorizontalAlignment(
        SwingConstants.CENTER);
    touchPanel.setBackground(Color.white);
    touchPanel.add(touchLabel);
    touchPanel.addMouseListener(mml);
    contentPanel.setLayout(new GridLayout(2,0));
    contentPanel.add(touchPanel);
}

class MyMouseListener extends MouseAdapter
{
    public void mouseEntered(MouseEvent e)
    {
        showStatus("Mouse entered Active Region");
    }
    public void mouseExited(MouseEvent e)
    {
        showStatus("Mouse exited Active Region");
    }
}
}
```

If you encountered difficulties in creating an inner-class, take another look at the example provided within the lab. As mentioned earlier, event handling is not considered an easy task; do not become discouraged if it seems like a complex task—it is a complex task!

b) Further modify the applet so that the *x* and *y* coordinates of the mouse pointer are displayed in the status area whenever the mouse is within the active region.

*Answer: Wouldn't it be great if life was simple and all the mouse event handlers were present in the same listener interface? Well, life is complex and so is the Java event delegation model. The handlers necessary for retrieving the current mouse coordinates are located within the **MouseMotionListener** interface. Now you must register a second listener with the active region panel.*

The **MouseMotionListener** interface defines the methods **mouseMoved** and **mouseDragged**. To determine the current mouse coordinates, you must track all movements of the mouse within the active region, and then report the current mouse location. Luckily, the current mouse *x* and *y* coordinates are available directly from the **MouseEvent** object, via the **getX** and **getY** methods.

Following is one possible solution to the problem. Your solution may not appear identical to that which is shown here. It is only important that your solution causes the desired outcome.

```
import javax.swing.*;
import java.awt.*;
import java.awt.event.*;

public class FocusApplet extends JApplet
{
    JPanel contentPanel = (JPanel)this.getContentPane();
    JPanel touchPanel = new JPanel();
    JLabel touchLabel = new JLabel("Active Region");
    MyMouseListener mml = new MyMouseListener();
    MyMouseMotionListener mmml = new MyMouseMotionListener();

    public void init()
    {
        touchLabel.setHorizontalAlignment(
            SwingConstants.CENTER);
        touchPanel.setBackground(Color.white);
        touchPanel.add(touchLabel);
        touchPanel.addMouseListener(mml);
        touchPanel.addMouseMotionListener(mmml);
        contentPanel.setLayout(new GridLayout(2,0));
        contentPanel.add(touchPanel);
    }

    class MyMouseListener extends MouseAdapter
    {
        public void mouseEntered(MouseEvent e)
        {
            showStatus("Mouse entered the Active Region");
        }
        public void mouseExited(MouseEvent e)
        {
            showStatus("Mouse exited the Active Region");
        }
    }
    class MyMouseMotionListener extends MouseMotionAdapter
    {
        public void mouseMoved(MouseEvent e)
        {
            showStatus("Mouse moved to location: x: "
                + e.getX() + " y: " + e.getY());
```

**LAB
8.2**

```
        }
        public void mouseDragged(MouseEvent e)
        {
            showStatus("Mouse dragged to location: x: "
                + e.getX() + " y: " + e.getY());
        }
    }
}
```

If you have completed the labs successfully to this point, congratulations—you are well along the path to event-handling mastery!

LAB 8.2 SELF-REVIEW QUESTIONS

In order to test your progress, you should be able to answer the following questions.

1) Corresponding adapter classes exist for all listener interfaces
    a) _____ True
    b) _____ False

2) Adapter classes provided within the JDK can be directly instantiated
    a) _____ True
    b) _____ False

3) Adapter classes make life easy because
    a) _____ They provide reasonable default implementations for all the methods within a listener interface
    b) _____ They prevent you from having to implement listener interface methods in which your program has no interest
    c) _____ They are optimized within the JVM to handle events much faster than standard classes
    d) _____ Chicks dig 'em.

4) A single anonymous inner-class can be used to handle events fired from multiple objects
    a) _____ True
    b) _____ False

5) Events can be fired only by graphical objects
    a) _____ True
    b) _____ False

Quiz answers appear in Appendix A, Section 8.2.

CHAPTER 8

TEST YOUR THINKING

In this chapter, we investigated how an object may register itself as a listener for particular event types and then act accordingly when events are received. We discussed various event types, listener interfaces, and adapter classes, and you were provided the opportunity to answer questions and demonstrate your newly acquired knowledge of events by writing and modifying actual code.

What was not discussed in this chapter, however, was the ability to register a component as a listener for *all* events that it fires, without registering listeners for each individual event type and without providing different handler methods for each event.

1) Rewrite **FocusApplet** from lab 8.2 so that the active region **JPanel** uses this new method to register itself for all of its own events, and then print the event type to the applet status bar.

One hint to set you off in the right direction—the method is named enableEvents. *Find the method description within the Java API Documentation and determine how it is used. Though it is rarely useful to capture all fired events in such a manner, it is yet another tool in your programming toolkit that may come in handy when least expected.*

CHAPTER 9

MULTIMEDIA

 Clothes make the man. Naked people have little or no influence on society.

Mark Twain

CHAPTER OBJECTIVES

In this chapter, you will learn about:

- ✔ Images
- ✔ Colors
- ✔ Sounds
- ✔ Fonts

Once upon a time, computers only dealt with numbers. Then numbers were used to represent letters, so *text* was born. Now computers can deal with pictures, sounds, and movies. Watch out for digital smells coming soon! In today's world, appearance is very influential, and it is important for a program or Web site to look as good as it can. Even if a program is fully functional, some people might not even bother with it if the graphics look primitive or old-fashioned. Java is specially designed to make it easy for you to spice up your program with sounds and images. This way, you can focus your attention on the details of your program instead of loading pretty pictures. In this chapter, we will refer to sound and image files that are available on the Web site for this book. You will need to save these files to your computer in order to run the examples and do the labs.

L A B   9 . 1

IMAGES

LAB OBJECTIVES

After this lab, you will be able to:

- Load and Display Images

The quickest and easiest way to spice up your program is with images. You can use images almost anywhere to improve your interface: in the background, as a header, even in a button. There are literally millions of public domain images out there to use. If you're talented, you can create your own. We will show you how to load and display images into a Java applet. Java understands how to read all of the common image formats like GIF, JPEG, and Bitmap, and then stores them in the generic **Image** class.

The image files for this chapter can be found at the following URL:

    http://www.phptr.com/phptrinteractive

LOADING AN IMAGE

Before you can use an image, you must first load it from a source file. Java, being the Internet-savvy programming language that it is, references all files as a URL (*Uniform Resource Locator*—i.e., a Web address). This is the same way you would reference any Web page, so using a URL, you can load any picture on the Web into your applet.

To load an image into an applet, use the **getImage()** method, which is part of the **Applet** class. There are two forms of this method, as follows:

```
public Image getImage(String url)
public Image getImage(String url, String name)
```

In this book, we will only use the second form of **getImage()**, and we'll see why in the exercises. The second form of **getImage()** will generate a new URL by appending **name** to the value of **url**.

For simplicity in the examples, we will assume that all of the required files are in the same directory as the applet class.

■ *FOR EXAMPLE:*

If we want to use the image file named **dogs.jpg** in the applet names *Dogs*, we would place **dogs.jpg** in the same directory as **Dogs.class**. Then, we can issue the following statement in an applet to load the image:

```
Image image = getImage(getCodeBase(), "dogs.jpg");
```

The **codeCodeBase()** method is a method that returns the base URL for the applet itself. Basically, this is a quick and easy way of telling **getImage()** to look for **dogs.jpg** in the same place as the applet's class file.

There is one last thing that you should do, and that is to create an **ImageIcon** from the **Image** object. The following code is all you need to do:

```
ImageIcon icon = new ImageIcon(image);
```

Now that you have the **ImageIcon**, you can put it into labels and buttons and display them in your program.

The Truth About the **ImageIcon**

The **ImageIcon** class is also a helper class that does some book-keeping for you behind the scenes. If you are loading the image from your local disk, then the loading will be very fast. But if the file is coming across the Web and through a slow network connection, then it may take some time. The **ImageIcon** will "watch" the download of the file and make sure your program doesn't try to use the image before the download is complete. You used to have to do this yourself, but no longer.

DISPLAY AN IMAGE

Once we have the picture in an **ImageIcon** object, displaying it is quite easy. You'll need to use the Swing components for this lab because the older AWT components can't use images this easily. The following constructors exist for the **JLabel** and **JButton** classes:

```
public JLabel(Icon icon)
public JButton(Icon icon)
```

So, all you need to do is pass in an **Icon** instead of a string and you'll have a button or label with a picture instead of text!

■ FOR EXAMPLE:

The following code will create an applet that displays a picture of a dog.

```
import java.applet.*;
import java.awt.*;
import javax.swing.*;
public class DogLabel
    extends JApplet
{
    public void init()
    {
            Image image;
            image = getImage(getCodeBase(), "dog.gif");
            ImageIcon icon = new ImageIcon(image);
            JLabel label = new JLabel(icon);
            Container pane = getContentPane();
            pane.add(label, BorderLayout.NORTH);
    }
}
```

The program looks like this when run:

It's just that simple to put an image into an applet. Almost every Swing component can use an **ImageIcon** wherever text can go. Some can even use both, as you'll see in the Exercises.

Figure 9.1 ■ Image displayed in Applet

LAB 9.1 EXERCISES

9.1.1 LOADING AND DISPLAYING IMAGES

For this exercise, you will need some image files to display. You can either use your own, or use the ones on the Web pages for this book:

        http://www.phptr.com/phptrinteractive

This page has instructions on how to save the files to your own computer. Remember that all image files should be in the same directory as your Java source and class files.

a) Change the **DogLabel** applet so that it creates a **JButton** instead of a **JLabel**. Call this program **DogButton**.

_____

_____

b) Change the image in your applet to be **dog2.gif**, or use any image file that you may have on your computer.

_____

_____

The `JButton` also defines two other icons: the *rollover* icon that is used when the mouse pointer is over the button, and the *pressed* icon, used when the button is pressed. Use the following `JButton` methods to set these values:

```
public void setRolloverIcon(Icon rolloverIcon)
public void setPressedIcon(Icon pressedIcon)
```

Use your program from question a for the next two questions.

> **c)** Assign `dog-roll.gif` to be the *rollover* image for the button. What happens when the mouse moves on and off the button?

> **d)** Assign `dog-press.gif` to be the *pressed* image for the button. What happens when the button is pressed?

The `JButton` can also have both an image and a text label by using the following constructor for the `JButton`:

```
public JButton(String text, Icon icon)
```

> **e)** Add a text label to your button using this new form of the `JButton` constructor. Where is the label displayed?

Add the following lines of code your program, after the `JButton` constructor.

```
button.setVerticalTextPosition(SwingConstants.BOTTOM);
button.setHorizontalTextPosition(SwingConstants.CENTER);
```

> **f)** Where is the label displayed now?

Let's quickly revisit something that we have been taking for granted. Add this line to your applet:

```
System.out.println("Code base is " + getCodeBase());
```

g) What is the output from this line?

_____

_____

LAB 9.1 EXERCISE ANSWERS

9.1.1 ANSWERS

a) Change the **DogLabel** applet so that it creates a **JButton** instead of a **JLabel**.

Answer: The following code creates an image in a button:

```
import java.applet.*;
import java.awt.*;
import javax.swing.*;
public class DogButton extends JApplet
{
    public void init()
    {
        Image image;
        image = getImage(getCodeBase(), "dog.gif");
        ImageIcon icon = new ImageIcon(image);
        JButton button = new JButton(icon);
        Container pane = getContentPane();
        pane.add(label, BorderLayout.NORTH)
    }
}
```

This code is virtually identical to the **DogLabel** code. The only difference is that the **JLabel** has been replaced with a **JButton**. Figure 9.2 shows the results of the code.

b) Change the image in your applet to be **dog2.gif**, or use any image file that you may have on your computer.

Figure 9.2 ■ JButton with an image.

Answer: The only change needed is the following code:

```
image = getImage(getCodeBase(), "dog2.gif");
```

The results of the change are shown in Figure 9.3.

The new image is now displayed.

c) Assign **dog-roll.gif** to be the *rollover* image for the button. What happens when the mouse moves on and off the button?

Answer: Add the following code to add a rollover image:

```
Image rollImage = getImage(getCodeBase(),"dog-roll.gif");
ImageIcon rollIcon = new ImageIcon(rollImage);
button.setRolloverIcon(rollIcon);
```

When the mouse pointer is over the button (but not pressing it), the button's image should change to the new image, as shown in Figure 9.4.

This feature can be used to give additional visual feedback to the user. A common usage is to highlight the button in some way. While you can use any image as the rollover image, it's best to use an image that relates to the original image, as we did in this example. Please note that you are not required to define a rollover image. Your program will work just fine without one.

Figure 9.3 ■ JButton with a new image.

Figure 9.4 ■ The JButton changes to the rollover image.

d) Assign **dog-press.gif** to be the *pressed* image for the button. What happens when the button is pressed?

Answer: Now the button's image changes when the button is pressed. Figure 9.5 shows the pressed button image. The code to implement this change follows.

Again, you don't *have* to use the pressed image. Java already darkens the background when you press the button, so the user already gets visual feedback when the button is pressed. However, only the border is darkened, so if you want the image itself to change, you should define the pressed image. A common usage for the pressed image is to use an image that is a darker version of the original button image. This improved the "pressed" look a bit.

In case you've gotten a bit lost, here is the entire **init()** code for the **DogButton** program that defines a button image, rollover image, and pressed image:

```
public void init()
{
Image image = getImage(getCodeBase(), "dog.gif");
ImageIcon icon = new ImageIcon(image);
JButton button = new JButton(icon);
Image rollImage =
      getImage(getCodeBase(), "dog-roll.gif");
ImageIcon rollIcon = new ImageIcon(rollImage);
```

Figure 9.5 ■ The JButton changes to the pressed image.

```
        button.setRolloverIcon(rollIcon);
        Image pressImage =
                getImage(getCodeBase(), "dog-press.gif");
        ImageIcon pressIcon = new ImageIcon(pressImage);
        button.setPressedIcon(pressIcon);
        getContentPane().add(button, BorderLayout.NORTH);
    }
```

e) Add a text label to your button using this new form of the `JButton` constructor. Where is the label displayed?

Answer: The following code will construct a button with both text and an image:

```
    JButton button = new JButton("Dog Button", icon);
```

The result of this code is shown in Figure 9.6. The text label is displayed to the right of the image, and is centered vertically. We had to resize the window to be a little bigger so that we could see the text.

It is usually a good idea to include text with your images. Not everyone can figure out what a button does just by a picture. Images should enhance your program, but not detract from its usability.

f) Where is the label displayed now?

Answer: The text label is now on the bottom-center of the button, as shown in Figure 9.7.

Figure 9.6 ■ **The JButton with picture and text.**

Figure 9.7 ■ **The JButton with the text centered on the
bottom.**

You can place the text label anywhere on the button relative to the
image. The default position of the text is on the right, which the authors
don't think is a very good place. The Swing set defines the following constants to modify the text's location:

For **setVerticalTextPostion:**
  • SwingConstants.TOP
  • SwingConstants.CENTER
  • SwingConstants.BOTTOM
For **setHorizontalTextPostion:**
  • SwingConstants.LEFT
  • SwingConstants.CENTER
  • SwingConstants.RIGHT

You can get nine different text positions using combinations of these values. We encourage you to play with these values and watch the results.

The following code summarizes all of the changes necessary to add a text
label to the image:

```
JButton button = new JButton("Dog Button", icon);
button.setVerticalTextPosition(SwingConstants.BOTTOM);
button.setHorizontalTextPosition(SwingConstants.CENTER);
// Same code as previously listed for the images.
```

g) What is the output from this line?

Answer: While your answer will most surely not be the same, the following is the authors' Java console output from the **getCodeBase()** *method:*

```
Code base is file:/C:/WINDOWS/jws/Chapter9/DogButton/
```

The preceding output is from using the *appletviewer* on a Windows 98 system. Your output will reflect the location of your applet. Because the output does change, your applet is now portable, meaning that it should be able to run from any location.

You might not recognize it as such, but a string like **file:/some/file** is a URL, just like **http://www.phptr.com/** is a URL. A URL, or Uniform Resource Locator, is a standard way of describing the location of something. Most people are familiar with the *http* version, since they see it on the Web all of the time. However, the *file* form is just as valid and just refers to a file on your local computer.

What **getCodeBase()** does is return the applet's URL up to, but not including, the applet name. If we were to run the applet using an *http* URL, then **getCodeBase()** would return the http-form of the URL.

It is also important to realize that **getCodeBase()** only exists in applets (it's a method of the **Applet** class). You won't be able to use **getCodeBase()** in a Java *application*, but you can still reference files using URLs.

LAB 9.1 SELF-REVIEW QUESTIONS

In order to test your progress, you should be able to answer the following questions.

1) Which of the follow is not a valid URL for a file that could be used by Java?
   a) _____ **http://phptr.com/file.jpg**
   b) _____ **file:/path/to/a/file.gif**
   c) _____ **phptr.com/file.jpg**
   d) _____ **file:/c:/path/to/a/file.jpg**
   e) _____ **http://www.phptr.com/images/file.jpg**

2) Which **Applet** method returns an applet's URL base?
   a) _____ **getCodeBase()**
   b) _____ **getURL()**
   c) _____ **getURLBase()**
   d) _____ **getAppletURL()**

3) Which classes can be constructed with images? Check all that apply.
- **a)** _____ **Button**
- **b)** _____ **Label**
- **c)** _____ **JButton**
- **d)** _____ **JLabel**

4) Which image class is used as a parameter to the Swing components?
- **a)** _____ **Image**
- **b)** _____ **Picture**
- **c)** _____ **Bitmap**
- **d)** _____ **ImageIcon**
- **e)** _____ **All of the above**

5) Which method defines the image that a **JButton** displays when the mouse moves over it?
- **a)** _____ **setMouseOverIcon()**
- **b)** _____ **setRolloverIcon()**
- **c)** _____ **setPressedIcon()**
- **d)** _____ **setPreviewIcon()**
- **e)** _____ **setMouseIcon()**

6) Which method defines the image that a **JButton** displays when the user clicks on the button?
- **a)** _____ **setClickedIcon()**
- **b)** _____ **setRolloverIcon()**
- **c)** _____ **setPressedIcon()**
- **d)** _____ **setSelectedIcon()**
- **e)** _____ **setActionIcon()**

7) You can mix text and images together on a **JLabel**.
- **a)** _____ **True**
- **b)** _____ **False**

8) Which **SwingConstants** value would you use to center you text on a **JButton**?
- **a)** _____ **CENTER**
- **b)** _____ **MIDDLE**
- **c)** _____ **BETWEEN**
- **d)** _____ **CENTRE**
- **e)** _____ **MIDPOINT**

Quiz answers appear in Appendix A, Section 9.1.

L A B   9 . 2

COLORS

LAB OBJECTIVES

After this lab, you will be able to:

- Change the Color of Components

Another way to bring some life into your programs is with color. Every component in Java has a *foreground* color and a *background* color, each of which can be changed from the default (and rather bland) value of "some kind of gray." An object's *foreground* color is the color used to draw text, or anything else in the "front" of an object. Not surprisingly, the *background* color is the color of the background of an object.

THE COLOR CLASS

As expected, Java represents *color* as an object using the **Color** class. You can define your own colors, or use some predefined colors that Java gives you.

■ *FOR EXAMPLE:*

The following code will set the foreground color of a button to *red*, and the background color to *blue*.

```
JButton button = new JButton("Hello");
button.setForeground(Color.red);
button.setBackground(Color.blue);
```

This creates a button where the word *Hello* is written in red on a blue background, as shown in Figure 9.8. Yes, the picture is in black and white, so you'll just have to trust us that it's a red-on-blue button. You'll see for yourself in the lab fairly soon.

**LAB
9.2**

Figure 9.8 ■ *A* JButton with red text on a blue background.

PREDEFINED COLORS

Table 9.1 lists all of the predefined colors that Java provides. You can use these values wherever a color is needed.

DEFINING YOUR OWN COLORS

As you can see, there are only 13 predefined colors and 3 of them are shades of gray! Fortunately, Java also let's us define our own colors. Java uses the RGB color model, which stands for *Red*, *Green*, and *Blue*. If you are familiar with optics (and who isn't!) then you know that these are the three primary colors of light. By mixing different amounts of red, green, and blue light, we can create any color in the world. We define the amount of each primary color by assigning a number between 0 and 255 to that color, with 0 meaning no color, and 255 meaning full color. Using this method, we can define 16,777,216 different colors!

By the way, do not confuse the three primary colors of light *with the three primary colors or* pigment, *which (as we all learned in kindergarten) are red, blue, and yellow.*

Table 9.1 ■ Predefined Java Color Values

Color.black	Color.red	Color.cyan
Color.darkGray	Color.green	Color.magenta
Color.gray	Color.blue	Color.pink
Color.lightGray	Color.yellow	Color.orange
Color.white		

■ *FOR EXAMPLE:*

Let's define our own color that has a *red* value of 200, a *green* value of 100, and a *blue* value of 0.

```
Color myColor = new Color(200, 100, 0);
button.setBackground(myColor);
```

We create the new color by passing in the RGB values into the constructor. We can then use **myColor** for any color. In reality, this is how all of the predefined colors are created. If you were to look "under the hood" of the **Color** class, you would see code like the following:

```
Color black = new Color(  0,   0,   0);
Color white = new Color(255, 255, 255);
Color gray  = new Color(128, 128, 128);
Color red   = new Color(255,   0,   0);
Color green = new Color(  0, 255,   0);
Color blue  = new Color(  0,   0, 255);
```

As you can see, there is no magic here. The predefined colors are just short cuts to basic colors that you can create yourself. Note that *black* is (0, 0, 0), which is no color, and *white* is (255, 255, 255), which is full color on all channels. If you didn't know, red light + green light + blue light = white light!

LAB 9.2 EXERCISES

9.2.1 CHANGING THE COLOR OF COMPONENTS

a) Create a button with blue text on a red background.

_____

_____

b) Set the background of your entire program to be yellow.

_____

_____

c) Create your own color and set a button's background to that color.

_____

_____

d) Create a `JLabel` and set its background color to red and the foreground color to green. Did anything unexpected happen?

LAB 9.2 EXERCISES

9.2.1 CHANGING THE COLOR OF COMPONENTS

a) Create a button with blue text on a red background.

_____

_____

b) Set the background of your entire program to be yellow.

_____

_____

c) Create your own color and set a button's background to that color.

_____

_____

d) Create a `JLabel` and set its background color to red and the foreground color to green. Did anything unexpected happen?

_____

_____

e) Create 11 buttons that range in shades of gray, starting at *black* and gradually increasing to *white*.

_____

_____

LAB 9.2 EXERCISE ANSWERS

9.2.1 ANSWERS

a) Create a button with blue text on a red background.

Answer: The following code creates this button:

```
JButton button = new JButton("Hello");
button.setForeground(Color.blue);
button.setBackground(Color.red);
```

Figure 9.9 shows the blue on red button.

This code is virtually identical to the code that produced Figure 9.8. All we have done is switched the foreground and background colors. The purpose of this question is to let you see actual color because the pictures in this book are black and white.

b) Set the background of your entire program to be yellow.

Answer: There are several ways of creating a yellow background.

The key is to remember that all *containers* are also *components*. So, to create a yellow background you need to set the background color of the container. However, you also need to remember that any objects placed in the container will cover the background. That may seem obvious, but it's an easy mistake to make.

Figure 9.9 ■ A JButton with blue text on a red background.

The following code sets the background color of a **JApplet** to yellow:

```
Container pane = getContentPane();
JButton button = new JButton("Hello");
pane.setBackground(Color.yellow);
pane.setLayout(new FlowLayout());
pane.add(button);
```

We reset the layout manager for **pane** to be a **FlowLayout()** so that the button would not be stretched, allowing you to see the actual background. Figure 9.10 shows the yellow background.

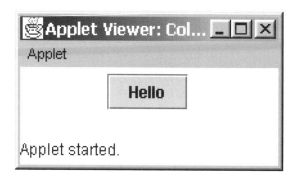

Figure 9.10 ■ A JApplet with a yellow background.

c) Create your own color and set a button's background to that color.

Answer: The following code creates a customized color and assigns it to be the background color of a button.

```
JButton button = new JButton("Hello");
Color swarthyPurple = new Color(240, 9, 200);
button.setBackground(swarthyPurple);
```

We created our own color using red, green, and blue values of 240, 9, and 200, respectively. We can then use this new color just like any of the predefined colors.

d) Create a **JLabel** and set its background color to red and the foreground color to green. Did anything unexpected happen?

Answer: While the foreground color changed the color of the text, the background color didn't seem to make a difference.

As you learned in Chapter 6, you need to set the label's opaque value to **true** for the background color to show through. By default, the **JLabel** is essentially a transparent object, setting the background color doesn't do anything because the label's main job is to just write the label text. This is a good feature because, more often than not, you want your labels to be the same color as the container.

If you need to change the background color of a label, use the following code:

```
// Code to create an orange label.
JLabel label = new JLabel ("Orange");
label.setBackground(Color.orange);
label.setOpaque(true);
```

e) Create 11 buttons that range in shades of gray, starting at *black* and gradually increasing to *white*.

Answer: To create a shade of gray, you must define a color where the red, green, and blue values are all equal to each other. The following code shows how to create the buttons:

```
Container pane = getContentPane();
for (int i=0; i<=10; i++)
{
   int grayLevel = (int) (255 * ((double) i / 10));
   JButton button = new JButton("Gray" + i);
   Color myGray =
        new Color(grayLevel, grayLevel, grayLevel);
   button.setForeground(Color.red);
   button.setBackground(myGray);
   pane.setLayout(new GridLayout(11, 1));
   pane.add(button);
}
```

The result of this code is shown in Figure 9.11.

The purpose of the *for* loop is just to generate even values between 0 and 255. You could have generated the values yourself, but why not just let the computer do the work for you? Once you have the values, you need to create **Color** objects based on those values. We set the button's foreground color to *red* so that the text's color is different from the

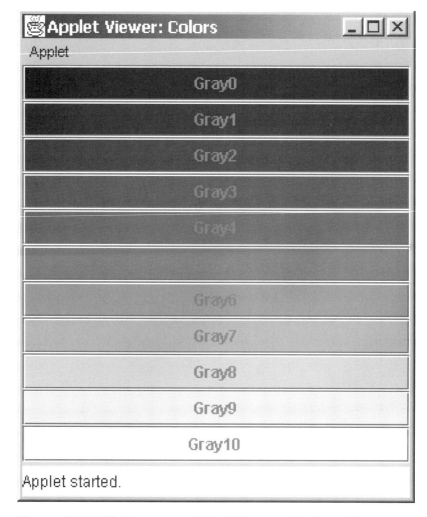

Figure 9.11 ■ Buttons with different shades of gray.

background, and can therefore still be seen. The *Gray5* color is close to the "gray" version of *red*, so that's why that label is a little hard to read.

LAB 9.2 SELF-REVIEW QUESTIONS

In order to test your progress, you should be able to answer the following questions.

1) In Java, what are the three primary colors? Check three.
   a) _____ **Red**
   b) _____ **Yellow**

c) _____ **Blue**

d) _____ **Green**

e) _____ **White**

f) _____ **Black**

2) Which color listed is **not** a predefined color?

a) _____ **Color.green**

b) _____ **Color.pink**

c) _____ **Color.cyan**

d) _____ **Color.purple**

3) Which method sets the text color of a **JButton**?

a) _____ **setForeground()**

b) _____ **setTextColor()**

c) _____ **setColor()**

d) _____ **setBackground()**

e) _____ **setFontColor()**

4) How many different colors can you define in Java?

a) _____ **none**

b) _____ **10**

c) _____ **One** *million* **colors!**

d) _____ **16.8 million**

e) _____ **32656**

5) Which method sets the background color of a component?

a) _____ **setBackgroundColor()**

b) _____ **setBackColor()**

c) _____ **setColor()**

d) _____ **setBackground()**

e) _____ **setComponentColor()**

6) A **JLabel** uses the background color of its container.

a) _____ **True**

b) _____ **False**

7) Which color listed represents a green color?

a) _____ **new Color(55, 0, 0)**

b) _____ **new Color (0, 255, 0)**

c) _____ **new Color (0, 0, 100)**

d) _____ **new Color (244, 0, 255)**

e) _____ **new Color (0, 0, 0)**

8) Which color listed represents a gray color?
   a) _____ **new Color(255, 255, 255)**
   b) _____ **new Color (10, 200, 100)**
   c) _____ **new Color (0, 100, 100)**
   d) _____ **new Color (0, 0, 0)**
   e) _____ **new Color (128, 128, 128)**

Quiz answers appear in Appendix A, Section 9.2.

LAB
9.2

L A B   9 . 3

SOUNDS

LAB OBJECTIVES

After this lab, you will be able to:

• Play Audio Clips

Java also provides the ability to easily play audio files on your computer. While you may not need to play audio files as often as displaying an image, it's good to know how for those times that you do.

Just like with the Images Lab, you will find sample audio files on the Web page for this book. You will need to save these files to your computer in order to run the examples and do the labs.

The audio files for this chapter can be found at the following URL:

http://www.phptr.com/phptrinteractive

All of the methods and classes pertaining to audio files are found in the **Applet** package, so you must have the following statement at the beginning of your code:

```
import java.applet.*;
```

This should be a standard line in all of your applet programs anyway, but since it's not obvious that the audio classes are contained in the applet package, the authors thought it wise to mention it.

AUDIO FILES

In the same way Java accessed image files, Java also references audio files as URLs. Java's **Applet** and **JApplet** classes understand how to load and play common audio formats such as WAV, AU, and SND. For this lab, you can use the audio files on this book's web page, or create your own using the software that comes with your computer. The same rules and suggestions apply for audio files as did with image files. That is, all audio files are assumed to be in the same directory as the class file.

AUDIO CLIPS

Java uses the class **AudioClip** to represent an audio file. Loading an **AudioClip** from a file is very similar to loading an **Image** from an image file.

■ *FOR EXAMPLE:*

The following applet code creates an **AudioClip** from a file:

```
AudioClip clip = getAudioClip(getCodeBase(), "hello.au");
```

Note that the **getAudioClip()** is a method from the **Applet** class.

Now that we have an **AudioClip** object, we can use it in our programs. There are three things we can do with a clip: *play*, *loop*, and *stop*.

PLAYING AUDIO CLIPS

To *play* an audio clip means to play it just one time. When you call the **play()** method, Java will open the audio device on your computer and send the audio information. At which time, you should hear the sounds coming from your computer. Of course, this assumes that your computer is capable of playing sounds.

■ *FOR EXAMPLE:*

The following code will play the audio clip from the previous example:

```
clip.play();
```

We hope that example wasn't too complicated for you! As you can see, Java is doing all of the work for you. If you were to play the **hello.au** file from the Web page, you would hear one of the authors saying "Hello" to you.

LOOPING AUDIO CLIPS

The second thing you can do with an audio clip is to *loop* it using the **loop()** method. Looping means to play the same clip over and over again. There are two reasons to do this. The first is to be very annoying, but the second reason is to get more mileage out of your audio files.

Audio files are quite large, and the longer the sound, the larger the file is. And, as you know, large files take longer to download over the Internet. If you *loop* a small audio file, it can sound long, even though it isn't. Realistically, however, only certain kind of sounds can be looped successfully.

■ FOR EXAMPLE:

Let's say we had a small audio file of ocean sounds. We could loop this clip and create a nice, meditation environment of ocean sounds. The following code demonstrates how we could accomplish this:

```
AudioClip ac = getAudioClip(getCodeBase(), "ocean.wav");
ac.loop();
```

Again, the method to loop is very simple. Note that the **loop()** method will return immediately. What it does is start the looping process in the *background*, and then returns control to your program.

Some other examples of sounds that could be looped are applause, rain, wind, engines, and daytime talk shows. Just a few repeated seconds of any of those will sound like the whole thing.

STOPPING AUDIO CLIPS

Okay, let's say we're tired of the ocean now, and we want it to stop. *For the love of Pete, please make it stop!* To stop a looping clip, we call the **stop()** method. This will tell the background process to stop playing the clip.

■ FOR EXAMPLE:

The following code will bring peace to the previous example:

```
ac.stop();
```

The **stop()** method tells the background process to stop playing the clip. The clip should stop playing immediately, as opposed to not repeating when the clip is finished. Also, if you started playing a long audio clip using the **play()** method, calling **stop()** will stop that clip immediately as well.

LAB 9.3 EXERCISES

9.3.1 PLAYING AUDIO CLIPS

For this exercise, you will need some audio files to play. You can either use your own, or use the ones on the Web pages for this book:

http://www.phptr.com/phptrinteractive

LAB
9.3

This page has instructions on how to save the files to your own computer. Remember that all audio files should be in the same directory as your Java source and class files.

> **a)** Create a button labeled "Play" that will play the `hello.au` audio clip when pressed. You should refer back to the *Events* chapter if you've forgotten how to take action when a button is pressed.

> **b)** Modify your program from question a by adding "Loop" and "Stop" buttons that will *loop* and *stop* the same audio clip. Also, change the audio clip to the `music.wav` file.

> **c)** For the program in question b, if you press *Loop* and then *Play*, what happens?

Go back to your `DogButton` program from Lab 9.1, question f, and make the following change:

> **d)** Modify `DogButton` so that it plays `bark.au` when the image button is pressed.

Lab 9.3 Exercise Answers

a) Create a button labeled "Play" that will play the **hello.au** audio clip when pressed.

Answer: The following code will do what we want.

```
import java.applet.*;
import java.awt.*;
import java.awt.event.*;
import javax.swing.*;

public class Sounds
    extends JApplet
{
    AudioClip clip;

    public void init()
    {
      clip = getAudioClip(getCodeBase(), "hello.au");
      JButton playButton = new JButton("Play");
      Container pane = getContentPane();
      pane.add(playButton);
      playButton.addActionListener(new ActionListener()
      {
          public void actionPerformed(ActionEvent ae)
          {
              clip.play();
          }
      });
    }
}
```

LAB
9.3

If you recall from the *Events* chapter, an **ActionListener** is an object that will react whenever the button is pressed (the button's *action*). All we have done here is call **clip.play()** from inside the **actionPer-formed()** method for the listener. Thus, whenever the button is pressed, the audio clip is played. In order to reference the **clip** variable, we need to define it in the global area of the applet by defining **clip** outside of the **init()** block.

b) Modify your program from question a by adding "Loop" and "Stop" buttons that will *loop* and *stop* the same audio clip.

Answer: The following modification will add the two new buttons:

```
public void init()
{
    clip = getAudioClip(getCodeBase(), "music.wav");
    JButton playButton = new JButton("Play");
    JButton loopButton = new JButton("Loop");
    JButton stopButton = new JButton("Stop");
    Container pane = getContentPane();
    pane.setLayout(new GridLayout(3, 1));
    pane.add(playButton);
    pane.add(loopButton);
    pane.add(stopButton);
    playButton.addActionListener(new ActionListener()
    {
            public void actionPerformed(ActionEvent ae)
            {
                clip.play();
            }
    });
    loopButton.addActionListener(new ActionListener()
    {
            public void actionPerformed(ActionEvent ae)
            {
                clip.loop();
            }
    });
    stopButton.addActionListener(new ActionListener()
    {
            public void actionPerformed(ActionEvent ae)
            {
                clip.stop();
            }
    });
}
```

This code just extends the answer from question a. We've only shown the **init()** code since nothing else changed. You should be able to play, loop, and stop the audio clip using the interface shown in Figure 9.12.

Figure 9.12 ■ **An applet that can play, loop, or stop an audio clip.**

c) For the program in question b, if you press *Loop* and then *Play*, what happens?

Answer: The clip will play one more time and then stop. The clip will stop looping.

The **AudioClip** object can only do one thing at a time. When you call the **play()** method, you are resetting the clip's mode from *loop* to *play*. The audio clip has no memory that it was looping before you pressed *Play*, so after it finished playing the clip, it stops.

d) Modify **DogButton** so that it plays the audio clip "bark.au" when pressed.

Answer: The following modification will work. We have only listed the modifications to the previous program. Where the code hasn't changed, we have inserted a comment stating that the code is the "same as before."

```
// Same as before
import java.awt.event.*;
public class DogButton extends JApplet
{
    AudioClip clip;
    public void init()
    {
```

```
                        clip = getAudioClip(getCodeBase(), "bark.au");
                        // Same as before
                        JButton button =
                               new JButton("Dog Button", icon);
                        button.addActionListener(new ActionListener()
                        {
                            public void actionPerformed(ActionEvent ae)
                              {
                              clip.play();
                            }
                   });
                   // Same as before
              }
          }
```

LAB
9.3

Your barking dog program is now complete! You can now amaze and astonish your friends!

LAB 9.3 SELF-REVIEW QUESTIONS

In order to test your progress, you should be able to answer the following questions.

1) Which Java class is used for sound files?
   a) _____ **Sound**
   b) _____ **Audio**
   c) _____ **SoundClip**
   d) _____ **AudioClip**
   e) _____ **SoundFile**
   f) _____ **AudioFile**

2) For the class from question 1, which method will play the sound file one time?
   a) _____ **playOnce()**
   b) _____ **play()**
   c) _____ **start()**
   d) _____ **startOnce()**

3) Which method will repeatedly play the sound file?
   a) _____ **loop()**
   b) _____ **repeat()**
   c) _____ **playMany()**
   d) _____ **startRepeat()**
   e) _____ **playRepeat()**

4) Which method stops the playing of a sound file?
- **a)** _____ **halt()**
- **b)** _____ **cancel()**
- **c)** _____ **stop()**
- **d)** _____ **end()**
- **e)** _____ **pause()**

5) Which Applet method will load an audio file?
- **a)** _____ **getAudioClip()**
- **b)** _____ **loadAudioFile()**
- **c)** _____ **getAudioFile()**
- **d)** _____ **getSoundFile()**

6) Audio files are referenced as URLs.
- **a)** _____ **True**
- **b)** _____ **False**

Quiz answers appear in Appendix A, Section 9.3.

L A B   9 . 4

FONTS

> ## LAB OBJECTIVES
>
> After this lab, you will be able to:
>
> • Change the Font of Components

If you have used a word processor before, then you probably know what fonts are. If you don't, fonts are characteristics that describe how text appears. For an example of different fonts, you don't have to go any further than this very page! There are several different fonts being used on this page alone. The lab number, the chapter title, and the very text you are reading now all look different from each other because each uses a different font.

FONT PROPERTIES

All fonts have the following properties: a *family name*, a *size*, and a *style*. We will first cover each of these properties, and then show you how to create a font and then assign it to a component.

FONT FAMILY NAME

The family name of a font defines the *shape* of the letters in the font. The family name of the font you're reading now is called *Stone Serif*. This is a common font used in newspapers and books (surprise!). Contrast this with the `Courier font family` and you can see the difference.

- Java is fun! (Stone Serif font)
- `Java is fun! (Courier font)`

Perhaps you'll recognize the Courier font; it's the font we have been using to show code examples. As you can see, not only are the individual letters drawn differently, but the spacing between the letters is also different. The Courier font is a fixed-width font, meaning that all of the letters have the same width. Conversely, the Stone Serif font is a variable-width (or proportional-width) font, meaning that the letters are spaced based on each letter's own width.

We will show you how to get a list of all the font family names later in this lab.

FONT STYLE

There are four font *styles* in Java, defined by field values from the **Font** class:

- Font.PLAIN (Plain)
- Font.BOLD (**Bold**)
- Font.ITALIC (*Italic*)
- Font.BOLD + Font.ITALIC (***Bold-Italic***)

Each of these styles modifies the basic font family shape to create a variation of the font that can be used to add emphasis to, or otherwise highlight, certain words.

FONT SIZE

The font size defines how big or small the letters are. The units of font size are called *points*, so sometimes font size is referred to as *point size*. The text you are reading now is 11-point text. Compare that to 14-point text, which is obviously bigger, and 9-point text, which is smaller. All of the text in this paragraph is still in the Times font family, the only difference is the point size.

JAVA FONTS

Now that we have defined the three font properties, we can show you how to define a font in Java. The constructor for the **Font** class is as follows:

```
public Font(String familyName, int style, int size)
```

Once we have a **Font** object, we can assign the font to a component using the following **Component** method:

```
public void setFont(Font font)
```

Let's look at an example.

■ *FOR EXAMPLE:*

The following code sets the font of a label to the "Helvetica" family, a bold style, and a 24-point size. This can be abbreviated as *Helvetica-Bold-24.*

```
public void init()
{
    Container pane = getContentPane();
    JLabel label =
        new JLabel("Time lost is never found again.");
    label.setHorizontalAlignment(SwingConstants.CENTER);
    Font font = new Font("Helvetica", Font.BOLD, 24);
    label.setFont(font);
    pane.add(label);
}
```

The result of this code is shown in Figure 9.13.

We have changed the label's font from the default font to our own font. The process would be exactly the same for any component with text, like buttons, and textfield objects.

LISTING ALL FONT FAMILY NAMES

So, now that you know how to create fonts, you might be asking yourself, "What fonts are available?" That's a good question, but unfortunately, we can't give you an exact answer in this book. We can, however, show you how you can get a list of all available font family names.

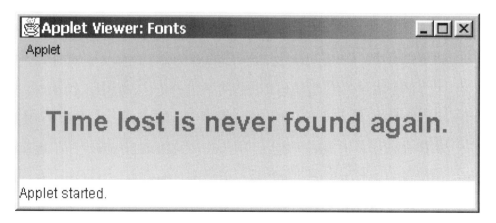

Figure 9.13 ■ JLabel with Helvetica-Bold-14 Font

The reason we can't tell you which fonts you have is because the answer depends on which fonts are installed on your system. We can tell you which fonts *we* have on *our* system, but that won't help you much.

The following code will print a list of all of the available fonts on your system:

```
GraphicsEnvironment ge =
    GraphicsEnvironment.getLocalGraphicsEnvironment();
String[] families = ge.getAvailableFontFamilyNames();
int numFonts = families.length;
System.out.println("You have " + numFonts + " fonts.");
for (int i=0; i<numFonts; i++)
{
    System.out.println(families[i]);
}
```

This code produces the following output for the authors:

```
You have 71 fonts.
Abadi MT Condensed Light
Arial
Arial Black
Arial Narrow
Bauhaus 93
Book Antiqua
Bookman Old Style
[. . . The list continues . . .]
```

The **GraphicsEnvironment.getLocalGraphicsEnvironment()** method produces a **GrapicsEnvironment** object, which describes the local system's graphical capabilities, which includes fonts. Using this object, you can get a list of font family names using the **getAvailableFontFamilyNames()** method, which returns an array of Strings containing the names.

At this point, you probably have just one more question. The answer to that question is "Yes, someone was paid good money to think up those method names."

LAB **9.4** EXERCISES

9.4.1 CHANGING THE FONT OF COMPONENTS

Because not all computers have the same set of fonts installed, there is a small possibility that some of the fonts required for the exercises may not be available to you. The authors have tried to select fonts that are common to most systems to decrease these odds. However, if you don't have one of the fonts required for a question, simply choose another font from the output of the program you will write for question a.

LAB 9.4

a) Use the `GraphicsEnvironment` class, as shown in the lab, to list all of the available font families on your system.

_____

_____

b) Create two `JButton` objects. Change the font for one of them to Arial-Bold-14.

_____

_____

c) Create a series of labels using the Times font. Have the font size for each label range from 10 to 20, increasing by 2 each time.

_____

_____

d) Create four labels using the Helvetica-14 font. Use the same text in each label, but give each label of the four styles: plain, **bold**, *italic*, and ***bold-italic***.

_____

_____

LAB 9.4 EXERCISE ANSWERS

9.4.1 ANSWERS

a) Use the **GraphicsEnvironment** class, as shown in the lab, to list all of the available font families on your system.

Answer: You should get a printout listing the number of fonts on your system, and a list of the font family names.

The purpose of this question is to give you a list of fonts that you can use in your programs. The actual code is listed in the chapter and won't be repeated here.

b) Create two **JButton** objects. Change the font for one of them to Arial-Bold-14.

Answer: The following code will create the two buttons:

```
Container pane = getContentPane();
JButton button1 = new JButton("Plain Button");
JButton button2 = new JButton("Arial Bold 14 Button");
Font arialBold14 = new Font("Arial", Font.BOLD, 14);
button2.setFont(arialBold14);
pane.setLayout(new GridLayout(2, 1));
pane.add(button1);
pane.add(button2);
```

The result of this code is shown in Figure 9.14.

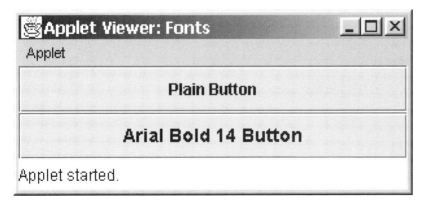

Figure 9.14 ■ Two buttons, one with a different font.

Fonts, like colors, are objects that can be used over again. If we needed to set the font of another object to Arial-Bold-14, we could just reuse the **arialBold14** variable. We would not have to create a second **Font** object.

c) Create a series of labels using the Times font. Have the font size for each label range from 10 to 20, increasing by 2 each time.

Answer: The following code will create the labels.

```
int min = 10;
int max = 20;
int inc = 2;
int numLabels = ((max - min) / 2) + 1;
Container pane = getContentPane();
pane.setLayout(new GridLayout(numLabels, 1));
for (int size=min; size<=max; size += inc)
{
    JLabel label =
        new JLabel("Times Font Point Size " + size);
    Font font = new Font("Times", Font.BOLD, size);
    label.setFont(font);
    pane.add(label);
}
setSize(300, 200);
```

The result of this code is shown in Figure 9.15.

While the authors got a little tricky with their answer, you didn't have to use a *for* loop to generate the fonts. You could just have easily created the six fonts and buttons by hand. The point of this question was to give you some perspective on point sizes.

d) Create four labels using the Helvetica-14 font. Use the same text in each label, but give each label of the four styles: plain, **bold**, *italic*, and ***bold-italic***.

Answer: The following code will create the four labels.

```
String msg = "Time lost is never found again.";
Container pane = getContentPane();
JLabel label1 = new JLabel(msg);
JLabel label2 = new JLabel(msg);
JLabel label3 = new JLabel(msg);
JLabel label4 = new JLabel(msg);
Font plain = new Font("Helvetica", Font.PLAIN, 14);
```

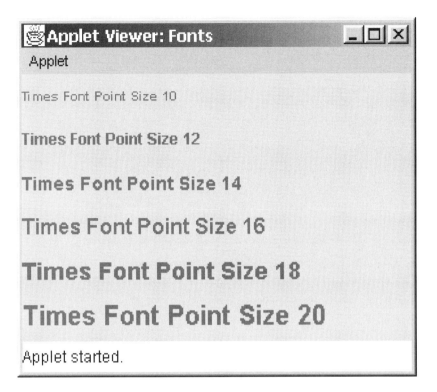

Figure 9.15 ■ Labels with increasing point size.

```
Font bold = new Font("Helvetica", Font.BOLD, 14);
Font italic = new Font("Helvetica", Font.ITALIC, 14);
Font boldItalic =
    new Font("Helvetica", Font.BOLD + Font.ITALIC, 14);
label1.setFont(plain);
label2.setFont(bold);
label3.setFont(italic);
label4.setFont(boldItalic);
pane.setLayout(new GridLayout(4, 1));
pane.add(label1);
pane.add(label2);
pane.add(label3);
pane.add(label4);
```

The result of this code is shown in Figure 9.16.

**LAB
9.4**

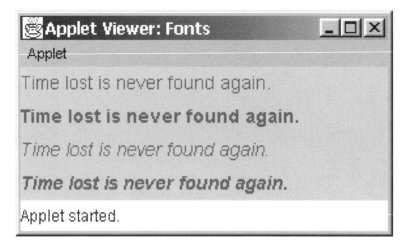

Figure 9.16 ■ Labels with different font styles.

You now have the skills to change the font for any component in Java. While a font won't make or break your program, you can improve the appearance of it.

LAB 9.4 SELF-REVIEW QUESTIONS

In order to test your progress, you should be able to answer the following questions.

1) Which font property changes the shape of the letters?
   a) _____ Style
   b) _____ Family
   c) _____ Size
   d) _____ Shape
   e) _____ Pattern

2) `Font.BOLD` is an example of which font property?
   a) _____ Style
   b) _____ Family
   c) _____ Size
   d) _____ Shape
   e) _____ Pattern

3) Font size is measured in what units?
   a) _____ pixels
   b) _____ dots
   c) _____ millimeters
   d) _____ points
   e) _____ inches

4) All computers are installed with the same set of fonts.

    a) _____ **True**

    b) _____ **False**

5) Which of the following is not a font attribute?

    a) _____ **Size**

    b) _____ **Family**

    c) _____ **Style**

    d) _____ **Color**

6) Which method sets the font of a component?

    a) _____ **setFont()**

    b) _____ **setTextFont()**

    c) _____ **setComponentFont()**

    d) _____ **None of the above, must set each property individually.**

LAB
9.4

7) You cannot reuse font objects.

    a) _____ **True**

    b) _____ **False**

    c) _____ **Depends**

Quiz answers appear in Appendix A, Section 9.4.

C H A P T E R   9

TEST YOUR THINKING

In today's high-tech world, people have come to expect a certain amount of flare and attractiveness in programs they use and from Web sites they visit. While images, sounds, colors, and fonts may not be vital to your program, they can enhance your program a great deal and encourage people to use it.

1) Why is it important that `getCodeBase()` return the applet's URL?

You have probably seen Web pages that use animated images. Technically, these are called GIF89 images, or animated GIFs, and are a collection of multiple images that can be played in sequence to create a motion effect.

2) Load an animated GIF into a button or label. What happens?

3) Write a program with a button and three text fields where a user can enter values for red, green, and blue. Then, change the color of the button to the color defined by values in the text fields. If you feel brave, try using sliders to define the color values.

4) Add images to the buttons in your play/loop/stop audio program. Some appropriate audio control images can be found on this book's Web site. Then, modify your program so that it will allow you to select any audio file and play it.

For the following question, use your program from Lab 7.1, question b (the touch-tone phone pad) and the twelve "touchtone" audio files on the Web page.

5) Modify your touch-tone phone program to play the corresponding touchtone audio file when each button is pressed.

6) Create a font selector program. Display a list of font names, styles, and sizes and allow the user to select one of each. Then display some text using that font.

CHAPTER 10

CREATING YOUR OWN CLASSES

We must become the change we want to see.

Mahatma Gandhi

CHAPTER OBJECTIVES

In this chapter, you will learn about:

✔ Designing and Implementing Classes
✔ Special Class Features
✔ Subclassing and Inheritance

Back in Chapter 2, we introduced you to the basic syntax of a Java program. Now it is time to learn the truth about Java, and to take a closer look at the insides of a Java class. In this chapter, we will show you how to make useful classes of your own. So far, the only classes you have made have been applications or applets. While these are technically classes, they serve a very specific purpose and cannot be reused in other programs. Conversely, this chapter will show you how to write specialized classes that can be used again and again in your other programs. We will also show you how to extend the abilities of existing classes by exploring the concepts of *subclassing* and *inheritance*. The goal of this chapter is to show you what it takes to take your programs out of the textbook and into the real world.

L A B   1 0 . 1

DESIGNING AND IMPLEMENTING CLASSES

LAB OBJECTIVES

After this lab, you will be able to:

- Create a Class that Contains Data

In your programs so far, you have been using classes like **Vector** and **JButton**, which were written by the makers of Java. It might surprise you to learn that those classes are themselves written in Java and use other classes that are also written in Java. This, of course, begs the question, *"How can Java be written in Java?"* How did it all begin? The answer is that the Java programming environment actually consists of two parts: a core Java language, and an archive of extensions. The core Java language consists of only the primitive data types, the mathematic operators, and the ability to create classes and extend itself. The archive consists of classes created from the core Java components. Later, more classes were added to the archive using the core Java and other classes already in the archive. Java, with its ability to extend itself, has grown to what it is today, and it's still growing.

The extensibility of Java is its true power. If something is missing, you can create it! If you don't like how something works, change it! This lab will show you how to create your own classes, and in later labs, we will show you how to extend and change them.

As always, we will show you a few simple examples, and then make you do something really hard in the exercises.

CREATING A NEW CLASS

Let's look at an example of creating a class so you can see how it's done. We'll then look at how this new class can be used in a program.

CREATING A CLASS THAT CONTAINS DATA

The simplest class is one that just holds a collection of data. Creating a data class can help organize the data and make it more useful and easier to manage.

■ *FOR EXAMPLE:*

We will create a new class called **FullName**, which can contain a person's *first* and *last* names. To create this class, we must first create a file called **FullName.java**. As with program names, all class names must match their source code file name. The contents of **FullName.java** are as follows:

```
public class FullName
{
    public String first;
    public String last;
}
```

That's it! That's the entire code for the **FullName** class. There's not much here, but let's take a closer look at what we did.

As you may recall from Chapter 2, the word **public** means that other classes have access to this class. Likewise, the variables defined in the main block are also **public**. In the next lab, we'll show you some other options besides **public**, but for now, always use **public**.

COMPILING THE CLASS

The next thing to do is compile the new class. Use the **javac** program to compile the file, just like every other program you've written so far. However, **do not run it**. This kind of class is not meant to be run; it's meant to be used. After compiling, you should now have a file called **FullName.class**.

USING THE NEW CLASS

Now we need to write a program that uses and tests the **FullName** class. The following program will do this for us.

```
import javax.swing.*;
public class TestName extends JApplet
{
    public void init()
    {
        FullName name = new FullName();
        name.first = "Nathan";
        name.last = "Detroit";
        System.out.println(name.last);
    }
}
```

Running the preceding program will yield the following output:

Detroit

When you compile and run the TestName *program, the* FullName.class *file must either be in the same directory (folder) as the* TestName.class *file, or the* FullName.class *file must reside in a directory specified in the* CLASSPATH *system variable.*

The **TestName** program doesn't do much in and of itself, but it does use a class that didn't exist until we created it. The **TestName** program is using the **FullName** class just like any of the built-in classes.

For the remainder of this lab, we will expand the **FullName** class and give it some of the features that you've seen in other Java classes.

CONSTRUCTORS

Every class has a *constructor* that is called whenever the **new** operator is used. When you see code such as the following:

```
Vector vec1 = new Vector();
```

the *constructor* for the **Vector** class is called to build a **Vector** object called **vec1**. If a class does not define a constructor, then a default constructor is called.

■ FOR EXAMPLE:

The code for a constructor looks almost like a method, except that there is no return value. Also, the name of the constructor must be the same as the class name. We have added two constructors to the **FullName** class, as follows:

```
public class FullName
{
    public String first;
    public String last;

    public FullName()
    {
        first = "no first name";
        last = "no last name";
    }

    public FullName(String f, String l)
    {
        first = f;
        last = l;
    }
}
```

LAB
10.1

A constructor with no parameters is called the *default constructor*. We have replaced the old default constructor, which did nothing, with a new constructor, which sets some default values for our object.

It's also possible to have a constructor with parameters, which is sometimes called an *initializer* because it initializes the object's values.

 Classes can have more than one constructor. The signature *that defines a constructor is its parameter list. The order and type of the parameters define the signature. You can have any number of constructors as long as all of the signatures are different.*

Let's make the following change to **TestName.java** to test the new constructors. Notice how we have created two instances of **FullName** objects using the different constructors.

```
public void init()
{
    FullName name1 = new FullName();
    FullName name2 = new FullName("Harry", "Truman");
    name1.first = "Bob";
    System.out.println(name1.first + " " + name1.last);
    System.out.println(name2.first + " " + name2.last);
}
```

When we recompile both files, the new output of **TestName** is as follows:

```
Bob no last name
Harry Truman
```

The values for **name1.first** and **name1.last** were both set in the default constructor. We then reset the value of **name1.first** to **"Bob"** later in the code. As a result, the string **"Bob no last name"** is printed. For **name2**, we initialized its values to be **"Harry"** and **"Truman"** so the end result is that **"Harry Truman"** is printed.

When you need to compile several Java files, you can compile then all at the same time, like this:

```
javac FullName.java TestName.java
```

The javac program will compile all of the files together.

METHODS

We are going to make one last change to the **FullName** class. We're going to add a method to it.

Currently, in order to print out the values in a **FullName** object, we've had to do something like the following:

```
System.out.println(name1.first + " " + name1.last);
```

This is a little cumbersome. Wouldn't it be nice if we could just do something like the following instead?

```
System.out.println(name1.getFullName());
```

Well, we can, since we have control of the **FullName** class.

■ *FOR EXAMPLE:*

Let's create the **getFullName()** method in the **FullName** class so we can use it later in the **TestName** program. Add the following code to **FullName.java**:

```
public String getFullName()
{
     String full = first + " " + last;
     return full;
}
```

We have added a method that will construct a **String** called **full**, which is the combination of the first and last names. We then return **full** back to whoever called **getFullName()**. Thus, we have created new data and made it available to users of the class.

Notice how the first line defines the return type as **String**, and how the last line then returns a value of type **String**. It's very important that you always return the proper type, otherwise the compiler will complain.

SUMMARY

You now know the basics for creating a new class. All of the classes that you have been using so far were written in Java using these same techniques. In the exercises, you will build on the **FullName** class. Additionally, you will learn how classes can manipulate their data, and also generate new data.

Here is the full code for the **FullName** class, as it stands now:

```
public class FullName
{
    public String first;
    public String last;

    public FullName()
    {
        first = "no first name";
        last = "no last name";
    }

    public FullName(String f, String l)
    {
        first = f;
        last = l;
    }

    public String getFullName()
    {
        String full = first + " " + last;
        return full;
    }
}
```

The **FullName** class has the following API definitions:

FIELDS

- `String first`
- `String last`

CONSTRUCTORS

- `FullName()`
- `FullName(String first, String last)`

METHODS

- `String getFullName()`

These API definitions are all that anyone needs to know to use your new class and are similar to those you will find in the Javadocs for the "normal" Java classes.

It's important to realize that by creating classes, you are now extending Java. While doing the following exercises, remember that you are using the same tools and techniques that the authors of Java used to create it. There is no longer any magic here, as we are opening the hood and showing you the truth about how Java works.

LAB 10.1 EXERCISES

10.1.1 CREATE A CLASS THAT CONTAINS DATA

 For these exercises, you will be using the `FullName` *class that was developed in this chapter. Most of the code you write for these exercises should be in a separate program, such as the* `TestName` *program. Only modify the source code to* `FullName` *if the question demands it. It's important to understand the difference between using a class, and modifying it.*

Use the following arrays for the next question:

```
String firstNames[] = {"Billy", "Peter", "Alison"};
String lastNames[] = {"Campbell", "Burns", "Parker"};
```

a) Write code to create an array of **FullName** objects using the **firstNames** and **lastNames** arrays.

_____

_____

b) Using the code from question a, cycle through the array and print out each name using the **getFullName()** method.

_____

_____

Modify the **FullName** class and add a method called **getLastNameFirst()** that returns a String in the form "Last, First".

c) Repeat question b using **getLastNameFirst()** to print each name.

_____

_____

d) Using the techniques used to create the **FullName** class, create your own version of the **Color** class, called **MyColor**. Remember a **Color** holds values for _red_, _green_, and _blue_ settings. Also, add a method called **getRGB()**, which returns a **String** version of the RGB values like **"[123, 22, 93]"** for easy printing.

_____

_____

e) Add a new constructor to the **MyColor** class. The parameter to this constructor should be another **MyColor** object. The goal is for the new object to duplicate the old one. What should the constructor code do with the parameter?

_____

_____

LAB 10.1 EXERCISE ANSWERS

10.1.1 ANSWERS

a) Write code to create an array of **FullName** objects using the **firstNames** and **lastNames** arrays.

Answer: The following code will create the array:

```
public void init()
{
    String firstNames[] = {"Billy", "Peter", "Alison"};
    String lastNames[] = {"Campbell", "Burns", "Parker"};
    FullName names[] = new FullName[3];
    for (int i=0; i<names.length; i++)
    {
        names[i] =
            new FullName(firstNames[i], lastNames[i]);
    }
}
```

Creating an array of our new object is just like creating an array of any other objects. Once the array has been created, we can assign values to each element using the initializing constructor. The point of this question is to show you that working with this new class is just like working with any of the classes that come with Java. The only difference here is that *you* created the **FullName** class yourself.

b) Using the code from question a, cycle through the array and print out each name using the **getFullName()** method.

Answer: The following code will print the values.

```
for (int i=0; i<names.length; i++)
{
    System.out.println(names[i].getFullName());
}
```

This would generate the following output:

```
Billy Campbell
Peter Burns
Alison Parker
```

The point of this question is to use the **getFullName()** method. Earlier, we had to construct the full name string by combining the **first** and **last** variables. This was cumbersome, so we added a new method to do this for us. We also gave the responsibility of formatting the "full name" to the object itself. The **FullName** object *owns* the data, so it should also *own* any methods that affects that data. This is the basic object-oriented model.

c) Repeat question b using **getLastNameFirst()** to print each name.

*Answer: To create the new method, add the following code to **FullName.java**:*

```
public String getLastNameFirst()
{
    return last + "," + first;
}
```

The new method will return a **String** like **"Smith,Bob"** that could be used in an alphabetical sorting routine.

To use the new method, we move back to the main program, and add the following code:

```
for (int i=0; i<names.length; i++)
{
    System.out.println(names[i].getLastNameFirst());
}
```

This produces the following output:

```
Campbell,Billy
Burns,Peter
Parker,Alison
```

This is just another example of how you can customize your objects.

d) Create your own version of the **Color** class, called **MyColor**.

*Answer: The following code creates the **MyColor** class.*

```
public class MyColor
{
    public int red = 0;
    public int green = 0;
    public int blue = 0;
```

```
public MyColor(int r, int g, int b)
{
        red = r;
        green = g;
        blue = b;
}

public String getRGB()
{
        return "[" + red + ", "
                + green + ", " + blue + "]";
}
}
```

Please note that **MyColor** is not a replacement for the real **Color** class. This was just a training exercise to give you experience with creating classes. The **MyColor** class requires that you save the values for red, green, and blue. It also has an initializing constructor and a method for printing its values. The actual **Color** class has similar code, plus a whole lot more.

Hopefully, you now have a feeling for how the **Color** class was created, as well as an appreciation for the work that was put into developing the Java language.

e) Add a new constructor to the **MyColor** class. The parameter to this constructor should be another **MyColor** object. The goal is for the new object to duplicate the old one. What should the constructor code do with the parameter?

Answer: The following is the code for the additional constructor:

```
public MyColor(MyColor mc)
{
     red = mc.red;
     green = mc.green;
     blue = mc.blue;
}
```

This is an example that is quite common in real life. With objects that contain data, it is customary to be able to copy an object by passing it as a parameter to the constructor of a new object, as follows:

```
MyColor c1 = new MyColor(33, 44, 55);
MyColor c2 = new MyColor(c1);
System.out.println(c2.getRGB());
```

The printout follows:

```
[33, 44, 55]
```

Constructors like this are sometimes called *clone* constructors, since they create a clone (copy) of an object. There are two reasons for doing this. The first is just to make things easier. Imagine if there were 100 pieces of data to be copied. It's nice to be able to do it in one step and not have to worry about it. The second reason (which will be made clearer in the next lab) is that it's possible to have "hidden" data in an object. If you left the copying up to the user, they wouldn't be able to copy it.

LESSONS TO BE LEARNED

Hopefully, these exercises have driven home the point that you have complete control of your objects. You can control how they are created and used. Conversely, if you know how you want to use your object, then you can customize the object to behave the way you want it to. This, too, is part of the object-oriented philosophy. Objects are defined by how they behave, rather than how they do their work. As long as an object does what it says it's going to do, you don't really care how it does it.

For example, recall some of the objects you have used already, like **Vector** and **AudioClip**. You know how to create and use those objects, but you have no idea how they work inside. To use a class, all you need are the API definitions for the class. This is why the Javadocs are so important, because they define the APIs for all of the Java classes.

DIVIDE AND CONQUER

Remember the *Divide and Conquer* strategy we discussed in Chapter 7? No? It's when you take a big problem and divide it into smaller ones, and then repeat the process with the smaller problems until you only have lots of little problems. Little problems are easier to solve than big ones, and you can then focus your efforts on the little problems. This approach is sometimes called the *Top-Down* approach, because you start at the top of problem and work your way down.

TOP-DOWN DESIGN

When you start to write a Java program, you should look at the big picture of what you want your program to do. Then, break your program up into smaller parts, let's call these parts *objects* (hint, hint), and then break each object into smaller objects if needed. Now, look at each object and ask yourself the following questions:

- What information does this object need to do its job?
- How do I use this object?

If your object is small and simple, then the answers to these questions should also be simple. Once you have these answers, you can begin to create your own class to build this object.In fact, if you can define the APIs for all classes in your program before you write a single line of code, you can save yourself a lot of trouble in the future. You can also assign different classes to different people to write. As long as everyone conforms to the API specifications, everything should fit together in the end.

LAB 10.1 SELF-REVIEW QUESTIONS

In order to test your progress, you should be able to answer the following questions.

1) If a class is named **MyWidget**, what is its source file named?
   a) _____ **MyWidget.src**
   b) _____ **MyWidgetSrc**
   c) _____ **MyWidget**
   d) _____ **MyWidget.java**
   e) _____ **Doesn't matter**

2) What would the default constructor for **MyWidget** look like?
   a) _____ **new MyWidget();**
   b) _____ **public MyWidget() {}**
   c) _____ **public class MyWidget**
   d) _____ **MyWidget {}**

3) How would the class definition for **MyWidget** begin?
   a) _____ **new MyWidget();**
   b) _____ **public MyWidget() {}**
   c) _____ **public class MyWidget**
   d) _____ **MyWidget {}**

4) Classes can have only one constructor.
   a) _____ **True**
   b) _____ **False**

5) You must always define a constructor.
   a) _____ **True**
   b) _____ **False**

6) The type and order of a constructor's parameters define its what?
   a) _____ **Signature**
   b) _____ **Usage**
   c) _____ **API**
   d) _____ **All of the above**

7) What restrictions are placed on user-created classes?
   a) _____ **Can only create one instance of them**
   b) _____ **Can only be used in Arrays, but not Vectors**
   c) _____ **Cannot be placed in Vectors or Arrays**
   d) _____ **Cannot be printed.**
   e) _____ **None**

   Quiz answers appear in Appendix A, Section 10.1.

LAB 10.2

SPECIAL CLASS FEATURES

LAB OBJECTIVES

After this lab, you will be able to:

- Use Public and Private Modifiers
- Use Static DataOverload Method Names

This lab will continue to explore the insides of Java classes. We'll start off by defining some terms that you've been using all throughout this book, but have only been doing so because we told you to. For example, you'll learn what **public** and **static** really mean, as well as a new term, **private**. Finally, we'll show you how to *overload* methods, which is one of the most powerful tools in Java.

PUBLIC VERSUS PRIVATE

So far, whenever you have defined a field or method, you have defined it as **public**. Everything has been either a *public* class, *public* variable, or *public* method. As we told you before, *public* means that any other class can access that item. Normally, that's what you would want, but there are times when something needs to be *private*. Something that is *private* is only accessible by the class itself. To any outside class, the private object does not exist.

PRIVATE DATA

To make any data field private, you just put the keyword **private** before the declaration.

■ *FOR EXAMPLE:*

We will define a new class, **PrivateParts**, with two data fields. One will be public, and the other private.

```
public class PrivateParts
{
    public String x;
    private String y;
}
```

In a different program, called **PrivateTest**, we have the following code:

```
PrivateParts pp = new PrivateParts(); // line 10
pp.x = "Hello";                       // line 11
pp.y = "Goodbye";                     // line 12
```

If we try to compile **PrivateTest**, we will get an error from the compiler that looks like this (your mileage may vary, depending on your software):

PrivateTest.java: 12 No variable y defined in class

This error means that on line 12, there is no variable named **y** defined. Whatever your exact error message is, the general message is that you are trying to use something that doesn't exist.

PRIVATE METHODS

Just as with private data, to make a method private, put the keyword **private** before the method definition.

■ *FOR EXAMPLE:*

We will add a private method to the **PrivateParts** class.

```
public class PrivateParts
{
    public String x;
    private String y;

    private void printY()
    {
        System.out.println(y)
    }
}
```

If any other class tried to access the **printY()** method for a **PrivateParts** object, it would generate a compiler error similar to the one previously shown.

WHY MAKE THINGS PRIVATE?

Something is made private when the users don't need to see it. When writing a class, there can be variables and methods that are for internal use only. Exposing them to the user only confuses and complicates things.

Please note that these examples are for educational purposes only; they are not useful as shown. It is possible to create public interfaces to the private data, and we'll explore this concept more in the exercises.

STATIC

If you were to look up the word *static* in a dictionary, you would see a definition along the lines of "unmoving" or "unchanging." This definition, while technically accurate, is also misleading in terms of Java. For Java, it's better to think of *static* as meaning "unique" or "shared."

STATIC VARIABLES

Remember when we first introduced the concept of classes? We compared a *class* to the blueprints for a house, and an *object* to the house built from those blueprints. Keeping that same analogy, imagine that we have 20 houses all built from the same blueprints. A normal variable would be something in one of the houses, like a door. Every house has its own door. If I open the door in one house, it doesn't affect any of the other doors in the other houses. However, a *static* variable would be something on the blueprint itself, like the name of the architect who built the homes. There is only one set of blueprints, therefore only one "architect" value. If someone were to write a new value on the blueprints, it would affect all of the houses.

A real example is worth a thousand words, so let's see a static variable in action.

■ *FOR EXAMPLE:*

We have created a new class called **House**, which has one "normal" variable and one *static* variable. To define a variable as being *static*, we inserted the keyword **static** before its type. This class also has a method that prints the values of its variables. The code for the **House** call follows:

```
public class House
{
    public String door;
    public static String architect = "Mike Brady";

    public House(String d)
    {
        door = d;
    }

    public void printValues()
    {
        System.out.println("door = " + door);
        System.out.println("architect = " + architect);
        System.out.println("------------");
    }
}
```

Likewise, we have a second class that uses the **House** class:

```
public class HouseTest extends Applet
{
    public void init()
    {
        House house1 = new House("Open1");
        House house2 = new House("Open2");
        // Before
        house1.printValues();
        house2.printValues();
        house1.door = "Closed1";
        house1.architect = "Archie Techt";
        // After
        house1.printValues();
        house2.printValues();
    }
}
```

If we run the **HouseTest** program, it generates the following output:

```
door = Open1
architect = Mike Brady
---------------------
door = Open2
architect = Mike Brady
---------------------
```

```
door = Closed1
architect = Archie Techt
------------------------
door = Open2
architect = Archie Techt
------------------------
```

As you can see, when we changed the values for **house1**'s variables, the changes to the **architect** variable were also reflected in **house2**. This is because there is only one **architect** variable that is shared by all objects of class **House**. Figure 10.1 attempts to show the location of the variables in this example.

Notice how there are two distinct variables named **door**, but only one named **architect**. Static variables are sometimes called *class variables* because they belong to the *class* and not to any object. The reason a static variable is called *static* is because its location doesn't change (it's always in the class), and therefore it is "unmoving." This is why we said the

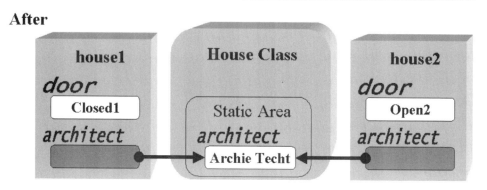

Figure 10.1 ■ Example of static variables.

"unchanging" definition of *static* was accurate, yet misleading. A static variable's value *can* change, but its location can't.

STATIC METHODS

Like variables, methods can also be declared *static*. However, for static methods, the whole house/blueprint analogy doesn't quite work, so we'll abandon that now (it would have to be a holographic blueprint that actually worked). In this case, an example is worth *ten* thousand words, so we'll revisit static methods in the Exercises.

OVERLOADING METHOD NAMES

The final topic we will cover is "overloading method names." In the same way, a class can have multiple constructors that are identified by their signature, so too can it have multiple methods of the same name. Each method is identified by its unique *signature*, which is defined by the method's name and the order and type of its parameters.

■ *FOR EXAMPLE:*

What follows is the complete code to a program called **Identify**. We have defined several methods, all called **identify()**. However, each method takes a different parameter type, and therefore has a different signature.

```
import java.applet.Applet;
public class Identify extends Applet
{
    private void identify(String s)
    {
        System.out.println("String: " + s);
    }

    private void identify(Integer i)
    {
        System.out.println("Integer: " + i);
    }
    private void identify(Double d)
    {
        System.out.println("Double: " + d);
    }

    public void init()
    {
```

```
            identify(new Double(42));
            identify("Help me, Mr. Wizard!");
            identify(new Integer(747));
            identify("3263827");
        }
    }
```

The output of this program is as follows:

```
Double: 42.0
String: Help me, Mr. Wizard!
Integer: 747
String: 3263827
```

We appear to call the same **identify()** method multiple times, but in reality, there are three different **identify()** methods:

```
    identify(String)
    identify(Double)
    identify(Float)
```

Java knows how to tell each method apart, and actually figures out which method to use while the program is running (a *run-time* decision). We'll see another example of this again in the Exercises.

Overloading is actually a very easy concept, and first-time programmers generally don't have any trouble picking it up. It's the veteran programmers of such languages as C and Fortran that get confused by this. In those languages, it was impossible to do overloading.

LAB 10.2 EXERCISES

10.2.1 USING PUBLIC AND PRIVATE MODIFIERS

Start with the following code for the exercises. You will be adding to this code.

```
    public class MinMax
    {
        private int min;
        private int max;

        public MinMax(int initValue)
        {
```

```
        min = initValue;
        max = initValue;
    }

    private void setMin(int testValue)
    {
        if (testValue < min)
            min = testValue;
    }

    private void setMax(int testValue)
    {
        if (testValue > max)
            max = testValue;
    }
}
```

The `MinMax` class will eventually keep track of the *minimum* and *maximum* values for a set of numbers.

> **a)** Since the **min** and **max** fields are private, there is currently no way to access them. Add two methods, **getMin()** and **getMax()** that return their respective values.

_____

_____

> **b)** Add a method, called **checkValue()**, which will take one **int** parameter (**value**) and reset the **min** and **max** values, if needed.

_____

_____

> **c)** What are the current API definitions for the **MinMax** class?

_____

_____

d) Use a `MinMax` object to calculate the minimum and maximum of the following numbers: 2, 5, 100, −5, −5, 300, 6, 10.

There is still one change that needs to be made to the `MinMax` class. As it stands now, the following code will still compile:

```
MinMax mm = new MinMax();
```

Since we didn't define a default constructor, Java created one for us. However, we don't want a default constructor, in this case, because it can cause problems.

e) Why is the default constructor dangerous (in this case) and what can we do about it?

10.2.2 USING STATIC DATA

Use the following code for questions a through d in this section.

```
public class Inventory
{
    private static int units = 100;
}
```

The function of the `Inventory` class will be to keep track of the number of items. You will be adding to this code.

a) Create the methods that allow a user to perform the following operations with the `Inventory` class: *get* the number of units available, *buy* units (increase the number), and *sell* units (decrease the number). That is, implement the following API for the Inventory class.

```
public int getUnits()
```

Returns the number of units.

```
public void buy(int newUnits)
```

*Increase unit count by **newUnits**.*

```
public void sell(int soldUnits)
```

*Decrease unit count by **soldUnits**.*

_____

_____

b) Test your code from question a by buying 50 units, and then selling 75 units. Make sure you use different **Inventory** objects each time to simulate different transactions.

_____

_____

As we said in the chapter, it is also possible to have static methods. To do so, simply insert the keyword **static** after the **public** or **private** declaration.

c) Convert all of the methods in the Inventory class to be static. Does your program run the same? Hint: Make sure you recompile your main program, too, or you might get some errors.

_____

_____

d) What happens if a program runs the following code? What does this mean?

```
Inventory.buy(50);
Inventory.sell(75);
int unitsLeft = Inventory.getUnits();
System.out.println("Units left = " + unitsLeft);
```

_____

_____

10.2.3 OVERLOADING METHOD NAMES

For question a, create a class called **NumberSum**, which will keep the sum total of all numbers of any type. For example, you should be able to use your new class as follows:

```
NumberSum sum = new NumberSum();
sum.add(10);     // an int
sum.add(11.5);   // a float or double
double total = sum.getSum();
System.out.println(total);
```

The output would be:

21.5

The **NumberSum** object was able to add two different types together.

a) Create the **NumberSum** class by overloading the **add()** method so that it accepts variables of the following types: **int**, **float**, and **double**. It should also have a **getSum()** method, which returns the total sum, as a **double**.

b) Augment the **NumberSum** class so that the **add()** method also accepts values of type **Integer**, **Float**, and **Double**. Test the **NumberSum** class using the following code:

```
NumberSum sum = new NumberSum();
sum.add(-8);
sum.add((float) 20.25);
sum.add((double) 3.125);
sum.add(new Integer(-3));
sum.add(new Float(11.75));
sum.add(new Double(1.5));
double total = sum.getSum();
System.out.println(total);
```

LAB 10.2 EXERCISE ANSWERS

10.2.1 ANSWERS

a) Since the **min** and **max** fields are private, there is currently no way of accessing them. Add two methods, **getMin()** and **getMax()** that return their respective values.

Answer: The following code will add the two methods:

```
public int getMin()
{
    return min;
}

    public int getMax()
{
    return max;
}
```

These methods may not look very exciting, but the important thing to notice is that they are defined as **public**. It's quite common to have public methods that access private data; in fact, it's recommended. While it may appear to be more cumbersome on the surface, this technique is essential to protect your data's integrity, as you'll see shortly.

b) Add a method, called **checkValue()**, which will take one **int** parameter and reset the **min** and **max** values, if needed.

*Answer: The following is the code for the **checkValue()** method.*

```
public void checkValue(int value)
{
    setMin(value);
    setMax(value);
}
```

Again, this method is **public** so that it is accessible outside of the class. The **checkValue()** method will then use the two private methods, **setMin()** and **setMax()** to check **value** and reset the **min** and **max** values, if necessary.

c) What are the current API definitions for the **MinMax** class?

*Answer: The API for **MinMax** would be as follows:*

Fields

- None

Constructors

- MinMax(int initValue)

Methods

- void checkValue(int value)
- int getMin()
- int getMax()

This is all the information that anyone needs to use the MinMax class. Notice how there are no field variables. The user doesn't need to know how the minimum and maximum values are stored. Only the essential information is exposed to the user. The rest of the details are hidden.

d) Use a **MinMax** object to calculate the minimum and maximum of the following numbers: 2, 5, 100, –5, –5, 300, 6, 10.

*Answer: The following code (in a different class) will use the **MinMax** class:*

```
public void init()
{
    int values[] = {2, 5, 100, -5, -5, 300, 6, 10};
    MinMax mm = new MinMax(values[0]);
    for (int i=1; i<values.length; i++)
        mm.checkValue(values[i]);
    System.out.println("Min = " + mm.getMin());
    System.out.println("Max = " + mm.getMax());
}
```

We create the new **MinMax** object called **mm** and initialize it with the first value in the list of numbers. We then check all of the other values in the array using **mm**. Finally, we query **mm** for the minimum and maximum values. Nowhere in this process do we need to know how the **MinMax** class works; we just use it.

The concept of knowing what an object does, but not how it does it, is know as *abstraction*. An abstract object can be described with words instead of functions. We can say, "The **MinMax** class determines the minimum and maximum number of any number it sees." Once you know this, you don't need to worry about the details and just assume that the object will do its job. This is very important for large projects that have many parts. Referring again to the *Divide and Conquer* technique, once we have abstracted an object's function, we no longer have to worry about its details.

e) Why is the default constructor dangerous (in this case) and what can we do about it?

Answer: The default constructor is dangerous for this class because it allows for a **MinMax** *object to exist without any initial values. This could lead to incorrect results.*

If we were to create an object as follows:

```
MinMax mm = new MinMax();
mm.checkValue(1);
mm.checkValue(2);
mm.checkValue(3);
System.out.println("Min = " + mm.getMin());
```

The result would be:

Min = 0

This result is not correct since we never tested 0. How did this happen? Since we never used the initializing constructor, the values for **min** and **max** were set to the default values for **int** variables, which is 0. Since 0 is less than 1, 2, and 3, the values for **min** never gets reset.

So, how do we fix this? The most elegant way is to prevent anyone from using the default constructor, and we accomplish this by making it private! All we need to do is add the following constructor:

```
private MinMax()
{
}
```

It is now impossible for anyone to use the default constructor, because it has been defined as private, and therefore, not available outside of the class.

Here is the complete code for the **MinMax** class:

```
public class MinMax
{
    private int min;
    private int max;
```

```
private MinMax()
{
}

public MinMax(int initValue)
{
      min = initValue;
      max = initValue;
}

private void setMin(int testValue)
{
      if (testValue < min)
            min = testValue;
}

private void setMax(int testValue)
{
      if (testValue > max)
            max = testValue;
}

public int getMin()
{
            return min;
}

public int getMax()
{
            return max;
}

public void checkValue(int value)
{
      setMin(value);
      setMax(value);
}
}
```

10.2.2 ANSWERS

a) Create the methods that allow a user to perform the following operations with the **Inventory** class: get the number of units available,
buy units (increase the number), and sell units (decrease the number).

Answer: The following code will add the methods:

```
public int getUnits()
{
        return units;
}
public void buy(int newUnits)
{
        units = units + newUnits;
}
public void sell(int soldUnits)
{
        units = units - soldUnits;
}
```

**LAB
10.2**

This is straightforward code that demonstrates that public methods can access private data, even when it's static. The **units** variable is static and is therefore shared by all instances of the class.

b) Test your code from question a by buying 50 units, and then selling 75 units. Make sure you use different **Inventory** objects each time to simulate different transactions.

*Answer: The following code will test the **Inventory** class:*

```
public void init()
{
        Inventory inv1 = new Inventory();
        System.out.println("Starting units = "
            + inv1.getUnits());
        inv1.buy(50);
        System.out.println("After buy: Units left = "
            + inv1.getUnits());
        Inventory inv2 = new Inventory();
        inv2.sell(75);
        System.out.println("After sell: Units left = "
            + inv1.getUnits());
}
```

This code will generate the following output:

```
Starting units = 100
After buy: Units left = 150
After sell: Units left = 75
```

Even though the *buy* and *sell* operations used different objects, each transaction updated the same data. While there could be many transactions, there is only one *inventory* of units (one warehouse, if you will). By defining **units** to be **static**, we have defined it to be unique. There is only one **units** variable, and instances of the **Inventory** class share this single variable.

LAB 10.2

c) Convert all of the methods in the Inventory class to be static. Does your program run the same?

Answer: The headers to the methods should now have the following look:

```
public static int getUnits()
public static void buy(int newUnits)
public static void sell(int soldUnits)
```

We changed all of the methods to be static by adding **static** after the **public** keyword. After this change, however, the program should run exactly the same as before. So why bother to make the methods static? What does this accomplish? Read the next answer to find out.

d) What happens if a program runs the following instructions? What does this mean?

Answer: The code has the following output:

```
Units left = 75
```

This answer is that same answer as the previous two questions: 100 units, plus 50 units, minus 75 units, equals 75 units. However, this time, we never used an actual instance of the **Inventory** class. So, what's going on? Here is the answer.

STATIC METHODS

Static methods, like static variables, are part of the class. Because they are part of the class, you can invoke the method from the class itself! You can access both field variables and methods directly from the class. You don't actually need an instance of the class to run the method.

One word of warning: static methods can only access static data. Because a static method exists in the class, it only had access to fields and methods that are also in the class. It cannot access nonstatic methods or fields. You will get a compiler error if you try and do this.

YOU'VE BEEN USING STATIC METHODS ALL ALONG

Perhaps the following code looks familiar:

```
System.out.println("Hello World!");
```

This was the first piece of code we had you run. That was 10 chapters ago and now we're finally going to define it! There is a class called **System**. In this class is a *static* field variable called **out**, and within the **out** variable is a method called **println()**. So, you have been accessing static data all along.

Static methods have their place, usually grouping together a collection of utility functions. Similar to the **System** class is the **Math** class, which contains many advanced math functions. In theory, you could write your entire program with static data and methods, but then you wouldn't have an object-oriented program anymore! Our final advice on using static methods and fields is to only use them when necessary. There are areas of Java, which are beyond the scope of this book, that expose some dangers of using static members in your programs.

10.2.3 ANSWERS

a) Create the **NumberSum** class by overloading the **add()** method so that it accepts variables of the following types: **int**, **float**, and **double**. It should also have a **getSum()** method that returns the total sum, as a **double**.

*Answer: The following code is one way of creating the **NumberSum** class. We will show you a second technique following a short discussion.*

```
public class NumberSum
{
    private double sum = 0.0;

    public double getSum()
    {
        return sum;
    }
    public void add(double d)
    {
        sum = sum + d;
    }
```

```
public void add(float f)
{
      sum = sum + (double) f;
}
public void add(int i)
{
      sum = sum + (double) i;
}
}
```

We have created three methods called **add()**, each of which take one of the primitive number types as a parameter. The program using the **NumberSum** class can now just invoke **add()** and Java will call the correct method.

And now, for an alternate answer, which uses a new technique called *reducing*.

REDUCING

A different way of approaching this problem uses a concept called *reducing* and better takes advantage of method overloading. *Reducing* is taking a problem and *reducing* it down to a known problem, one that you can solve. For example, if you were driving around town and get lost, you would try and find some known landmark to get your bearings. Once you can get to the landmark, you can find your way home because you know how to "get home from there." This same principle can apply to programming as well.

■ *FOR EXAMPLE:*

Using this technique, we have created the *new and improved* **NumberSum** class, as follows:

```
public class NumberSum
{
    private double sum = 0.0;

    public double getSum()
    {
          return sum;
    }
    public void add(double d)
    {
          sum = sum + d;
    }
```

```
      public void add(float f)
      {
            add((double) f);
      }
      public void add(int i)
      {
            add((double) i);
      }
}
```

The only things that have changed are the **add(float)** and **add(int)** methods.

As we said, reducing is taking one problem and reducing it to a known problem. In this case, the **add(double)** method is the *known problem*. This problem is easy to "solve" since the variable **sum** is a **double**, and adding a **double** to a **double** is easy (you just add them). Our goal now is to *reduce* the other methods to use the **add(double)** method. For the **add(float)** and **add(int)** methods, we cast their parameters to a **double**, and then call **add(double)**.

What benefits does this have? The main advantage is that you *centralize* the actual *work* that your object does. Compare the two versions of **NumberSum**. The first version had essentially the same "*sum = sum + something*" code in all three **add()** methods. In this example, the *work* is only one line of code. But in the real world, that *work* could be thousands, or millions of lines of code. Suddenly, it's much more efficient to reduce everything else down to a centralized *work* method.

In the next answer, we will show how much easier it is to make modifications using the *reducing* technique.

b) Augment the **NumberSum** class so that the **add()** method also accepts values of type **Integer**, **Float**, and **Double**.

*Answer: The code for **NumberScan** now appears as follows:*

```
public class NumberSum
{
    private double sum = 0.0;

    public double getSum()
    {
          return sum;
    }
```

```
public void add(double d)
{
      sum = sum + d;
}
public void add(float f)
{
      add((double) f);
}
public void add(int i)
{
      add((double) i);
}
public void add(Double D)
{
      add(D.doubleValue());
}
public void add(Float F)
{
      add(F.floatValue());
}
public void add(Integer I)
{
      add(I.intValue());
}
}
```

Testing this class, using the given code, yields the following result:

25.625

This code uses the *reducing* technique introduced in the answer to question a. In this case, we use two levels of reducing. The **add(Integer)** method is reduced to **add(int)**, which is then reduced to **add(double)**. Reducing is another example of the *Divide and Conquer* strategy. You can now divide your problems in to smaller problems, or into known problems.

LAB 10.2 SELF-REVIEW QUESTIONS

In order to test your progress, you should be able to answer the following questions.

1)   Which of the follow methods would be accessible outside of the class?
     a) _____ **public void getValue()**
     b) _____ **private void getValue()**
     c) _____ **void pubic getValue()**
     d) _____ **void private getValue()**

2) Private data cannot be accessed directly.
 a) _____ **True**
 b) _____ **False**

3) Public methods cannot access private data.
 a) _____ **True**
 b) _____ **False**

4) Which line defines a static variable?
 a) _____ **public static int i;**
 b) _____ **static public int i;**
 d) _____ **public int static i;**
 e) _____ **int public static i;**
 f) _____ **static int public i;**
 g) _____ **int public static i;**

5) Only static methods can access static fields.
 a) _____ **True**
 b) _____ **False**

6) Static methods can access nonstatic fields and methods.
 a) _____ **True**
 b) _____ **False**

7) Which definition overloads the method `add()`?
 a) _____ **public overload void add(int value)**
 b) _____ **overload public void add(int value)**
 d) _____ **overload void add(int value)**
 e) _____ **None of the above**

8) Overloaded methods are identified by their what?
 a) _____ **Name**
 b) _____ **Parameter types**
 c) _____ **Parameter order**
 d) _____ **All of the above**
 e) _____ **None of the above**

Quiz answers appear in Appendix A, Section 10.2.

L A B   1 0 . 3

SUBCLASSING AND INHERITANCE

LAB OBJECTIVES

After this lab, you will be able to:

- Extend a Class
- Override Methods

Now that you have learned how to create your own classes, it is time to learn how to extend and modify existing classes. We don't mean modifying the source code for a class. When you extend a class, you create a new class, which is a *subclass* of the original class. The subclass *inherits* all non-private fields and methods from the original class, which is also called the *superclass* or *parent* class. Figure 10.2 illustrates the concept of subclassing.

The subclass inherits fields and methods from the superclass, and then can add fields and methods of its own. Likewise, the subclass can change the behavior of any existing method by overriding it. You will see more on that topic later.

CREATING A SUBCLASS

You have already created a subclass, several, in fact. Each time you created an applet, you extended the **Applet** class. Every one of your applet programs is a subclass of the **Applet** class. Thus, your programs inherited methods such as **add()** and **getAudioClip()** from the **Applet** class. You were then able to use these methods from within your program.

This may not all make sense right now, but keep it in mind as we walk through an example of subclassing.

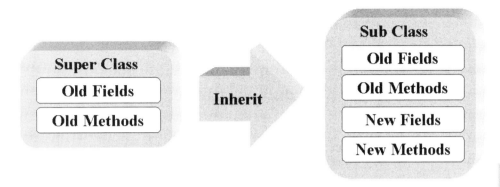

Figure 10.2 ■ A subclass inheriting from its parent class.

■ FOR EXAMPLE:

We will create two classes. The first class, called **Ball**, will be the starting class. The second class, called **ColorBall**, will extend **Ball**. **ColorBall** will therefore be a subclass of **Ball**.

The code for the **Ball** class follows:

```
public class Ball
{
    private double radius;

    public Ball(double r)
    {
        setRadius(r);
    }
    public double getRadius()
    {
        return radius;
    }
    public void setRadius(double r)
    {
        radius = r;
    }
    public double getVolume()
    {
        return Math.PI * radius*radius*radius * 4 / 3;
    }
}
```

Ball is a straightforward class with one private field (**radius**) and several public methods that access that field. All balls have a single property, which is their radius (the distance form the center to the surface).

We now want to extend the concept of a ball, and add the property of color. However, we don't want to change the original **Ball** class, so we extend it with **ColorBall**. The code for **ColorBall** follows:

```
import java.awt.*;
public class ColorBall extends Ball
{
    private Color color;

    public ColorBall(double radius, Color c)
    {
        super(radius);
        setColor(c);
    }
    public Color getColor()
    {
        return color;
    }
    public void setColor(Color c)
    {
        color = c;
    }
}
```

Note the keyword **extends** as part of the class declaration. This tells the Java compiler to use the **Ball** class as a starting point, and then add our new code to create a new class.

THE SUPER CONSTRUCTOR

If you look at the constructor for **ColorBall**, you will see that it calls something called **super()**. The *super constructor* is a reference to the superclass's constructor. Since **ColorBall** extends **Ball**, the **ColorBall** constructor must call the **Ball** constructor with a call to **super()**.

It is the responsibility of the subclass to create its superclass. The call to **super()** *must be the first statement in the subclass's constructor.*

Notice how **ColorBall** passes in the value of **radius** to the super constructor. If you take a look back at the **Ball** constructor, you will see that takes a *radius* parameter. If the superclass has multiple constructors, then the subclass can call any one of the constructors by using the correct parameters.

INHERITENCE

As we said earlier, subclasses inherit fields and methods from their parent class. Figure 10.3 illustrates how the **ColorBall** class has inherited its methods from the **Ball** class.

The following code shows how a **ColorBall** object also behaves as a **Ball** object:

```
ColorBall sb = new ColorBall(10, Color.red);
System.out.println("Color = " + sb.getColor());
System.out.println("Volume = " + sb.getVolume());
```

The output of this code is:

```
Color = java.awt.Color[r=255,g=0,b=0]
Volume = 4188.790204786391
```

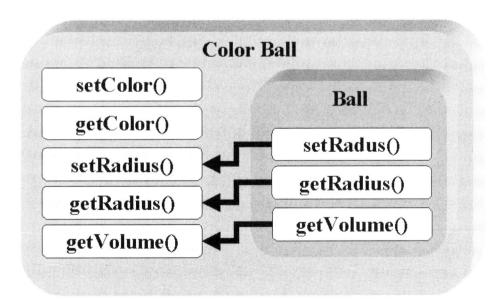

Figure 10.3 ■ ColorBall inherits methods from Ball.

You would expect to be able to call **getColor()**, since you can see **getColor()** defined in the code for **ColorBall**. However, you can also call **getVolume()** because **ColorBall** has inherited it from **Ball**.

Remember how we said that all of your applet programs were subclasses of the **Applet** class? Your applets can call methods like **getAudioClip()** because they exist in the Applet class. Your subclass (the program) inherits **getAudioClip()**, and other methods, from **Applet**, and can then use it as if it were one of your own.

PUBLIC, PRIVATE, AND PROTECTED

What about the **radius** field? Did **ColorBall** inherit it as well? The answer is *no*, and the reason is that **radius** was declared **private** in **Ball**. The subclass does not inherit fields and methods that are private. In this example, **ColorBall** must use the **getRadius()** and **setRadius()** methods, just like any other class.

This may lead to the question, "Is there anything in between *public* and *private*?" This time, the answer this is *yes*! There is the **protected** declaration. A field or method that is *protected* behaves as *private* to outside classes, but behaves as *public* to any subclasses. A protected item will be inherited by a subclass, but still remain hidden from the outside.

Table 10.1 summarizes the behavior of public, private, and protected items.

OVERRIDING METHODS

A subclass also has the ability to change the behavior of any method that it inherits by *overriding* that method. When you override a method, you essentially replace the old method with a new method. However, you can still access the old method if you want to, as we'll show you.

Table 10.1 ■ public, private, and protected behavior

	public	private	protected
Accessible by class	yes	yes	yes
Accessible by outside classes	yes	no	no
Accessible by subclasses	yes	no	yes
Inherited by subclasses	yes	no	yes

■ FOR EXAMPLE:

We will override the **setRadius()** method in **ColorBall**. As inherited from **Ball**, the **setRadius()** method will change the value of **radius** to a new value. The change we are about to make will restrict all radius values to be positive, since a **ColorBall** can't have a negative radius.

We have added the following code to the **ColorBall** class:

```
public void setRadius(double radius)
{
    if (radius < 0)
    {
        Strig error = "Can't have negative radius!";
        System.out.println(error);
    }
    else
    {
        super.setRadius(radius);
    }
}
```

Notice how the signature of this method matches the signature of the **setRadius()** method in the **Ball** class. This is important since Java must replace the old method and needs the signature to identify it. If the method's name and parameters do not match, then the subclass will not override the method in the superclass.

Also notice that we still used the original **setRadius()** method from the **Ball** class by referencing it as **super.setRadius()**. Just like the **super()** constructor is a reference to the superclass's constructor, **super.*method-name*()** is a reference to a method in the superclass called *method-name*. Thus, **super.setRadius()** calls the **setRadius()** method in the original **Ball** class.

■ FOR EXAMPLE:

The following code demonstrates the use of the overridden **setRadius()** method:

```
public void init()
{
    ColorBall cb = new ColorBall(10.0, Color.red);
    System.out.println("Radius = " + cb.getRadius());
    cb.setRadius(-5.0);
```

```
        System.out.println("Radius = " + cb.getRadius());
        cb.setRadius(2.0);
        System.out.println("Radius = " + cb.getRadius());
}
```

The output of this code follows:

```
Radius = 10.0
Can't have negative radius!
Radius = 10.0
Radius = 2.0
```

As you can see, the value of **−5.0** is rejected by the new **setRadius()** method, but the value of **2.0** is accepted. We have overridden the method and changed its behavior. Remember that this can be done with any class, including those that come with Java, like **Vector**, and **JButton**.

In the Exercises, you will be extending the **JButton** and modifying its behavior. You will also be creating your own classes, and then extending them so you can see how the **protected** declaration works, as well as concepts like *overriding*.

LAB 10.3 EXERCISES

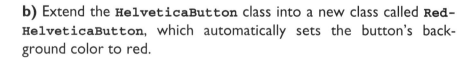

10.3.1   EXTENDING A CLASS

a) Create a new class called **HelveticaButton**, which extends the **JButton** class and automatically sets the font to Helvetica-Bold-18.

_____

_____

b) Extend the **HelveticaButton** class into a new class called **Red-HelveticaButton**, which automatically sets the button's background color to red.

_____

_____

Use the following class for questions c and d:

```
public class Witness
{
    public String caseNumber;
    protected String name;

    public Witness(String cn, String n)
    {
        caseNumber = cn;
        name = n;
    }
}
```

c) As written, how would you get the value of **name** from a **Witness** object?

_____

_____

d) Create a new class called **WitnessProtectionProgram**, which extends **Witness** and provides access to the **name** field.

_____

_____

10.3.2 OVERRIDING METHODS

All graphical components, like buttons, labels, and panels, are subclasses of the **Component** class. This allows them all to share methods like **setFont()**. The **Panel** class, as a subclass of Component, can also call **setFont()**, but it normally has no effect. You're about to change that.

a) Create a new class called **FontPanel**, which extends the **Panel** class. Override the **add()** method so that it sets the font of the component being added to the panel's font. The API for the **add()** method is as follows:

```
public Component add(Component comp)
```

_____

_____

Use the `ColorBall` class from this chapter for the next two questions.

b) What is the output of the following code?

```
ColorBall cb = new ColorBall(4.0, Color.blue);
System.out.println(cb);
```

_____

_____

Modify the `ColorBall` class by adding the following method to it:

```
public String toString()
{
    return "radius=" + getRadius() + ", Color=" + color;
}
```

c) Repeat question b: What is the output of the following code?

```
ColorBall cb = new ColorBall(4.0, Color.blue);
System.out.println(cb);
```

_____

_____

d) Recall the `FullName` class from Lab 10.1 and add a `toString()` method that uses the `getLastNameFirst()` method for its return value. Redo question c from Lab 10.1.1, except that lines that used to look like this:

```
System.out.println(names[i].getLastNameFirst());
```

Should now look like this:

```
System.out.println(names[i]);
```

<hr>

<hr>

LAB 10.3 EXERCISE ANSWERS

10.3.1 ANSWERS

a) Create a new class called **HelveticaButton**, which extends the **JButton** class and automatically sets the font to Helvetica-Bold-18.

Answer: The following code will create the HelveticaButton class:

```
import java.awt.*;
import javax.swing.*;

public class HelveticaButton extends JButton
{
    public HelveticaButton(String label)
    {
        super(label);
        setFont(new Font("Helvetica", Font.PLAIN, 18));
    }
}
```

We changed the button's font by adding some code to the button's constructor. We first called the **super()** constructor, passing in the **label** value, to create the **JButton**. Then we set the font using the **setFont()** method. Since we are extending the **JButton** class, we can call the **setFont()** method as if it were one of our own methods (which it is!).

To use this new class, we just use is as if it were a **JButton** (which it is!). The following applet code will use our new class:

```
import java.applet.Applet;
import java.awt.*;
import javax.swing.*;
public class Exercises extends Applet
{
```

```
public void init()
{
        add(new HelveticaButton("Hello Helvectica!"));
        add(new JButton("Normal JButton"));
}
}
```

We created the **HelveticaButton** just like a **JButton** (which it is!), and we can use it just like a **JButton** (say it with us, "which it is!"). We also added a regular **JButton** for comparison. Figure 10.4 shows the result of this code.

Did we mention that the **HelveticaButton** can be treated just like a **JButton**?

b) Extend the **HelveticaButton** class into a new class called **Red-HelveticaButton**, which automatically sets the button's background color to red.

Answer: The code for the RedHelveticaButton follows:

```
import java.awt.*;

public class RedHelveticaButton
    extends HelveticaButton
{
    public RedHelveticaButton(String label)
    {
        super(label);
        setBackgroud(Color.red);
    }
}
```

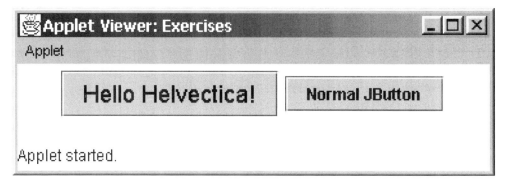

Figure 10.4 ■ HelveticaButton subclassed from JButton

This answer is very similar to the previous answer to question a. Notice how we have extended **HelveticaButton**. The **RedHelveticaButton** class is now a subclass of **HelveticaButton**.

You should also notice how we didn't need to import the *Swing* classes anymore (**javax.swing.***). Even though **HelveticaButton** is a subclass of a **JButton** (which is part of *Swing*), we don't need to worry about that anymore. Extending **HelveticaButton** gives us that link.

The point of this question was to show that any class can be both a subclass, and a superclass. The **HelveticaButton** is a subclass of **JButton**, and a superclass of **RedHelveticaButton**. This is quite common, and if you look at the *Javadoc* API manual, you will see the *class hierarchy* that exists for all classes. On the documentation pages for each class, you will find that class' lineage listed. The lineage will show you from which other classes a particular class was derived.

c) As written, how would you get the value of **name** from a **Witness** object?

Answer: You can't.

The **name** field is declared as **protected**, and there are no **public** methods to access it. So, no other class can get to it. The only way to access **name**, in this case, would be to extend the class, as the next question demonstrates.

d) Create a new class called **WitnessProtectionProgram**, which extends **Witness** and provides access to the **name** field.

Answer: The following code creates the new class:

```
public class WitnessProtectionProgram extends Witness
{
    public WitnessProtectionProgram(String cn, String n)
    {
        super(cn, n);
    }
    public String getName()
    {
        return name;
    }
}
```

Okay, so the class names are a little silly, but this exercise does show how a subclass can access a **protected** field. The **getName()** method returns

name, but there is no visible declaration of the **name** variable in the preceding code. The reason this works, of course, is because **name** is declared within the **Witness** class. **WitnessProtectionProgram** inherits **name**, and can therefore access it.

10.3.2 ANSWERS

a) Create a new class called **FontPanel**, which extends the **Panel** class.

Answer: The following code creates the FontPanel class:

```
import java.awt.*;

public class FontPanel extends Panel
{
    public Component add(Component comp)
    {
        comp.setFont(getFont());
        return super.add(comp);
    }
}
```

The important thing to remember is that in order to override a method, you must match the method's signature exactly. While a method's return value is technically not part of the signature, Java won't let you change it either. So, the return value must match, otherwise you will get an error from the Java compiler. The easiest way to return the right value is to return the superclass's method value, as we did in our answer. Unlike the **super()** constructor, a "super.method()" does not have to be called first, or even at all (but only do so if you know what you're doing).

The following code will use the new **FontPanel** class.

```
import java.applet.Applet;
import java.awt.*;
import javax.swing.*;

public class FontPanelTest extends Applet
{
    public void init()
    {
```

```
FontPanel fp = new FontPanel();
fp.setFont(new Font("Arial", Font.ITALIC, 20));
fp.setLayout(new GridLayout(3, 1));
fp.add(new JButton("First Button"));
fp.add(new JButton("Second Button"));
fp.add(new JButton("Third Button"));

add(fp);

setSize(250, 150);
    }
}
```

**LAB
10.3**

We set the font for the **FontPanel**, and then add the buttons. Since we have overridden the **add()** method, all of the buttons get added, and have their font values changed.

Figure 10.5 shows the three buttons with the italic font.

The Container class actually has several add() methods. If you really wanted this behavior, you would need to override all of the add() methods.

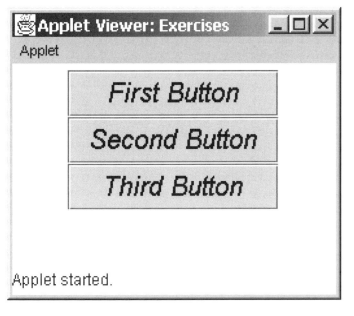

Figure 10.5 ■ The new FontPanel in action.

b) What is the output of the following code?

Answer: The following output is generated:

```
ColorBall@56b66dd
```

This ugly looking string is what the **System.out.println()** method prints out for most classes. It's basically the class name followed by a unique number (which only has meaning to Java itself). While this value is mildly helpful, it can be improved upon. Read the next answer to find out how.

c) Repeat question b: What is the output of the following code?

Answer: The output has changed to the following:

```
radius=4.0, Color=java.awt.Color[r=0,g=0,b=255]
```

So, how did adding a method to the **ColorBall** class change how the object is printed? Allow us to explain.

THE OBJECT CLASS

When we first introduced you to Java, we said that everything in Java is an object, and now we're going to prove it. The reality is that every class in Java is an *extension* of the **Object** class. Really! The **ColorBall** is an extension of the **Ball** class. That's easy to see, since the code says **extends Ball**. However, the **Ball** class would appear not to extend any class, but the truth is that Java secretly makes it extend the **Object** class. The result is that the **Object** class then becomes the *ancestor* of every other class in Java.

One of the advantages of having an **Object** class is that every class will inherit every method in the **Object** class. That way, you can always count on certain methods being available. One such method is the **toString()** method. By default, it will return the "ugly string" we saw in question b. However, if we override it (as we did in question c) then we change the output. Methods like **System.out.println()** only need to call an object's **toString()** method and let the object itself determine how it should be printed.

d) Recall the **FullName** class from Lab 10.1 and add a **toString()** method that uses the **getLastNameFirst()** method for its return value. Redo question c from Lab 10.1.1.

Answer: Add the following code to the FullName class to override the toString() method:

```
public String toString()
{
        return getLastNameFirst();
}
```

If you haven't already, read the answer to question c so you'll understand what is going on.

We are overriding the default **toString()** method again, this time returning the value of the **getLastNameFirst()** method that already exists. Now, code that looks like this:

```
FullName name = new FullName();
name.first = "Nathan";
name.last = "Detroit";
System.out.println(name);
```

will generate output like this:

Detroit,Nathan

instead of this:

FullName@79c77c7

If you ever wanted to change the object's printout behavior, you would just change its **toString()** method.

LAB 10.3 SELF-REVIEW QUESTIONS

In order to test your progress, you should be able to answer the following questions.

1) What keyword is used to subclass a class?
   a) _____ subclass
   b) _____ augment
   c) _____ modify
   d) _____ extend

2) What is the original class from which a subclass is created called?
   Check all that apply.
   a) _____ Superclass
   b) _____ Parent class
   c) _____ Master class
   d) _____ Grand class
   e) _____ Grand Master Funky-C

3) What does a subclass inherit? Check all that apply.
   a) _____ **Constructors**
   b) _____ **Fields**
   c) _____ **Methods**
   d) _____ **All of the above**

4) How does a subclass refer to its parent class's constructor?
   a) _____ **parent()**
   b) _____ **master()**
   c) _____ **upper()**
   d) _____ **constructor()**
   e) _____ **super()**
   f) _____ **It can't**

5) Which keyword allows a method to be inherited but not accessible to the public?
   a) _____ **public**
   b) _____ **private**
   c) _____ **super**
   d) _____ **protected**
   e) _____ **inherit**
   f) _____ **propagate**

6) Which keyword allows a subclass to override a method?
   a) _____ **override**
   b) _____ **replace**
   c) _____ **new**
   d) _____ **displace**
   e) _____ **All of the above**
   f) _____ **None of the above**

7) If a class subclasses **JButton**, then the new class can still be considered a **JButton**.
   a) _____ **True**
   b) _____ **False**

8) Which method should you override to change how an object is printed?
   a) _____ **toString()**
   b) _____ **print()**
   c) _____ **printObject()**
   d) _____ **printString()**
   e) _____ **objectString()**

Quiz answers appear in Appendix A, Section 10.3.

C H A P T E R   1 0

TEST YOUR THINKING

Building your own classes is what being a Java programmer is all about. Lots of people can code, but not as many can engineer great classes. The planning and design of a class can be more important than the code. As with all things, skill comes from practice, so here are some exercises to give you that practice.

1) Create classes to manage baseball players and their batting averages. You'll need classes that associate a name with a batting average, as well as the ability to store multiple records.

2) Create a graphical interface where you type in a player's name, hits, and at bats, and it calculates their average. Save the data in the structure from question 1.

3) To your program from question 2, add the ability to search for a player's name. It will then search through all records and display any matches that it finds.

Two of the fundamental container objects in computer science are the *stack* and the *queue*. Both are used as a temporary holding area for things waiting to be processed.

However, each handles its items differently.

A *stack* is like a stack of books. You can *push* an item onto the stack, which would be like placing a book on top of the stack. You can also *pop* an item off of the stack, which would be like taking a book off the top of the stack. The key is that the most recently added item (the one on top) is first one to be removed. The term for this is LIFO, which stands for Last-In-First-Out.

A *queue*, on the other hand, is like a waiting line, where the first person in line is the next one to be processed. This is known as First-In-First-Out, or FIFO. When you *add* an item to a queue, it is added to the "back." Similarly, when you *remove* and item from a queue, it is removed from the "front."

4) Build stack and queue classes. The stack should have *push* and *pop* methods to add and remove items. Likewise, the queue should have *add* and *remove* methods. Both classes should return items in the correct LIFO or FIFO order. Make sure to hide all fields and methods that the user doesn't need to use.

5) Convert the **DogButton** applet from Chapter 9 into a class that extends **JButton**. Thus, you could add a **DogButton** anywhere. Note, this problem is a little tricky since you'll have to use other methods to load your pictures and sound files than the ones in the **Applet** class. Read the Javadoc pages for the **Image** and **ImageIcon** classes for information.

CHAPTER 11

ERRORS AND EXCEPTIONS

Freedom is not worth having, if it does not include the freedom to make mistakes.

Mahatma Ghandi

CHAPTER OBJECTIVES

In this chapter, you will learn about:

✔ Error-Handling with Return Values
✔ Error-Handling with Exceptions
✔ Throwing and Catching Exceptions
✔ Creating Your Own Exceptions

L et's face it, things do not always go as planned—especially when it comes to software. Users might input values other than what your program expects, a full filesystem may prevent your program from being able to save a file to disk, or (GASP!) your program may contain a bug. In these cases, it is important that your program be able to discern errors and handle them to the best of its ability without simply crashing and losing the user's data.

In this chapter, we will explore how you can detect error conditions within your programs and handle them appropriately, experimenting with return values and Java's powerful exception-handling facility. Once finished with this chapter, you will be able to detect and handle error conditions within your programs in a user-friendly manner.

417

L A B   1 1 . 1

ERROR-HANDLING WITH RETURN VALUES

LAB OBJECTIVES

After this lab, you will be able to:

- Use Return Values to Signal Generic Error Conditions
- Use Return Values to Signal Specific Error Conditions

So, how do we write software that is able to inform itself when an error has occurred? Up to this point, the examples in this workbook have not directly addressed error-handling, but this is never a safe assumption in the real world of software. Many issues that arise during the runtime of a program are out of the engineer's control, such as invalid user input or exhaustion of system resources such as memory or storage. The best we can do is to allow the program to check itself as it runs, and be able to recognize errors during runtime.

The classic method for discerning errors is to have each method return a status indicating whether or not (or to what degree) the method successfully did its job. This return value can then be checked by the caller of the method to ensure that everything has been done to satisfaction. If you have done even the least bit of programming in a language such as C or the UNIX shell, you are probably quite familiar with this concept.

Let's jump right in and examine a simple example of using a return value for error-detection.

■ FOR EXAMPLE:

Let's write a function which iterates through an e-mail address String and returns the index of the '@' within the address. This method will return the integer index where the '@' is located, or –1 if there is no '@' present:

```
public int getIndexOfAtSign(String emailAddr)
{
    int index;
    int length = emailAddr.length();
    for(index = 0; index < length; index++)
    {
        if(emailAddr.charAt(index) == '@')
        {
            return(index);
        }
    }
    return(-1);
}
```

In the preceding method, the string **emailAddr** is searched for the first occurrence of '@' and returns the index within the String where it is located. If the '@' is not present in the String this method will return −1. Since index values cannot ever be −1, this return value cannot be confused with a proper index value. Although quite basic, this method does encompass the basics of error-checking.

Consider the following calls to this method:

```
int retVal = getIndexOfAtSign("java.joe@sun.com");
```

The input String **"java.joe@sun.com"** contains the '@' sign at index 8, so **retVal** would contain the value 8. Alternatively, let's say the method was called in the following manner:

```
int retVal = getIndexOfAtSign("com!sun!java.joe");
```

The input String **"com!sun!java.joe"** does not contain '@', and your method would return **retVal** with a value of −1. Your method has just informed you, in its own special way, that there was an error with the input value.

We can also apply this same type of error checking to a method which normally returns an Object upon success. We can modify the preceding example to return a String that represents all the characters following the '@', and still be able to discern erroneous input.

■ FOR EXAMPLE:

Here is a rewrite of the previous method that returns a String instead of an integer value. Take notice of the return value if '@' is not present.

```
public String getEMailHost(String emailAddr)
{
    int index;
    int length = emailAddr.length();
    for(index = 0; index < length; index++)
    {
        if(emailAddr.charAt(index) == '@')
        {
            return(emailAddr.substring(index +1));
        }
    }
    return(null);
}
```

In this example, we iterate through the input String until '@' is found. If '@' does not exist within the input String, we return **null** instead. Consider the following calls to this method:

```
String retString = getEMailHost("java.joe@sun.com");
```

The input String **"java.joe@sun.com"** does contain '@', so the value of **retString** is returned as **"sun.com"** in this instance. However, the following call to this method passes an erroneous value—it does not contain '@':

```
String retString = getEMailHost("com!sun!java.joe");
```

In this case, the value of **retString** would be **null**. Methods that return null values for Objects are quite common and can be very useful tools for error notification.

 If you design a method to return a null Object upon error, be sure you document this well; failure to check for a null value can lead to a runtime error called a NullPointerException, which we will discuss later in this chapter.

Now let's turn our attention to a slightly more complex way to use return values for error checking. In the previous example, only one type of error was possible—the omission of '@' from the input value. What if several errors were possible, each of which needed to be recognized and handled by your program? Let's investigate how we might use return values to indicate more than one type of error condition.

■ *FOR EXAMPLE:*

The following method takes a String as input and validates the length of the String against an acceptable range of lengths. In this case, we wish to be alerted either when the provided String length is too short or too long. Notice that we define global variables outside the method, so that callers of this method can refer to these variables when checking return values. We will discuss this in greater detail in the next section.

```
public static final int VALID      = 0;
public static final int TOO_SHORT = 1;
public static final int TOO_LONG  = 2;
Public int validateStringLength(String inputString)
{
    int min = 10;     // minimum valid String length
    int max = 15;     // maximum valid String length
    if(inputString.length() < min)
    {
        return(TOO_SHORT);
    }
    if(inputString.length() > max)
    {
        return(TOO_LONG);
    }
    return(VALID);
}
```

This method now has the ability to discern two error conditions in addition to a valid condition. Take a look at the following invocations of this method, followed by the respective return values:

```
int retVal = validateStringLength("this is valid");
```

retVal contains the value 0, also represented by the variable **VALID**.

```
int retVal = validateStringLength("short");
```

retVal contains the value 1, also represented by the variable **TOO_SHORT**.

```
int retVal = validateStringLength("this is too long");
```

retVal contains the value 2, also represented by the variable **TOO_LONG**.

Your method is able to successfully detect values that are too short or too long, and can provide appropriate return values for each condition. Using this methodology, you will be able to create methods that detect errors and report them with enough detail that your program is able to take appropriate action.

As we have demonstrated, return values can be an excellent method of error notification; however, these return values can be worthless if not thoroughly checked. Be sure you are aware of all possible return values and check for them in your program. Consider the following fragment of code related to the previous example:

```
int ret = validateStringLength("some input text here");
if(ret == TOO_SHORT)
{
    System.err.println("The input length is too short");
}
else
{
    // continue with program flow
}
```

This code does not check for the **TOO_LONG** return value, and the error condition is not detected and dealt with appropriately. For methods that may have several return values that indicate error conditions, it may be beneficial to check the return value against the known non-error value or against the negation of the non-error value. By checking the "good" return value in such a manner, you can effectively "trap" any return values that indicate error and deal with them as appropriate.

■ FOR EXAMPLE:

Such an approach to the preceding example would have caught the return value implicitly:

```
int ret = validateStringLength("some input text here");
if(ret != VALID)
{
    System.err.println("The input length is not valid");
    // Perhaps check for more specific error type here.
}
```

LAB 11.1 EXERCISES

11.1.1 SIGNAL THE PRESENCE OF A GENERIC ERROR CONDITION

Create a method that checks an array of integers for the first entry that contains a value greater than 20. It should return either the index into the array that first matches the criteria, or −1 if no match is found. Use the following method signature as your guide:

```
public int checkIntArrays(int[] inputArray)
```

a) What is the method that you have created?

_____

_____

Using your method as a reference, what is returned when the input is:

b) { 2, 4, 6, 8, 10, 12, 14, 16, 18, 20 }

_____

_____

c) { 1, 2, 3, 4, 5, 6, 7, 8, 9, 10 }

_____

_____

d) { 20, 40, 60, 80, 100 }

_____

_____

11.1.2 SIGNAL THE PRESENCE OF A SPECIFIC ERROR CONDITION

In the preceding exercise, you created a method that was able to detect an error condition when none of the input integer values was greater than 20. Modify the preceding example to return 0 if one entry exists with a value greater than 20 (no error), 1 if no entries contain a value greater than 20, and 2 if more than one entry contains a value greater than 20. Use the same method signature as in Exercise 11.1.1, as follows:

```
public int checkIntArrays(int[] inputArray)
```

a) What is the method that you have created?

_____

_____

Using your previous method as a reference, what is returned when the input is:

b) { 2, 4, 6, 8, 10, 12, 14, 16, 18, 20 }

_____

_____

c) { 5, 10, 15, 20, 25 }

_____

_____

d) { 20, 40, 60, 80, 100 }

_____

_____

LAB 11.1 EXERCISE ANSWERS

11.1.1 ANSWERS

a) What is the method that you have created?

Answer: Your answer may very well differ from what is displayed here, so use the following as a reference when checking your answers to the other Exercises in this section:

```
public int checkIntArrays(int[] inputArray)
{
    int aryIndex;
    int arySize = inputArray.size;
    for(aryIndex = 0; aryIndex < arySize; aryIndex++)
    {
        if(inputArray[aryIndex] > 20)
        {
            return(aryIndex);
        }
    }
    return(-1);
}
```

Double-check that your comparison is correct and that you are returning the proper error value, −1, if none of the array elements have a value greater than 20.

b) { 2, 4, 6, 8, 10, 12, 14, 16, 18, 20 }

Answer: Your method should return −1, because none of the individual values exceed 20.

In the array provided, none of the individual values was greater than 20. Your method should have iterated through the array and "dropped" through to the bottom where it would return −1.

c) { 5, 10, 15, 20, 25 }

Answer: Your method should return 4, because the fifth element of the provided array contains the value 25.

The fifth element of this array has a value greater than 20. Your method should have detected this value and returned the index of the fifth element, which is 4. As you will recall, array indexes always begin with 0, not 1.

d) { 20, 40, 60, 80, 100 }

Answer: Your method should return 1, because the second element of the provided array contains a value greater than 20.

The second element of this array is the first to contain a value greater than 20. Your method should have detected this value and returned the index of the second element, which is 1.

11.1.2   ANSWERS

a)   What is the method that you have created?

Answer: Your answer may very well differ from what is displayed here, so use the following as a reference when checking your answers to the other exercises in this section. Do note, however, that the possible return values are declared outside the method so that they may be referenced elsewhere:

```
public static final int VALID       = 0;
public static final int NO_MATCH    = 1;
public static final int MULTI_MATCH = 2;
public int checkIntArrays(int[] inputArray)
{
    int aryIndex;
    int matchCount = 0;
    int arySize = inputArray.size;
    for(aryIndex = 0; aryIndex < arySize; aryIndex++)
    {
        if(inputArray[aryIndex] > 20)
        {
            matchCount++;
        }
    }
    if(matchCount == 1)
    {
        return(VALID);
    }
    if(matchCount == 0)
    {
        return(NO_MATCH);
    }
    return(MULTI_MATCH);
}
```

There are countless solutions to appropriately modifying this method, and so long as the return values are identical to the method shown here you are on the right track. The answers to the following Exercises should indicate your success.

b)   { 2, 4, 6, 8, 10, 12, 14, 16, 18, 20 }

Answer: Your method should return 1, or NO_MATCH, because none of the individual values exceed 20.

In the array provided, none of the individual values was greater than 20. Your method should have iterated through the array and "dropped" through to the bottom where the number of matches would be zero upon completion.

c) { 5, 10, 15, 20, 25 }

Answer: Your method should return 0, or VALID, *because the fifth element of the provided array contains the value 25.*

The fifth element of this array has a value greater than 20. Your method should have detected only one integer with a value greater than 20, returning the appropriate value.

d) { 20, 40, 60, 80, 100 }

Answer: Your method should return 2, or MULTI_MATCH, *because every element of this array except the first are greater than 20.*

All elements of this array except the first have a value greater than 20. Your method should have counted more than one integer value greater than 20 and returned the appropriate value.

LAB 11.1 REVIEW QUESTIONS

In order to test your progress, you should be able to answer the following questions.

1) Return values must be integers.
   a) _____ True
   b) _____ False

2) If a method returns a value, it is important to do which of the following?
   a) _____ Check the value for any defined error conditions
   b) _____ Discard the value; it may be a false warning
   c) _____ Inform the user that an error has occurred
   d) _____ Immediately exit the program

3) If a method that returns a String object needs to reflect an error condition, which type of return value should be used?
   a) _____ A value of "-1"
   b) _____ A value of "0" or "zero"
   c) _____ An empty String
   d) _____ A null String

4) All methods return a possible error value.
  a) _____ True
  b) _____ False

5) A value of –1 always means an error.
  a) _____ True
  b) _____ False

Quiz answers appear in Appendix A, Section 11.1.

LAB 11.2

ERROR-HANDLING WITH EXCEPTIONS

> ## LAB OBJECTIVES
>
> After this lab, you will be able to:
>
> • Understand the Concept of Exceptions
> • Understand Exception Flow

In the previous section, we investigated how methods can be written to return diagnostic return values. In many instances, however, no clear distinction can be made between a valid return value and a return value that would indicate an error condition. In such cases where an error occurs, the error can be considered "out of the ordinary," or an "exceptional" condition. The Java language has a facility for dealing with such exceptional conditions called, understandably, *exception-handling*. During the course of this section, we will take a look at exception-handling and how you can safely use methods that make use of this error-handling mechanism.

When things go dreadfully wrong within a method, it is nice to know that you can pull the emergency brake. In Java parlance, this is called "throwing an *exception*." In Java, of course, exceptions are objects defined by the **Exception** class. Once an *exception* is thrown, the normal flow of your method stops immediately and the Java Virtual Machine attempts to find a *handler* that can "catch" and then deal with the particular exception. The method that has thrown the exception does not return a value, nor does it resume normal operation; instead, the exception object encapsulates the error information.

If a *handler* cannot be located, the **Exception** object will propagate upwards through the program; first through the enclosing blocks of the current method and then through the called methods until it reaches the

main() method, at which point the JVM will give up on trying to locate a handler—a stack trace of the program will be printed to standard error (most likely, your screen) and the program will exit.

■ FOR EXAMPLE:

Without getting into the syntax involved with throwing and catching exceptions, let's focus on how an exception propagates upwards through the code blocks and methods within a program. Take a look at the following example:

```
public class ExceptionTest1
{
    int[] intArray = { 1 };
    public ExceptionTest1()
    {
        // nothing needs to be done here
    }
    public static void main(String[] argv)
    {
        System.out.println("Main Called");
        ExceptionTest1 etest = new ExceptionTest1();
        etest.doMethodA();
    }
    public void doMethodA()
    {
        // something safe-no Exceptions thown here
        System.out.println("Method A Called");
        // call doMethodB here
        doMethodB();
    }
    public void doMethodB()
    {
        System.out.println("Method B Called");
        // something careless-access past end of array
        for(int i = 0; i <= intArray.length; i++)
        {
            System.out.println("Index " + i +
                " Value: " + intArray[i]);
        }
        System.out.println("Method B Done!");
    }
}
```

Figure 11.1 illustrates the programmatic flow. One method calls another, creating a program *stack*.

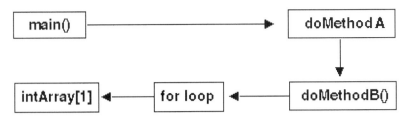

Figure 11.1 ■ Programmatic flow of ExceptionTest1

Notice that within the **for** loop, there is a reference to **intArray[i]**. The array **intArray** only has one element in it (**intArray[0]**), however, the **for** loop is poorly written and will try to access **intArray[1]**, which doesn't exist. So, now what happens?

The answer is that an *exception* will be thrown and the JVM will attempt to locate a handler for the exception. It will start at the bottom of the stack and then works its way up the stack looking for a handler.

When an exception is thrown during the **for** loop, the enclosing **for** block is given a chance to handle the exception. If the **for** block does not contain a handler for the exception, it is then passed upwards to **doMethodB()**, then to **doMethodA()**, and finally to the **main()** method of the class—then the buck stops here, as they say. We will actually examine the output from this class later within the lab. For now, it is important only that you understand the upward traversal of exceptions through a class.

SO WHAT EXACTLY IS AN EXCEPTION?

In simplest terms, an **Exception** is a class that is subclassed from the **Throwable** class. If you take a look at the Java API Documentation, you'll see the following heredity for an Exception, as shown in Figure 11.2.

There are two subclasses of **Throwable**—**Error** and **Exception**. The **Error** class indicates a *severe* problem within the JVM during the execution of your program. Suffice it to say that in most circumstances, you should not attempt to deal with a thrown **Error**. An **Error** primarily indicates an abnormal condition within the JVM that should not occur during normal operations. Your code should let the **Error** pass and be reported.

The **Exception** class, however, can indicate many general error conditions that should be dealt with in some manner. Notice that there are

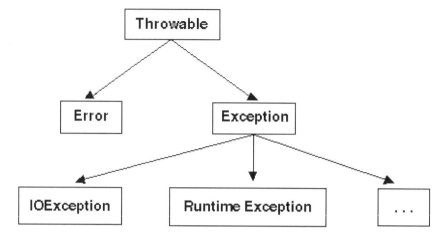

Figure II.2 ■ Lineage of the Exception object

many subclasses of **Exception**. Basically, these can be broken down into two categories—subclasses of **RuntimeException**, and all the other subclasses of **Exception**. The **RuntimeException** subclasses represent conditions attributable to programming errors, such as careless indexing past the end of an array, or calling methods on a null object. Similar to the **Error** class, you should not attempt to deal programmatically with a **RuntimeException**. When a subclass of **RuntimeException** is thrown, it indicates that the programmer is at fault and the program needs to be fixed. In short, a **RuntimeException** is Java's way of telling you to fix a bug in your program! It is considered bad programming to catch a **RuntimeException**.

The other subclasses of **Exception** indicate general error conditions that should be addressed. You are free to use these subclasses yourself, and we will discuss in a later lab how you can create your own subclasses of **Exception** to meet your specific needs.

■ *FOR EXAMPLE:*

Let's take a closer look at an **Exception**. In **ExceptionTest1**, shown previously in this lab, we carelessly index past the end of an array. This will cause an **ArrayIndexOutOfBoundsException**, which is a subclass of **RuntimeException**.

When you run this class, you will see output similar to the following:

```
Constructor Called

Method A Called

Method B Called

Index 0 Value: 1

Exception in thread "main"
java.lang.ArrayIndexOutOfBoundsException: 1

       at ExceptionTest1.doMethodB(ExceptionTest1.java:27)

     at ExceptionTest1.doMethodA(ExceptionTest1.java:18)

     at ExceptionTest1.main(ExceptionTest1.java:11)
```

Why did we not see the message "Method B Done"? This is because an exception had been thrown previously, so the method exited immediately and the JVM began the search for an appropriate handler. You can see from the stack trace (this is the "dump" from the JVM) the order in which the program was searched for a handler—the fact that your program terminated with a stack trace indicates that no appropriate handler was found.

When viewing a stack trace, you may find that the line numbers have been replaced with the words "compiled code." This indicates that the Java Runtime is using a "Just In Time" compiler, or JIT for short. The JIT offers tremendous performance improvements over the standard runtime because it is able to compile Java bytecodes into native code as the program runs. The downside to this technology is that stack traces do not always contain line numbers where errors occurred, which makes the debugging of runtime exceptions more difficult. We recommend that you disable the JIT when you are developing your programs so that all stack traces will provide you with ample debugging information. You can disable the JIT by adding the following parameter to your java or jre command line:

```
-Djava.compiler=NONE
```

So, instead of running a program with the following command line:

```
java ExceptionTest1
```

use the following instead:

```
java -Djava.compiler=NONE ExceptionTest1
```

LAB 11.2 EXERCISES

11.2.1 UNDERSTANDING EXCEPTIONS

a) Under what conditions could you expect a program to throw an `Error`?

_____

_____

b) Under what conditions could you expect a program to throw a subclass of `RuntimeException`?

_____

_____

c) Briefly describe how subclasses of `RuntimeException` differ from the other subclasses of `Exception`.

_____

_____

11.2.2 UNDERSTANDING EXCEPTION FLOW

Use the following stack trace to answer the questions in this section:

```
Exception in thread "main" java.lang.ArithmeticException: / by zero
        at ExceptionTest2.getDivisionResult(ExceptionTest2.java:12)
        at ExceptionTest2.doDisplayResults(ExceptionTest2.java:19)
        at ExceptionTest2.main(ExceptionTest2.java:24)
```

a) What is the name of the `Exception` that was thrown?

_____

_____

b) Within what class was the `Exception` thrown? Which method?

_____

_____

c) On what line number is the operation that caused the `Exception` to be thrown?

_____

_____

d) List sequentially the names of the methods that were called until the `Exception` was thrown.

_____

_____

e) What is the superclass of the thrown `Exception`? What does this tell you about the thrown `Exception`?

_____

_____

LAB 11.2 EXERCISE ANSWERS

11.2.1 ANSWERS

a) Under what conditions could you expect a program to throw an `Error`?

Answer: `Error` *is a subclass of* `Throwable` *that indicates a serious or abnormal error was encountered by the JVM. Circumstances under which such an exception would be thrown include system resource exhaustion or the inability of the JVM to locate a referenced class.*

As mentioned earlier, an `Error` is rarely thrown during the course of a program. However, it is possible you might see this occur if your system has low amounts of memory or if classes that are referenced in your application are not part of the JDK and are located within packages not referenced within your CLASSPATH environment variable. In any case, there are very few reasons why you might attempt to deal programmatically with such exceptions, and there is not very much you can do once these types of errors occur.

b)   Under what conditions could you expect a program to throw a subclass of **RuntimeException**?

Answer: **RuntimeException** *is a subclass of* **Exception** *that indicates a programmer-induced error has occurred. Circumstances under which such an exception would be thrown include dividing by zero, attempting to put the wrong type of object into an array, accessing past the end of an array or casting an object to an incompatible type.*

When a subclass of **RuntimeException** is thrown, you can be reasonably sure that it is caused by programmer error. Accesses past the end of an array, division by zero, bad casts, and the multitude of other errors that cause subclasses of **RuntimeException** to be thrown should be corrected within the program. Think of these exceptions as learning opportunities.

c)   Briefly describe how subclasses of **RuntimeException** differ from the other subclasses of **Exception**.

Answer: When a **RuntimeException** *is thrown, it indicates a programming error. The other exceptions, which do not subclass* **RuntimeException**, *indicate errors that occur for reasons outside the control of the programmer.*

Exception handling is a very powerful tool for dealing with errors in a logical fashion. As we progress further with Exceptions, you will see how the exception-handling mechanism allows you to focus on your program structure rather than on error detection and trapping. Perhaps the concept has been beaten to death, but the take-home message of this question is "If it is a **RuntimeException**, it is your fault!"

11.2.2 ANSWERS

Use the following stack trace to answer the questions in this section:

```
Exception in thread "main" java.lang.ArithmeticException: / by zero
        at ExceptionTest2.getDivisionResult(ExceptionTest2.java:12)
        at ExceptionTest2.doDisplayResults(ExceptionTest2.java:19)
        at ExceptionTest2.main(ExceptionTest2.java:24)
```

a)   What is the name of the **Exception** that was thrown?

Answer: ArithmeticException or, specifically, java.lang.ArithmeticException

The name of the exception that was thrown is displayed prominently in the stack trace on the first line, following the name of thread from which the exception was thrown. Do not confuse the "/ by zero" as part of the exception name; the stack trace appends the exception name with text (known as the *message*) which describes the exception in more details. We will cover this *message* in greater detail later.

b) Within what class was the exception thrown? Which method?

Answer: **ExceptionTest2**, *within the method named*
getDivisionResult().

As we discussed in the lab, the stack trace prints the hierarchy, or stack, of methods that lead to the thrown exception. From this, we can determine that the exception was thrown within **getDivisionResult()** because that is the method listed on the "top" of the stack. As shown in the stack trace, the listing of methods is what can be called a LIFO (last-in first-out) stack—the most recently called method is on top.

c) On what line number is the operation that caused the exception to be thrown?

Answer: *The operation that caused the exception is located on line 12*

Each method listed within the stack trace is appended with the class name and line number from which the method was called. In the case of the method that caused the exception, the listing is of the class and line number from which the responsible operation was called.

Figure 11.3 shows the structure of each method listed in the stack trace.

d) List sequentially the names of the methods that were called until the exception was thrown.

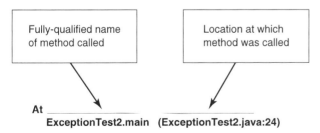

Figure 11.3 ■ **The breakdown of an exception.**

Answer:
  main()
  doDisplayResults()
  getDivisionResult()

Since the stack trace prints out all the methods that were called, you simply need to traverse the list from the bottom (least recent) to the top (most recent).

e) What is the superclass of the thrown exception? What does this tell you about the thrown exception?

Answer: The superclass of **ArithmeticException** *is* **RuntimeException.** *This tells you the exception was due to programmer error; specifically, it was due to a divide-by-zero error.*

Yep, the **RuntimeException** take-home message has been beaten to death. Enough said.

LAB 11.2 REVIEW QUESTIONS

1) Which of the following conditions could cause an *Error* to be thrown?
    a) _____ Division by zero
    b) _____ Memory exhaustion
    c) _____ Creating an array with a negative index size
    d) _____ Calling a method of a null object

2) Which of the following is information not present in a stack trace? Assume that a JIT was not in use during runtime.
    a) _____ Line number at which the exceptional condition occurred
    b) _____ Method within which the exceptional condition occurred
    c) _____ Class within which the exceptional condition occurred
    d) _____ Version of the JVM under which the program was run

3) After an exception is thrown:
    a) _____ The method completes as programmed
    b) _____ The error code "0" is returned by the method that caused the exception
    c) _____ The method stops immediately and the JVM attempts to find a handler for the exception
    d) _____ The program immediately exits

4) The Exception class is a subclass of what class?

    a) _____ Error

    b) _____ Throwable

    c) _____ Problem

    d) _____ Snafu

5) All Errors are Exceptions.

    a) _____ True

    b) _____ False

Quiz answers appear in Appendix A, Section 11.2.

**LAB
11.2**

L A B   1 1 . 3

THROWING AND CATCHING EXCEPTIONS

LAB OBJECTIVES

After this lab, you will be able to:

- Throw an Exception
- Catch an Exception
- Safely Call Methods which Throw Exceptions

In the previous lab, we examined exceptions and learned how the JVM uses exceptions to signal error conditions. In this lab, we will take exceptions one step further and learn how we can leverage exceptions and exception-handling within our own programs. Without further ado, let's throw some exceptions!

ADVERTISING AN EXCEPTION

Remember that a method has only two pathways through which it can exit—it can return successfully, or it can terminate immediately with an exception. For the same reason you must inform the compiler what type of object your method will return, you must also inform the compiler that your method throws an exception.

■ *FOR EXAMPLE:*

The syntax for declaring a method that throws an exception is quite straightforward. The following example is the signature of a method that can throw an **InvalidArgumentException**:

```
public void myMethod() throws InvalidArgumentException
```

This method signature is not very different that what you have already seen. The difference is the **throws** keyword, along with the specific exception class to be thrown. This is known as an *exception specification*. This modified signature does not indicate that the method **will** throw and exception, only that is **may** throw and exception. This becomes very important later, as it takes a special syntax to safely call methods that may throw exceptions.

Ah yes, we can hear your next question now: "What if I would like my method to advertise *two* exceptions that can be thrown?" No problem—take a look at the following method signature:

```
Public void myMethod()
    throws InvalidArgumentException, IOException
```

To advertise multiple exceptions, simply place them in a comma-delimited list following the **throws** keyword. In this preceding example, we broke the method signature into two lines for readability, though it is not a requirement.

 Exceptions that inherit from **Error** *do not need to be advertised, and you should not throw them from within your methods. These exceptions are thrown because of conditions beyond the control of the programmer and could be thrown at any time during the execution of a program.*

As well, exceptions that inherit from **RuntimeException** *do not need to be advertised, either. These exceptions are thrown because of errors that are completely preventable by the programmer—don't advertise that they may occur, don't throw them, just fix the problem.*

If you intend on throwing a multiple exceptions, all of which subclass from a common parent exception, you need only advertise the parent exception within the method signature. As an example, if you are designing a method that can throw a **FileNotFoundException** and an **EOFException**, the following method signature is perfectly valid:

```
public String myMethod() throws IOException
```

This declaration will cover all of your bases since both **FileNotFoundException** and **EOFException** are subclasses of **IOException**.

This is not a two-way street, however. If, in the previous signature, you advertised only **FileNotFoundException**, you could neither throw an **EOFException** nor a generic **IOException**.

THROWING AN EXCEPTION

Now that you know how to provide an *exception specification*, let's take a look at how an exception gets thrown. The first step in this process is determining which exception best suits your needs. The Javadocs are a great place to investigate which exceptions might be a good fit—if the Java API documentation is not already your best friend, it soon will be. Next we will use the keyword **throw** to throw the exception.

■ *FOR EXAMPLE:*

Let's say you are writing a method that parses a colon-delimited String for the value of a particular field:

```
public String myFieldParser(String inputStr)
{
    // does some stuff here to parse for a given field
    return(parsedField);
}
```

This all seems fine, but what if the String passed into the method is not colon-delimited? If this is a serious enough problem that an exception should be thrown, which exception should you use? If you were to look through the Javadocs, you'll find **java.text.ParseException**, which is annotated with "Signals that an error has been reached unexpectedly while parsing." This seems like a pretty good fit—let's use it.

First, we advertise that we that our method may throw a **ParseException**:

```
public String myFieldParser(String inputStr)
    throws ParseException
```

Now we actually insert code to throw the exception:

```
public String myFieldParser(String inputStr)
    throws ParseException
{
    if(input.indexOf(':') == -1) // simple test for ':'
    {
        throw new ParseException(
            inputStr, inputStr.length() -1 );
    }
    // found a colon, we are safe to continue parsing
    ...
    return(parsedString);
}
```

Notice how the exception was instantiated. The constructor for **Parse-Exception** expects a String as an error message and an integer offset within the String where the error was located. In our example, the error was found at the end of the String when it was determined that no colon was present. In your method, it may be wise to include a more verbose message than we have provided in the previous example.

Now that you are proficient at throwing exceptions, heed this one piece of advice—a Java program should never be exception-driven. This means that no part of your normal program runtime should ever depend upon an exception being thrown. Fight the urge to replace proper flow control with exception-handling code, and don't attempt to catch subclasses of **RuntimeException** *unless you have a very specific reason for doing so.*

CATCHING EXCEPTIONS

Up to this point, we have ambiguously referred to the *handler* that catches exceptions and, somehow, deals with them appropriately. Now that you understand how exceptions can be thrown, we can tackle the issue of how an exception can be caught.

To setup a handler, you must implement a *try/catch* block. The syntax can be quite simple, as shown here:

```
try
{
    // some code here which may throw and exception
}
catch(Exception ex)
{
    // do something intelligent about the exception
    // This IS your handler
}
```

This is how it all comes together. If any code within the **try** block throws an exception that is specified by the **catch** block, the rest of the try block is skipped and the code within the **catch** block is executed. The rest of the code within the **try** block is not executed. If all goes well and no exception is thrown within the **try** block, the entire **catch** block is skipped.

You can also specify multiple **catch** blocks, sequentially, to handle different possible exceptions in different ways:

```
try
{
    // some code here which may throw IOException,
    // ParseException, or both...
}
catch(IOException ioex)
{
    // do something with this exception
}
catch(ParseException pex)
{
    // do something with this exception
}
```

The preceding case allows you to handle multiple types of exceptions differently. Keep in mind, however, that you must provide a **catch** block that is able to handle each type of exception that can be thrown. If you do not do so, the compiler will generate an error similar to the following:

```
Parse.java:19: Exception java.text.ParseException must be caught,
    or it must be declared in the throws clause of this method.
```

This is a not-so-subtle hint that you are calling a method that throws an exception for which you have not provided a **catch** block.

If the exceptions that may be thrown from within your catch block are all subclasses of a common class, you can simply **catch** the common superclass. In the following example, we'll assume that the code within the **try** block may throw both **MalformedURLException** and **UnknownHostException**; both are subclasses of **IOException**.

```
try
{
    // code which may throw MalformedURLException
    // and/or UnknownHostException
}
catch(IOException ex)
{
    // do something intelligent here
}
```

Yes, I know what you must be thinking: "If all exceptions are subclasses of **Throwable**, can I simply catch a **Throwable**?" The answer is *yes*, but that would pretty much guarantee that you would win the "World's Worst Programmer" award. To be blunt: *Don't do that!*

As we discussed previously, you should never attempt to catch a thrown **Error,** and there are extremely few instances where it would ever make sense to catch a **RuntimeException**. These exception types are not advertised because they could potentially occur at any time, and you should not need to include error-handling provisions for such oddball occurrences. There is a compromise, and although it is ugly it may be appropriate in many circumstances—catch the **Exception**:

```
try
{
    // code which may generate a few different exceptions
}
catch(Exception ex)
{
    // do something with the exception
}
```

Though you lose the fine-grained control over how you handle the thrown exception, this might well meet your needs. Consider this the *catchall* of catch blocks.

HANDLING THE EXCEPTION

Now that you have caught the exception, you must decide how to best to cope with the situation. Since this highly depends upon your program, it would be difficult to offer any hard and fast rules on how things *should* be done; in fact, you can ignore the exception altogether (not recommended in many circumstances) or even rethrow the exception so that it is passed up the method hierarchy.

Ignoring the exception is easy:

```
try
{
    // code which generates some type of exception
}
catch(Exception ex)
{
    // do nothing
}
```

In the preceding example, if an exception were thrown within the try block, the catch block would silently ignore it. If you must ignore an exception, do others a great favor and place a comment within the catch block indicating that you are purposefully doing nothing. Otherwise, folks reading your code will assume either that you forgot to handle the exception or you didn't know how to handle the exception.

 Though you can silently ignore exceptions by doing nothing within the catch block, we would not recommend doing this. Either deal with the exception locally, or rethrow the exception up the method stack until some handler can be found to deal with it properly. In the case of exception-handling, silence is most definitely not golden.

**LAB
11.3**

Sometimes you may decide to catch an exception and rethrow it so that it travels up the method hierarchy. Most often, this would be done if you need to do a little error-induced housekeeping within your method, but you still wish another method to receive the notification:

```
try
{
    // some code which may throw an exception
}
catch(Exception ex)
{
    // do some local housekeeping, such as
    someBoolean = false;
    // re-throw the exception to a method that
    // knows better how to handle it
    throw ex;
}
```

In fact, it is not even necessary that you rethrow the same exception that you caught. If you ever find yourself in the position of dealing with somebody else's buggy classes, over which you have no control, you can catch the exception and then propagate it as another type of exception which can be caught somewhere up the method hierarchy:

```
try
{
    // buggy code which throws runtime exceptions
}
catch(RuntimeException ex)
{
    throw new Exception("Argh! Buggy code again!");
}
```

It is very important to note that if you rethrow an exception, the method that contains the handler **must** advertise that it throws an exception. The only case in which you would not need to advertise would be if you are rethrowing a subclass of **Error** or **RuntimeException**, but you know better, don't you?

FINALLY . . .

No discussion of exception handling would be complete without mentioning the **finally** block. In conjunction with **try** and **catch**, you may also provide a **finally** block which will execute under *all* circumstances. Most likely, you will not find much use for this within the average program, but it can be useful if you need to do local cleanup whether or not an exception was caught; or if control was transferred from the try block via a **return**, **break**, or **continue**.

**LAB
11.3**

The functionality of **finally** is as follows:

- If no exceptions are generated within the **try** block, the **finally** block is executed.
- If control leaves the **try** block because of a **return**, **break**, or **continue**, the **finally** block is executed *before* the **try** block relinquishes control.
- If an exception is generated within the **try** block, the appropriate **catch** block is executed, and then the **finally** block is executed.

In all cases, your **finally** block will be executed.

LAB 11.3 EXERCISES

11.3.1 THROW AN EXCEPTION

a) Which types of exceptions (subclasses of **Throwable**) must be advertised by methods that may throw them?

_____

_____

b) Which types of exceptions (subclasses of **Throwable**) do not need to be advertised by methods that may throw them?

_____

_____

c) Under what circumstances may you advertise only one exception type when multiple exceptions may be thrown?

_____

_____

11.3.2 CATCH AN EXCEPTION

For the following questions, use the this method signature as your guide:

```
public void doSomethingDangerous()
    throws HearNoEvilException, SeeNoEvilException
```

a) Write a method which calls **doSomethingDangerous()**. Be sure you include the proper error-handling blocks, though they need not contain actual code.

_____

_____

b) If both **HearNoEvilException** and **SeeNoEvilException** are subclasses of **SpeakNoEvilException**, how could you write more succinct code than you did for the previous question?

_____

_____

c) If your code must set the **Boolean** variable **finishedHere** to **true** after **doSomethingDangerous()** is called, regardless of whether or not an exception has occurred, how can this be done without setting the variable at two separate locations?

_____

_____

LAB 11.3 EXERCISE ANSWERS

11.3.1 ANSWERS

a) Which types of exceptions (subclasses of **Throwable**) must be advertised by methods that may throw them?

Answer: Any subclass of **Exception** *that is not a subclass of* **RuntimeException**, *must be advertised by a method that may throw it.*

As you may recall, any subclass of **Exception** that is not a **RuntimeException** must be advertised within the method signature. The compiler must be made aware that the method can throw an exception that must be caught.

b) Which types of exceptions (subclasses of **Throwable**) do not need to be advertised by methods that may throw them?

Answer: **Error** *and* **RuntimeException** *do not need to be, and should not be, advertised by methods that may throw them.*

The **Error** and **RuntimeException** exceptions are implicit exceptions, meaning that they are not advertised and can be thrown at any time during the execution of a program. Good programming dictates that you not throw subclasses of **Error** ever, and you'd better have a really good reason for throwing a subclass of **RuntimeException**.

c) Under what circumstances may you advertise only one exception type when multiple exceptions may be thrown?

Answer: If all the exceptions that can be thrown by a method have a common superclass, you may simply advertise the superclass if you so choose.

It is not mandatory, but you may decide to advertise only the common superclass of the thrown exceptions. In such a case, the code that calls this method will not be able to catch the specific subclasses that are thrown, but must instead catch the superclass. Often, such an approach makes sense; other times, you might desire the granularity available through catching the individual exceptions.

a) Write a method which calls **doSomethingDangerous()**. Be sure you include the proper error-handling blocks, though they need not contain actual code.

Answer: Because doSomethingDangerous() advertises two exceptions, you must call this method from within a try block and provide catch blocks for both types of exceptions.

**LAB
11.3**

Your answer should look similar to the following:

```
...
try
{
    doSomethingDangerous();
}
catch(HearNoEvilException he)
{
    // do something here
}
catch(SeeNoEvilException se)
{
    // do something here
}
```

In this instance, it does not matter whether or not you provided code within your catch blocks, but you should have at least included a comment. If you did not, shame on you. Go do that now.

b) If both **HearNoEvilException** and **SeeNoEvilException** are subclasses of **SpeakNoEvilException**, how could you write more succinct code than you did for the previous question?

Answer: Since both exceptions share the same superclass, you can provide only one catch block that specifies the superclass.

The more succinct approach to the calling the method should look similar to the following:

```
...
try
{
    doSomethingDangerous();
}
```

```
catch(SpeakNoEvilException ex)
{
    // do something here
}
```

Whether or not you choose to catch only the superclass highly depends upon your program. Keep in mind that this is not a requirement, but can make life a bit easier at times.

c)   If your code must set the **Boolean** variable **finishedHere** to **true** after **doSomethingDangerous()** is called, regardless of whether or not an exception has occurred, how can this be done without setting the variable at two separate locations?

Answer: A **finally** *block can be employed to set* **finishedHere** *regardless of the outcome from calling* **doSomethingDangerous()**.

Because the **finally** block is guaranteed to be executed regardless of what occurs within the **try** block, you can set **finishedHere** within the **finally** block and still be able to sleep at night. If you included a code fragment, it should look similar to the following:

```
...
try
{
    doSomethingDangerous();
}
catch(SpeakNoEvilException ex)
{
    // do something here
}
finally
{
    finishedHere = true;
}
```

Using the **finally** block is strictly optional. In most cases, it will be of little use; however, it is another tool in your bag of tricks which may come in handy when you least expect it.

LAB 11.3 REVIEW QUESTIONS

1) Which of the following method signatures is syntactically correct for a method that throws an IOException?
   a) _____ public void doSomething(); throws IOException
   b) _____ public void doSomething() throws new IOException()
   c) _____ public void doSomething() throws IOException
   d) _____ public void doSomething()

2) The code within a `finally` block
   a) _____ will be executed before any error-handling is attempted
   b) _____ will not be executed unless an exception is thrown within the preceding try block
   c) _____ Is not guaranteed to be executed at any certain time, but will be called prior to garbage-collection by the JVM
   d) _____ Is guaranteed to be executed regardless of whether or not an exception is thrown within the try block

3) For every `try` block
   a) _____ There must be exactly one catch block
   b) _____ There must be at least one catch block
   c) _____ There must be a finally block
   d) _____ There must be at least one catch block or one finally block
   e) _____ There must be a `try-try-again` block

4) You can catch an Exception by catching its superclass
   a) _____ True
   b) _____ False

5) You can catch Errors and Throwables.
   a) _____ True
   b) _____ False

6) You *should* catch Errors and Throwables.
   a) _____ True
   b) _____ False

Quiz answers appear in Appendix A, Section 11.3.

LAB 11.4

CREATING YOUR OWN EXCEPTIONS

LAB OBJECTIVES

After this lab, you will be able to:

- Create Your Own Exceptions

Oftentimes, your code may encounter an error condition for which there is no adequate exception already defined. In such cases, you can create your own exception.

To create your own exception, you may either subclass **Exception** or a specific subclass of **Exception** generally applicable to the situation at hand. To follow convention, it is highly recommended that you provide at least two constructors for your class:

- An empty constructor
- A constructor that takes a single String used for a verbose message

Though not required, this is the convention to which all exceptions defined within the JDK adhere. Because your exception will ultimately be a distant subclass of **Throwable**, it is conceivable that the handler for this exception may wish to call the **getMessage()** method of **Throwable** (and thus, of your new exception class) for a detailed description of what went wrong.

■ *FOR EXAMPLE:*

Referring to the parsing examples from the previous lab, let's take a look at how we could create our own subclass of **ParseException** that better fits our predicament.

```
import java.text.ParseException;
public class ColonParseException extends ParseException
{
    public ColonParseException()
    {
        super();
    }
    public ColonParseException(String message)
    {
        super(message, message.length() -1);
    }
}
```

Now we have an honest-to-goodness exception that we can advertise and throw instead of the more ambiguous **ParseException**. Best of all, since the exception is ours, we can "hard-code" the index value because it is unimportant to us and to the handler in this instance.

We can even go one step further, and remove that index value entirely. If we subclass **Exception** instead of **ParseException**, we needn't even bother with an index value at which the parse error occurred.

```
public class MissingColonException extends Exception
{
    public MissingColonException()
    {
        super();
    }
    public MissingColonException(String message)
    {
        super(message);
    }
}
```

The name of the exception was changed so that it will not be confused for a subclass of **ParseException**, and because it better fits the error that we would encounter within our program. Extending **Exception** is fairly straightforward, and nothing prevents you from adding more methods to your exception for which your handlers might find a use.

Throwing exceptions of your own creation is no different than throwing the standard exceptions. Likewise, you will provide **try**, **catch**, and **finally** blocks in the same manner as you would for any exception.

LAB 11.4 EXERCISES

11.4.1 CREATE YOUR OWN EXCEPTIONS

In the computer world, **IO** stands for Input and Output. Whenever Java encounters a problem reading or writing information, it throws an **IOException**.

a) Create your own exception as a subclass of **IOException** that could be used for a more specific **IO** problem.

**LAB
11.4**

LAB 11.4 EXERCISE ANSWERS

11.4.1 ANSWERS

a) Create your own exception as a subclass of **IOException**.

Answer: As long as your exception is syntactically correct, you have answered correctly. The following is one correct example.

```
import java.io.IOException;
public class EIEIOException extends IOException
{
    public EIEIOException ()
    {
        super();
    }
    public EIEIOException (String message)
    {
        super(message);
    }
}
```

If you have not yet done so, attempt to compile your answer to this question. The Java compiler is the final word on whether or not your syntax is correct. If it does not compile, make adjustments to your syntax using the previous lab as a guide and check it again.

The new exception could be used as follows:

```
if (!moo.here() && !moo.there() && !moomoo.everywhere())
{
    throw new EIEIOException("Trouble on the farm!");
}
```

LAB 11.4 REVIEW QUESTIONS

1) What difference is there between throwing an exception included within the JDK and throwing an exception of your own creation?
   a) _____ None. Both are thrown using the same syntax
   b) _____ If you have subclassed an existing **Exception** class, you must catch both the your own exception and the superclass of your exception

2) You can only subclass the **Exception** class.
   a) _____ True
   b) _____ False

3) You are not required to call the **super()** constructor when you extend the **Exception** class.
   a) _____ True
   b) _____ False

4) User-defined exceptions cannot be caught.
   a) _____ True
   b) _____ False

5) The authors of this book have a dorky sense of humor.
   a) _____ True
   b) _____ False

Quiz answers appear in Appendix A, Section 11.4.

C H A P T E R　11

TEST YOUR THINKING

A well-written program is one third "program" and two-thirds error checking. Far too many programs are written with the assumption that everything is going to work fine. You've probably heard of Murphy's Law: *Whatever can go wrong, will go wrong*. There are also those who say that Murphy was an optimist. Those people are right. Just as a person's true character is revealed under duress, the same is true for a computer program. Your well-written programs should always consider what should be done if the unexpected, or even impossible, should occur.

1) Create a new exception called **NoMoreElementsException**, which is a subclass of **Exception**.

2) Modify the **Stack** and **Queue** classes created in Chapter 10 (Test Your Thinking) so that the **pop()** and **remove()** methods will throw a **NoMoreElements-Exception** if you try to pop an empty stack, or remove an item from an empty queue.

APPENDIX A

LAB SELF-REVIEW ANSWERS

Lab 1.1 Self-Review Answers

Question	Answer	Comments
1)	b	The Java Virtual Machine interprets the bytecode.
2)	d	*javac* stands for **java c**ompiler.
3)	a	*java* is the interpreter.
4)	b	*appletviewer* will run an applet.
5)	b	JDK is the Java Developer's Kit.

Lab 2.1 Self-Review Answers

Question	Answer	Comments
1)	c	Classes are used to build objects.
2)	c, d	The terms *variable* and *field* can be used interchangeably.
3)	a	Objects are a collection of fields and methods.
4)	b	Methods perform a task. While answer d is a specific task performed by a method, *printing* is not the purpose of all methods.
5)	a	Fields hold data.
6)	c	Java needs to know which other classes it needs to use for your program.

LAB 2.2 SELF-REVIEW ANSWERS

Question	Answer	Comments
1)	b	False; there are certain restrictions on variable names.
2)	c	The terms *field* and *variable* are interchangeable.
3)	b	You can "define and assign" a variable in one line.
4)	d	A variable only exists within a certain scope.
5)	a	If you can define it, a variable can hold it.
6)	a	Technically, there are no global variables in Java.

LAB 2.3 SELF-REVIEW ANSWERS

Question	Answer	Comments
1)	a	The method *accesses* the variable.
2)	b	*Mutator* sounds more professional than *changer*.
3)	c	The method has an effect.
4)	b	The parameter list changes the method's *signature*.
5)	b	thisNamingConventionIsOptionalButRecommended
6)	d	Example modifiers are **public** and **private**.

LAB 3.1 SELF-REVIEW ANSWERS

Question	Answer	Comments
1)	d, e	Both float and double can contain decimal numbers.
2)	a, d, e	All of these number types can store the number 10.
3)	d, e	**float** is fine for such a value, but **double** is good, too.
4)	e	For values like *pi*, you would want high precision.
5)	b, d	All **char** values must be in single quotes. The *character* "5" is a legal **char**, but the *number* 5 is not.

| 6) | a, b | A boolean must be either **true** or **false**. These words have special meaning to Java so you can't use quotes. While many languages use 1 for true and 0 for false, Java does not. |
| 7) | a | The result is truncated to 9. |

Lab 3.2 Self-Review Answers

Question	Answer	Comments
1)	b, c, e	(a) is missing its double quotes, and (d) uses single quotes. Choice (c) is a valid String, just an empty one.
2)	c	The two Strings are combined as is.
3)	b	The first character has index 0.
4)	e	There is no *bloom* in *chocolate*!
5)	b	String uses the length().
6)	a	Substring from index 10 up to, but not including, 14.

Lab 3.3 Self-Review Answers

Question	Answer	Comments
1)	d	The square brackets [] denote an array.
2)	c	None of the other methods will work.
3)	d	The first element has index 0.
4)	c	The last element's index one less than the length of the array.
5)	e	You can make an array out of any type or class.
6)	b	No. The println() method needs help before it can print the contents of an array.
7)	b	An array cannot change size once defined.

LAB 3.4 SELF-REVIEW ANSWERS

Question	Answer	Comments
1)	b, d, f	Only objects can be stored in a Vector.
2)	b	false, you can mix and match any types in a Vector.
3)	a	Put the boolean in a Boolean and add it to the Vector.
4)	d	charValue() is the correct method.
5)	a	add() places the new object at the end of the list.
6)	b	You can cycle though a Vector's contents.
7)	b	An Enumeration never affects a Vector.
8)	b	You can have as many Enumerators as you can handle.

LAB 4.1 SELF-REVIEW ANSWERS

Question	Answer	Comments
1)	d	Answer a is just wrong. Answer b is for objects only (not ints). Answer c is an assignment.
2)	c	Just because they're reversed, doesn't mean it doesn't work.
3)	f	Answer a is wrong because this statement will not test the numeric values of **f1** and **f2**; it will only compare f1 and f2 as objects. Answer b is an assignment not a test.

4)	a	This is a shortcut for
		
		`boolean b;`
		
		`b = (x ==y );`

5)	b	The less-than operator requires primitive types.

LAB 4.2 SELF-REVIEW ANSWERS

Question	Answer	Comments
1)	a	The test is false, so the else-clause (**y = 30**) is executed.
2)	d	Choice c is the **else** keyword, but the else-clause is the statement following the word "**else**."
3)	a	This is a nested *if* statement. **z** will be assigned the value 10 if **x > 10** and **y < 10**.
4)	b	We wish it was required, but we can only recommend that you do.
5)	b	This is the best answer. While answer c could be correct, it is not necessarily the case; the statement could also be executed after the then-clause. All of the other answers are definitely not correct.

LAB 4.3 SELF-REVIEW ANSWERS

Question	Answer	Comments
1)	b	The value of y is 10 since the loop is repeated 10 times.
2)	a	When x gets to 0 the test is false, so the loop exits.
3)	d	These are all ways of saying the same thing. You must have an exit condition (one that returns false) or else you will get an infinite loop.
4)	b	Only boolean values are allowed here.
5)	b	No, this code will repeat forever. Since **moreWorkToDo** starts as **true**, and the value of **moreWorkToDo** does not change inside the loop, so there is nothing to stop the loop.

LAB 4.4 SELF-REVIEW ANSWERS

Question	Answer	Comments
1)	b	Any *for* loop can be rewritten as a *while* loop. The *for* loop just makes it a little more convenient.
2)	b	The code will loop 10 times, with the value of **i** ranging from 0 to 9. When **i** reaches 10, the loop will exit.
3)	d	The variable **i** is define inside the for loop, so it does not exist outside of the loop (and therefore can't have a value).
4)	c	The **i++** command is the "modification statement" of the *for* loop. The modification statement is automatically executed at the end of each loop after the last command in the loop block.
5)	b	The **i < 10** test is performed at the beginning of each loop. If the result is **false**, then the program flow skips to end of the loop.
6)	a	The **int i = 0** instruction is executed once at the very beginning of the *for* loop, even before the first **i < 10** test.

LAB 4.5 SELF-REVIEW ANSWERS

Question	Answer	Comments
1)	b, d	int and char are the only valid choices.
2)	c	Example: **case 1:**
3)	a	No comment.
4)	d	**break** is optional, but it can signal the end.
5)	b	Only "two" is printed.
6)	c, d	Both "three" and "four" are printed because there is no **break** statement in the **case 3:** block.
7)	e	There is no match, so the default block is used.

Lab 5.1 Self-Review Answers

Question	Answer	Comments
1)	c	&& is the symbol for AND.
2)	b	! is the symbol for NOT.
3)	a	true AND true is true.
4)	d	^ is the symbol for XOR.
5)	b	This is the behavior of the OR operator.
6)	c	Make sure to use the "pipe" characters || and not exclamation points.

Lab 5.2 Self-Review Answers

Question	Answer	Comments
1)	c	"The order in which things are done."
2)	a	Only boolean operators in boolean expressions
3)	b	Evaluate left to right:
4)	a	The expression inside the parentheses is evaluated separately. The result is: `true || (false)` which is true.
5)	b	It doesn't matter what the value of **x** is, the result of this expression is **false** since AND requires both values to be **true** to have a **true** result.
6)	a	Again, it does matter what the value of **x** is, the result will be **true**.
7)	a	Same logic as previous two answers.
8)	d	Always celebrate your achievements! Also, test your code by trying sample values to see if the results are valid.

LAB 6.1 SELF-REVIEW ANSWERS

Question	Answer	Comments
1)	c	The pieces of a GUI are components and containers.
2)	c	A dialog box is a container.
3)	a	A label is a component.
4)	a	Containers can contain containers.
5)	c	The JWindow is meant to pop up and pop down by it-self.
6)	b	The JDialog is meant to pop up and bring critical info to the user.
7)	a	The JFrame is the standard "program" window.
8)	c	All of the other classes have content panes.

LAB 6.2 SELF-REVIEW ANSWERS

Question	Answer	Comments
1)	c	Applets get treated like panels because they are placed inside other things, like a Web browser.
2)	a	Sometimes the obvious answer is correct!
3)	c	The applet is stopped whenever it's not being used.
4)	b	Use the PARAM tag.
5)	b	Applets do not need a main() method.

LAB 6.3 SELF-REVIEW ANSWERS

Question	Answer	Comments
1)	c	JLabels can display both.
2)	c	There is no constant called DEFAULT.
3)	b	False, use the setText() method.

4)	b	Default value is SwingConstants.LEFT
5)	d	You can set the background color.

LAB 6.4 SELF-REVIEW ANSWERS

Question	Answer	Comments
1)	c	AbstractButton defines the behavior of any button.
2)	c	Good for all two-value inputs.
3)	b	The JRadioButton will automatically deselect all other buttons.
4)	b	False. A ButtonGroup just lets links buttons together.
5)	d	By default.

LAB 6.5 SELF-REVIEW ANSWERS

Question	Answer	Comments
1)	c	JTextComponent defines characteristics of all text components.
2)	b	This hides the typed text from prying eyes.
3)	a	True, use the setHorizontalAlignment() method.
4)	b	It is supported. Use the setWrapStyleWord() method.
5)	b	False. Use something like textArea.setText(null) instead.

LAB 7.1 SELF-REVIEW ANSWERS

Question	Answer	Comments
1)	e	The layout manager controls all other attributes.
2)	b	The BorderLayout uses compass points to signal direction.
3)	c	The full class name is java.awt.BorderLayout.

4)	a, b, c	The *West* and *East* do not stretch horizontally.
5)	c, d, e	Likewise, the *North* and *South* do not stretch vertically.
6)	b	The *West* and *East* will only touch the bottom if there is no *South* region. Likewise for the top and the *North* region.
7)	e	You cannot do a corner with the BorderLayout.

LAB 7.2 SELF-REVIEW ANSWERS

Question	Answer	Comments
1)	a	rows is the first parameter.
2)	b	cols is the second parameter.
3)	d	vgap is the fourth parameter.
4)	e	The maximum number of components is 18, but you can't tell how many have been added.
5)	a	The upper-left.
6)	a	true!

LAB 7.3 SELF-REVIEW ANSWERS

Question	Answer	Comments
1)	b	False, it is possible, and usually necessary.
2)	b	False, you can nest until the cows come home.
3)	b	False, all layout managers are independent of each other.
4)	a	True, technically, a container is a component.
5)	b	False, the order does not matter.
6)	b	False, while it's common, it's not required.

LAB 7.4 SELF-REVIEW ANSWERS

Question	Answer	Comments
1)	b	GridBagConstraints control the layout behavior.
2)	b	False, but you can if you want to.
3)	a	Setting gridwidth to GridBagConstraints. REMAINDER signals the end of a row.
4)	c	weightx will contribute to the proportional spacing.
5)	d	With fill set to NONE, a component will move, but never resize and always be as small as it can be.
6)	e	Set anchor to one of the nine anchor points.
7)	b	Uses gridy (and gridx) will explicitly set the grid position.

LAB 8.1 SELF-REVIEW ANSWERS

Question	Answer	Comments
1)	d	All events have common properties.
2)	b	Since there are so many events, it's best to only handle the ones we care about.
3)	c	Don't count on any determined order.
4)	a	This is a very common technique.
5)	b	Limits on scope apply.

LAB 8.2 SELF-REVIEW ANSWERS

Question	Answer	Comments
1)	b	The idea is that they adapt.
2)	b	The actual functionality must be implemented.
3)	b	Both chicks *and* dudes dig 'em.

4)	b	The anonymous class only handles events for the one object.
5)	b	False, although it's usually true, just not always.

LAB 9.1 SELF-REVIEW ANSWERS

Question	Answer	Comments
1)	c	Unlike a browser, Java will not prepend the http:// for you.
2)	a	getCodeBase() returns the URL base.
3)	c, d	Only the Swing components have image constructors.
4)	d	The components take the Icon class, and its subclasses.
5)	b	The *rollover* icon is the image displayed when the mouse *rolls over* the button.
6)	c	The pressed icon is displayed when the button is pressed.
7)	a	True, the JLabel is just like the JButton when it comes to images.
8)	a	Sometimes these questions are as easy as they look! CENTER can be used to center either horizontally or vertically.

LAB 9.2 SELF-REVIEW ANSWERS

Question	Answer	Comments
1)	a, c, d	Java uses RBG colors, red, green, and blue.
2)	d	There is no purple define. Use "magenta" instead.
3)	a	setForeground() will set the text color.
4)	d	256 * 256 * 256 = 16,777,216
5)	d	setBackground() will set the background color.

6)	a	True. JLabels are transparent and have no background of their own.
7)	b	Java uses RGB color, so Color(0, 255, 0) is red=0, green=255, blue=0.
8)	e	All shades of gray have equal values for red, green, and blue. Values near 0 or 255 will look black or white, so a real gray should be a mid-range value.

LAB 9.3 SELF-REVIEW ANSWERS

Question	Answer	Comments
1)	d	The AudioClip class is used to store and play sound files.
2)	b	play() will play the audio clip one time.
3)	a	loop() will play the audio clip in a repeating loop.
4)	c	stop() will immediately stop the playing of an audio clip.
5)	a	getAudioClip() will load an audio clip from a URL.
6)	a	True. All files, including audio files, are URLs.

LAB 9.4 SELF-REVIEW ANSWERS

Question	Answer	Comments
1)	b	The Font family name describes the look of the font.
2)	a	Font.BOLD is a Font style.
3)	d	This text is a 10-point font.
4)	b	False. While there is a set of common fonts that most computers have, every computer could be different.
5)	d	Color is not a Font attribute.
6)	a	Nice and easy.
7)	b	False. You can reuse Font objects.

LAB 10.1 SELF-REVIEW ANSWERS

Question	Answer	Comments
1)	d	Class and file names must match, and have a .java extension.
2)	b	Constructor definitions look like methods, but do not have a return type.
3)	c	Classes are defined with the class keyword.
4)	b	False. You can have any number of constructors, as long as the signatures are different.
5)	b	False. If you don't define one, you get the default constructor.
6)	d	API stands for Application Programming Interface.
7)	e	No restrictions. User-created classes are just like any other Java class.

LAB 10.2 SELF-REVIEW ANSWERS

Question	Answer	Comments
1)	a	Only public methods are accessible. Answers c and d have the wrong syntax.
2)	a	True. Private objects don't exist outside.
3)	b	False. Public methods for private data is common and recommended.
4)	a	Just add static after the public or private declaration.
5)	b	False. Any method can access static fields and methods.
6)	b	False. Static methods can only access static fields and methods.
7)	b	No special keyword is needed. Just define add() with a different parameter signature.
8)	d	A method's signature is its name and the type and order of its parameters.

LAB 10.3 SELF-REVIEW ANSWERS

Question	Answer	Comments
1)	d	Example: public class NewClass extends OldClass
2)	a, b	If you checked e, seek help!
3)	b, c	Constructors are not inherited.
4)	e	super() must always be called first.
5)	d	public allows the method to be accessed, and private does not allow inheritance.
6)	f	No special keywords needed. Just use the same signature.
7)	a	True (which it is!)
8)	a	toString() is inherited from the Object class.

LAB 11.1 SELF-REVIEW ANSWERS

Question	Answer	Comments
1)	d	A *runtimeException* is the programmer's error.
2)	a	It's always important to check for errors.
3)	d	The other values could be valid String values.
4)	b	Not all do, so read the Javadocs.
5)	b	It depends on the method, so again, read the Javadocs.

LAB 11.2 SELF-REVIEW ANSWERS

Question	Answer	Comments
1)	b	The other answers are all exceptions.
2)	d	To get the JVM version, run "java –version"
3)	c	What happens next is up to the programmer.

4)	b	If you said "d" we'd like to sell you a bridge.
5)	b	Errors and Exceptions are not the same thing, but both are subclasses of Throwable.

Lab 11.3 Self-Review Answers

Question	Answer	Comments
1)	c	Could be broken into two lines.
2)	d	The *finally* code is always executed.
3)	b	You need to catch all of the possible exceptions that could be thrown inside the *try* block.
4)	a	You can do this, but you lose the ability to differentiate between Exceptions.
5)	a	Yes, but . . .
6)	b	You shouldn't catch the Errors and Throwables.

Lab 11.4 Self-Review Answers

Question	Answer	Comments
1)	a	It's all the same.
2)	b	You can subclass any class.
3)	b	Just like any subclass, you need to create your super-class.
4)	b	What would be the point?
5)	a	This was probably the easiest question in this book!

A P P E N D I X   B

JAVA RESERVED WORDS

This section lists all of the *reserved* words in Java, also called *keywords*. You cannot use these words as variable (field) names, method names, or class names since they have special meaning in Java. To be considered a keyword, the word must appear in a stand-alone form. Likewise, you can use keywords inside the value of a String or Java comment.

■ *FOR EXAMPLE:*

If the keyword is "finally" then the following are **NOT** acceptable:

```
int finally;
public void finally()
public class finally
```

However, the following examples are legal uses of the word "finally."

```
int isFinallyDone;
public double getFinallyValue()
String s = "I'm finally done with this book!";
// This is a comment with the word finally in it.
/* This is also a comment with finally in it. */
```

LIST OF JAVA KEYWORDS

The following words are the Java reserved keywords:

abstract	catch	default	final
boolean	char	do	finally
break	class	double	float
byte	const	else	for
case	continue	extends	goto

if	native	short	throws
implements	new	static	transient
import	package	super	try
instanceof	private	switch	void
int	protected	synchronized	volatile
interface	public	this	while
long	return	throw	

The following words are technically not keywords (they are *literals*), but for all intents and purposes, they should be treated as keywords.

true

false

null

INDEX